Leadership in Educational Reform

This book is printed on recycled paper. ♻

Leadership in Educational Reform

An Administrator's Guide to Changes in Special Education

by

Daniel D. Sage, Ed.D.
Professor Emeritus
Special Education Administration
Syracuse University

and

Leonard C. Burrello, Ed.D.
Professor
Educational Leadership and Policy Studies
School of Education
Indiana University

·P A U L·H·
BROOKES
PUBLISHING Cº

Baltimore • London • Toronto • Sydney

Paul H. Brookes Publishing Co.
P.O. Box 10624
Baltimore, Maryland 21285-0624

Copyright © 1994 by Paul H. Brookes Publishing Co., Inc.
All rights reserved.

Typeset by Brushwood Graphics, Inc., Baltimore, Maryland.
Manufactured in the United States of America by
The Maple Press Company, York, Pennsylvania.

Library of Congress Cataloging-in-Publication Data

Sage, Daniel D.
Leadership in educational reform : an administrator's guide
   to changes in special education / by Daniel D. Sage and
   Leonard C. Burrello.
      p.   cm.
   Includes bibliographical references and index.
   ISBN 1-55766-149-9
   1. Special education—United States—Administration.
2. Handicapped children—Education—United States—
Administration. 3. Mainstreaming in education—United
States.   4. Educational change—United States.   I. Burrello,
Leonard C., 1942–   . II. Title.
LC3981.S34   1994
371.9′042′0973—dc20   93-51071
                                                            CIP

British Library Cataloguing-in-Publication data are available
from the British Library.

Contents

Preface

Educators in the 1990s are feeling increasing pressure to modify the way they view their world. The challenge presented by critics of existing systems of education is to shake loose many of the most familiar assumptions about how our institutions should be organized. The call for restructuring involves more than a popular buzzword, and more than an invitation for tinkering; it is a demand for a paradigm shift of dramatic proportions. The elements that professionals are expected to examine, question, and probably change include curricula, instructional methods, styles of leadership, and governmental policies at all levels regarding the organization and support of our schools.

Concurrent with this general call for restructuring is an expression of concern about the manner in which services for students with special needs have evolved into a system that is perceived as parallel, separate, and (although very expensive) largely unequal. The debate in the professional community over the validity of these perceptions and the nature of necessary changes has been intense. Proposed remedies have been advanced in the form of a variety of vaguely understood concepts with confusing names—mainstreaming, integration, the regular education initiative, and inclusion. A common thread that has been recognized by much of the leadership within both the special and general education communities is the need for a truly *unified* system that includes *all* students, without an emphasis on classification and separation as a prerequisite for securing their rights as citizens. A unified-system framework assumes an inclusive strategy for educating all students with special needs and places responsibility for their education at the doorstep of the local schoolhouse.

The intersection of the call for restructuring and the call for a *unified* system provides the conceptual core of this book, and we believe that the study of these intersecting issues is critical to the professional practice of leadership personnel in educational settings. In addition to different sets of beliefs and assumptions, we believe that an inclusive school's philosophy requires different structures, policies, and practices. School superintendents, building principals, and supervisors of both general and special education programs are all confronted with the issues that we have endeavored to illuminate in this book. This volume draws upon our two previous works—

Leadership and Change in Special Education (1979) and *Policy and Management in Special Education* (1986)—but here we examine the issues surrounding special education within the context of the paradigm shift that is changing our perceptions of public education as a whole. This volume begins with a discussion of paradigms for restructuring, then proceeds to an extended discussion of several issues concerning the field of special education, including its scope and its various sources of organizational and fiscal support. The proper use of outcome-based education with students with disabilities is then examined, followed by discussions of the respective leadership roles of principals and special educators, and, finally, of issues surrounding program evaluation.

Both in academic settings and in practice, our professional lives have been spent at the junction between the special education and educational administration communities. We hope and believe that our perspectives from this vantage point will be useful to both scholars and practitioners.

REFERENCES

Burrello, L.C., & Sage, D.D. (1979). *Leadership and change in special education.* Englewood Cliffs, NJ: Prentice Hall.

Sage, D.D., & Burrello, L.C. (1986). *Policy and management in special education.* Englewood Cliffs, NJ: Prentice Hall.

Acknowledgments

We are indebted to a number of people who provided assistance in different ways in the preparation of this, our third joint publication. Dr. Karen Waldron, of Trinity University in San Antonio, Texas, provided us with an opportunity to step into the "New Paradigm of Practice" and to test the validity of our proposals. Dr. Carl Lashley, of the State University of New York at New Paltz, co-authored a series of preliminary papers that led to two of the chapters included here. Pam Wright and Judith Hughes, students at Indiana University, provided feedback on all chapters and especially aided in research for Chapter 7.

to
Doris and Sheila

Leadership in
Educational Reform

Paradigms for Restructuring

A Perspective for Special Education

Writing in a time of dynamic change is difficult. To frame a chronicle of special education leadership and policy issues within a specific time period or perspective is futile. The purpose of this chapter is to describe the evolving context of special education. We begin with a brief introduction to the driving forces of change in our society and their relationship to school restructuring. We define a *paradigm shift* and highlight those aspects of the present shift that have become increasingly important for educators to consider as they reinvent schools. We also explore emerging practices and discourse about the restructuring of public education and identify their implications for students with disabilities and for special services personnel. The specific assumptions, values, and practices underlying the paradigm shift in special education are also presented to flesh out our description of the current and emerging agenda for leaders in education. Throughout this volume, we return to the themes introduced here. In later chapters, we review historical and contemporary contexts to illustrate the leadership and policy choices that are presently available to administrators at the state and local levels. And finally, we describe the future that we envision.

THE CONTEXT OF CHANGE

A *paradigm shift* is a change in the way that people view the world, including the institutional practices in economic, political, and social systems. Paradigms are mental models that we use to put opportunities and problems in perspective. These models determine what information people perceive as relevant and useful in understanding and resolving the discrepancy between their actual situations and their goals. A paradigm shift predicted by Thomas Kuhn (1970) has been chronicled by Barker (1986), Osborne and Gabler (1992), Perelman (1987), Peters (1985, 1987), and Peters and Waterman (1982). These writers suggest that the power of paradigms lies in their ability to influence what we perceive. They are powerful conceptual lenses that filter our individual views of reality. According to Peters (1987), the paradigm shift in education includes changes in perceptions of how people are viewed and valued in organizations, how those organizations are structured (and, in particular, how they are changing from centralized to decentralized semi-autonomous workplaces), and how leadership inspires self-management and continuous improvement fostered by a shared vision for the future. Finally, Barker (1986) concludes that people can and do change their paradigms. In light of new evidence, which generally comes from the fringes of an organization, or from outside of it, people are influenced to adopt new models for viewing the world and their place in it.

In the fields of education and public administration—in contrast with business applications—Kearns and Doyle (1988), Osborne and Gabler (1992) and Perelman (1987) argue that the information-based society of the near future will force administrators to entirely restructure schools—not merely extend the school year or require more credits for graduation. The essential problem, they suggest, is that the hierarchically organized bureaucracy of the public schools has destroyed the trust between administrators, teachers, and the lay public. This trust has instead been replaced by the rules and regulations mandated in federal and state laws. Staff accomplishments are measured only by student performances on objective, standardized state and national tests, reported annually in the media. Branson (1987) has argued that no single factor can ensure high quality and greater productivity in schools. The quick fixes of the past have yielded only limited and temporary results, he argues, because the traditional models of management, organization, resource allocation, and innovation have become outmoded. Conventional fixes are single-variable remedies that often fail to lead to changes in the basic strategies of teaching and learning. Nor do they focus on individualized valued student outcomes. The problem, he continues, is not poor execution or insufficient resources; it is a flawed system design. "Little further improvement can be made in the traditional model of education without fundamental redesign; the productivity function in American schools is near the upper attainable limit of achievement" (Branson, 1987, p. 16).

The search for ways to change the organizational design of public schools has tempted educators and noneducators alike to look to management transformations in Japanese and European private enterprises. Deming's system of total quality management, the prescription being touted in the 1990s, is valuable but limited (National LEADership Network study group on restructured schools, 1993). Perelman (1987) suggests that studying the ways in which private-sector organizations are actually instituting changes in management strategies is more valuable than studying the specific changes being made. Peters (1987) agrees that today there are no longer any excellent companies, that there are only good exemplars of organizations that are value and quality driven, that accept change and uncertainty as constants, and that are engaged in ongoing, continuous improvement. The challenge for educators is to determine which factors within the control of individual school districts create obstacles to productive change and which factors support innovative, cooperative, choice-oriented work contexts for students, teachers, and school leaders.

Advocates for restructuring are meeting resistance as they introduce their plans into the cultures and program regularities of the schools. Central-office and school fiscal managers are resisting school-centered decision making within local school councils that include community participation because it threatens the prerogatives of their power. Multi-age grouping and attempts to eliminate tracking by ability are being resisted by teachers because they threaten traditional practices and by parents because they feel that students with special needs will slow their children down. Instructional innovations like team teaching and cooperative learning are being resisted because they threaten teacher authority and the self-image of the educator (Sarason, 1971, 1982). Professionals bound within their maturing bureaucracy subscribe to a paradigm of schooling that is based on a machanistic, mass-production model.

Changing paradigms of teaching and learning requires a knowledge of which changes are inherently compatible with the local culture, which ones are not, and which ones can, over time and with support, be reinvented to fit evolving norms of practice. Senge (1990) suggests that in addition to engaging in systems-level thinking, faculty members must confront their own shared vision of schooling. He argues that until teachers are given the opportunity to engage in open dialogues about the future while realistically examining the current state of schooling, they will thwart any change. It would be foolish to believe that teachers will adopt any new model of schooling without this dialogue. It is only when we come to understand the strongly held values of members of school faculties and of communities at large that we can begin to understand how to change them. The call for change, Johnson (1990) argues, will command the attention of teachers to the extent that it supports or compromises their current instructional practices. In her study of high school teachers in 16 districts, Johnson found that educators believed that the power to change their workplaces rested not in the hands of state-level policy-makers, but in their local schools and districts—among peers, princi-pals, parents, and district administrators. Reformers who assume a mutability of values are likely to fail. For a change process to begin, there must be creative tension between the current reality and future alternatives. The task for leaders is to create conditions for the school and community debate that lead to a consensus that either reaffirms current reality or suggests a need for change.

Once the difference between the real and the hoped-for is defined and a school community can begin to build a shared vision of what they hope to create, a restructured learning organization can begin to emerge. A learning organization should be founded on principles of personal mastery and every member should find meaning in the com-mon vision of the organization and their place in it (Senge, 1990). Shared visions grow out of new mental models of practice, which in turn are based on a commitment to team learning. If schools are to truly become learning organizations, they must cast off the mistrust common to professional bureaucracy, which is governed by contracts and rules, and move toward becoming an organization bound by a shared vision. Teachers and school leaders must design their own mental models or paradigms of practice using team learning and systems-level thinking and action. They must come to understand that the systems they create, like the ones that they inherited, de-mand constant evaluation and revision to eliminate negative rein-forcing behaviors that may have unintended side effects.

A PARADIGM SHIFT IN EDUCATION

In their chapter on organizing for the future, Burrello and Lashley (1992) describe an educational paradigm shift first proposed by Bur-rello and Gregory (1990). Burrello and Gregory drew from the works of several other researchers (Barker, 1986; Goodlad, 1984; Gregory & Smith, 1987; Kantor, 1989; Kearns & Doyle, 1988; Perelman, 1987; Peters, 1987; Senge, 1990). An outline of this shift is included here to illustrate the set of factors we believe should be considered in any restructuring debate within a school or school district.

A new mental model of schooling might involve the changes pre-sented in Table 1; they are included to illustrate the assumptions and beliefs that show where the creative tension lies between what was or is and what must be. The factors depicted in the paradigm shift need to be considered in relation to one another, not merely as isolated in-terventions. They need to be viewed as interacting elements that sup-

Table 1. The future of schooling

Factor	Was/is	Must become
1. Identity	Schools are defined by their formal structures, rules, roles, functions, and "rational bonds."	Schools are defined by shared purposes, values, and histories.
	Formal structures serve to regulate individual behavior.	Purpose integrates constituent groups into a harmoniously focused community.
2. People	Hierarchical structure is used to control people.	Human resources are continuously reorganized to achieve personal mastery and student lifelong learning goals.
	Specialization of personnel leads to separate programs and fragmentation of expertise and practices.	Staff self-selects to join teams of choice, which increases their responsibility for one another and for the school as a whole.
	Rewards are based on status.	Rewards are based on contributions to team learning.
3. Structure	Communication is top–down and hierarchical, emphasizing a "chain of command."	Functional barriers are removed and communications emphasize participation in a community of peers in pursuit of a common purpose.
	Power relationships are defined by one's place in the hierarchy.	Collegial self-governance is fostered by school-level leaders who support self-managed teams.
	Schools are functionally driven by state and federal mandates and administered bureaucratically, reducing discretion and creativity.	Schools are driven by outcomes, emphasizing discretion, innovation, and flexibility in adjusting to student learning styles and life situations.
4. Leadership and control	Leadership is based on position in the hierarchy.	Leaders develop shared values and beliefs leading to culturally tight and managerially loose organizations.
	Planning is centralized; the agenda is set and resources allocated accordingly.	School leadership is developed in autonomous teams, each led by a teacher.
	Special interest groups operate as political entities serving individual groups' interests.	Leadership includes designing opportunities for growth, serving as a steward and coach in a culture of inclusiveness.
	Control is other-directed.	Control is self-directed and is expected of all staff and students.

(continued)

Table 1. (*continued*)

Factor	Was/is	Must become
	Size of units means that fears of losing control limits program flexibility.	Units are small enough to permit students to be trusted and, consequently, teachers are freed to employ different teaching strategies.
5. Innovation	Motivation to innovate is external, driven by state and federal mandates and initiatives.	Innovation is a response to student needs. Local flexibility encourages risk-taking and entrepreneurship.
	Change is reactive in nature; emphasis is on short-term "fixes."	Change is developmental, and is sustained by shared concerns and a common vision among all stakeholders.
	Change efforts are most often technical in nature, seldom affecting the basic structure of the organization.	Change can be technical in nature, but it can also be cultural, affecting not only the surface structure of the organization, but also its deep structure.
6. Organizing for instruction	A mass training model using four tracks—college prep, vocational, special, and general education addresses minimum requirements within traditional age-based grade levels.	Organizational units are empowered to act autonomously. The focus is on learning.
	Curriculum and instruction are organized around: • the individual's capacity to achieve • competition • teacher-directed lessons • order and conformity • prevention of cheating • dispensing of information, leading to passive learning	Teaching and learning are based on: • the group members' supporting one another to achieve valued ends • cooperation • group sharing of each member's knowledge and skill • trying and helping one another to succeed • sharing • active learning
	Teachers practice their craft in isolation and hold sole responsibility for preparation and student progress. Problem students are referred outside of the main program to specialists and the dropout rate among the disenfranchised is high.	Because the learning community accepts shared responsibility for its students, those failing are a team concern within each program unit.

(*continued*)

Table 1. (*continued*)

Factor	Was/is	Must become
7. Technology	Information processing is centralized and inflexible, and its constraints determine what kinds of information are valued.	Integrated information resources provide access to outside information, breaking the physical and psychological boundaries of the classroom and of the school.
	Access is usually limited to a few specialists; group or lab teaching by computer specialists dominates student use.	Computers and software are flexible, accessible tools integrated into the total educational program.
	Information processing for state and federal reporting and grade and assessment reporting are centralized. Procedures are long-lived despite rapidly changing technical capabilities.	Integrated software and hardware environments enhance communication throughout the organization, as well as facilitating individualized and self-paced instruction for all learners.
8. Financial management and control	Budgeting is a centralized function, and allocation decisions are made in a climate of conflict and competition between administration, teachers' unions, and constituencies concerned about tax rates.	Budgeting is a cooperative function and allocation is planned from the bottom up. Building-level decisions integrate allocation needs and the revenue constituencies in a joint learning-community effort.
9. Marketing the schools	Central determination of student school assignments places a strong onus on the schools to maintain rigid program uniformity, with the private sector being the primary source for alternative programs.	The school is a service provider offering a range of different programs to meet different student needs; students and parents (the consumers) select the service provider from among schools articulating clear purposes for their respective programs with the knowledge that program participation represents a mutual commitment between the consumer and the school.
10. Standards of accountability	Nominal accountability requires meeting state standards, while political accountability is based on the achievement of students and the school's graduation rates and average SAT scores as compared with those of surrounding districts.	Accountability is measured against standards established locally and reflective of the learning community and its constituency's values and goals. Student accountability is individually defined and measured at an individual level for teachers, administrators, board members, and consumers.

port movement toward building a collegial culture for staff and students who are constantly redefining the structure of schools (Little, 1982, Little & McLaughlin 1993).

SPECIAL EDUCATION REFORM

The Regular Education Initiative

Since the 1980s, the field of special education has been characterized by a significant reform effort referred to as the regular education initiative (REI). The prevailing theme of this initiative is a call to encourage greater social and academic integration of students with disabilities by placing them in general education classrooms. Skrtic (1991b) has completed a comprehensive analysis of the professional debate on REI. As special educators examine the paradigm underlying REI, Skrtic (1988) has argued that its "anomalies should lead them to conclude that the end of mass produced schooling and the beginning of an era of respect for and the nurturance of each student as a unique and ultimately valuable individual is at hand" (p. 517). PL 94-142 and the recent Section 504 amendments recognize and respect the uniqueness of the individual. At the same time however, Skrtic (1991b) finds the authors of the law unable to reconcile the conflict between respect for the individual and the reality of schools as groupings of professional or machinistic bureaucracies that are typically in conflict with one another. He contends that the law requires schools to be adhocracies (i.e., problem-solving organizations in which teams of regular and special education professionals collaborate reciprocally in the interests of individual students), . . . something they cannot be without a total reorganization of their fundamental operation. By approaching change as if schools were machine bureaucracies—through new rules and regulations inserted into the existing formalization—PL 94-142 fails to recognize that the existing formalization in school organization is decoupled from the actual work (pp. 170–173).

The net effect of this conflict, coupled with the intent of the law to decrease the stigma attached to disability while promoting integration within the general education classroom, has been to increase the distance between programs, staff, and students. Skrtic (1991b) describes in great detail how the bureaucratic value orientation in schools and the procedural requirements of the law itself have resulted in an increase in the number of students classified as having disabilities, a disintegration of instruction, and a decrease in personalization in both general and special education classrooms. He contends that on the basis of evidence collected to date, there are five assumptions that must be called into question. The first assumption is that students with even mild disabilities, particularly learning disabilities, are pathological. Both advocates and opponents of the REI[1] agree that "a number of definitional and measurement problems, as well as problems related to the will or capacity of teachers and schools to accommodate student diversity, . . . [suggest that] many students identified are not truly disabled" (Skrtic, 1991b, p. 154–155) in an inherent and chronic sense.

The second assumption is that an accurate diagnosis is both possible and useful in educational programming. Skrtic (1991b) contends that diagnosis is unreliable, inconsistent, excessively costly, and of little instructional value, and that it does not result in "objective distinctions, either between the disabled and non-disabled students or among the three mild disability categories" (p. 155).

The third assumption is that special education is a rational and coordinated system of referral, identification, eligibility, individual educational planning, program placement, and reintegration, where appropriate, into the mainstream. While both proponents and opponents of REI agree that the only adequate rationale for special education is that it brings instructional benefits to students with disabilities, most also agree that these benefits have yet to be realized:

> Proponents believe that, given the weak effects of special education instructional practices and the social and psychological costs of labeling, the current system of special education is, at best, no more justifiable than simply permitting most students to remain unidentified in regular classrooms and, at worst, far less justifiable than regular classroom placement in conjunction with appropriate in-class support services. (Skrtic, 1991b, p. 156)

Special education is not a rationally conceived and carefully planned and coordinated system of services. Rather, it evolved through the combined efforts of advocates, parents, and professionals with mutual interests in serving students with disabilities. The general system of education left special educators and parents with little alternative but to create a parallel system with its own rules and regulations.

The fourth assumption is that special education, with the help of technology, is undergoing incremental improvements in diagnostic and instructional practices. Those who favor the REI proposals con-

[1]REI proponents include: Gartner and Lipsky (1987); Pugach and Lilly (1984); Stainback, S., and Stainback, W. (1984, 1987); Stainback, S., Stainback, W., and Forest (1989); Wang, Reynolds, and Walberg (1986, 1987). REI opponents include: Braaten, S.R., Kauffman, Braaten, B., Polsgrove, and Nelson (1988); Bryan, Bay, and Donahue (1988); Council for Children with Behavioral Disorders (1989); Kauffman, Gerber, and Semmel (1988); and Keogh (1988).

tend, "why invest in a flawed system?", while opponents believe that with more research we can develop a better understanding of the manner in which students with disabilities learn.

The fifth assumption underlying the REI debate is that an integrated educational system as codified in PL 94-142 is justified on political grounds. Such a system would allow all students to benefit from targeted resources formerly made available only to students with disabilities. Opponents fear that targeted resources would be lost entirely and that attempts to improve special education services would not be realized in a merged or unified system of education. According to Skrtic, REI opponents believe that:

> although special education is not an instructionally rational system in its current form, it is a politically rational system. This is so, they maintain, because the nonadaptability and political inequality of the general education system makes the pull-out logic of mainstreaming and the targeting function of EHA absolute necessities if designated students are to receive instructional assistance in school, even though the assistance they receive does not appear to be effective. (1991b, p. 156)

But in spite of these difficulties, Skrtic argues that PL 94-142 should not be abandoned—nor should the ideal of a free, appropriate public education in the least restrictive environment (LRE) be compromised. Sarason (1991) concluded that PL 94-142, because it mandates parental veto power, is one of the two most significant changes, along with the growth of teachers' unions, in public education in the last 50 years. Both came about through political action. Both Sarason (1991) and Skrtic (1991b) conclude that schools organized as professional bureaucracies cannot change without significant pressure from the outside. Without the drastic measures mandated by PL 94-142, including parental vetoes, there may not have yet been any change at all in the education of students with disabilities.

Full Inclusion

Like their partners in the REI initiative, special educators concerned with students who require the most extensive services have been calling for increased participation in age-appropriate home-school environments. Sailor (1991) has chronicled the movement from the early 1970s, when a great deal of research was concerned with how and what to teach students with significant or multiple disabilities. In the 1980s, the focus shifted from how and what to teach to *where* to teach, on the ways in which the general education setting affected the social development of these students. Simultaneously, school administrators had started to interpret the LRE provisions of the law in new ways. For the first time, students with multiple disabilities were being considered for placement within the typical classroom as the starting point of programming, rather than being tracked somewhere along the continuum of placements that had existed for the past 4 decades:

> Most recently, the emphasis in the literature pertaining to integration of students with severe disabilities has shifted from a discussion of approaches that exemplify special class models within regular schools, where integration occurs primarily in extraneous school settings such as assemblies, recess, and lunch time involving peer tutors, friendship relationships, etc., to a discussion of "full inclusion" models that exemplify placement of these children in the regular classroom with some program time in other environments, as needed. (Sailor, 1991, p. 9)

The significance and growth of the "full inclusion" movement is demonstrated by the fact that the International Council of Administrators of Special Education, Inc. (CASE) has changed its own position statement since 1989–1990 and five states—Colorado, (McNulty, 1990), Vermont (Williams et al., 1986), Iowa (Hamre-Nietupski, Nietupski, & Maurer, 1990), New Mexico (New Mexico Department of Education, 1991), and Michigan (Michigan Department of Education 1993)—have proclaimed their support for full inclusion as a goal in the education of all students with disabilities. The impetus for an increasing number of state positions on full inclusion has been the position statement issued by the National Association of State Boards of Education, entitled *Winners All* (1992). Several Canadian models of inclusion have also emerged in Ontario and New Brunswick (Forest & Lusthaus, 1989; Porter & Richler, 1991; and Vandercook, York, & Forest, 1989). The reader is also referred to discussions of the inclusion issue in Biklen (1985), Falvey (1989), Forest and Lusthaus (1989), Stainback and Stainback (1990), Stainback et al. (1989), and Thousand and Villa (1989).

According to Sailor (1991), the basic components of a full inclusion model are:

1. All students attend the school to which they would go if they had no disability.
2. A natural proportion (i.e. representative of the school district at large) of students with disabilities occurs at any school site.
3. A zero-rejection philosophy exists so that typically no student would be excluded on the basis of type or extent of disability.
4. Age and grade-appropriate school and general education placements, with no self-contained, special education classes operative at the school site.
5. Significant use of cooperative learning and peer instructional methods in general instructional practice at the school site.

6. Special education supports provided within the context of the general education class and in other integrated environments. (Sailor, 1991, p. 8)

The "common denominator" in these two special education reform efforts lies in the principle of LRE (Sailor, 1991, p. 11). Bauwens, Hourcade, and Friend (1989) add that education reform, both at the policy and programmatic levels, requires statutory and regulatory changes that better reflect a more diverse and vulnerable student population and recognize the need for universal outcomes and for curricular, instructional, and technological improvements.

In summary, what was to have been an impetus for change and an increase in instructional equity and benefits to students with disabilities (PL 94-142), has unintentionally resulted in a system that: 1) encourages labeling and has led to categorical programming; 2) legitimizes exclusion through the preservation of the concept of placement along a continuum from least to most restrictive environment; 3) builds subsystems for managing defects, rather than preventing them; 4) reduces opportunities to achieve valued student outcomes, including acceptance by an age-appropriate peer group, by segregating students based on ability; and 5) allows other forms of discrimination and permits school professionals to treat labeled students in ways that would not otherwise be tolerated.

The net result is an educational system so structured that it is failing more and more students. The predominant pull-out model of instruction within parallel systems for students determined to be at-risk, bilingual students, and students with disabilities requires expanding the mainstream of education to make it inclusive of all students.

RECONSTITUTING THE
MAINSTREAM BY RESTRUCTURING THE SCHOOLS

Restructuring Defined

Since the emergence of research on effective schools in the 1970s, the school as an individual community entity has become the focal point of attempts at organizational change in education. The present focus of restructuring efforts is almost always school based. Most writers and commentators argue that school restructuring cannot be achieved by a simple initiative, but instead must be a series of acts designed to embrace a diversity of learners at the level of the individual school. All agree that restructuring must include changes in the manner in which decisions are made. The process definition of restructuring to which we subscribe includes:

Integrating the work of students with planning, goal setting, and evaluation of student learning
Involving internal and external audiences in clearly defined roles, relationships, and governance structures
Focusing on the actual functions of teaching and learning

It is best to think of restructuring not as a single categorical event, but as having multiple dimensions along a continuum. The single most significant category, however, that most agree must be the first target of change, is the actual function of teaching and learning.

The Wisconsin Center on Restructuring has developed a framework with four arenas comprising a total of 38 criteria that they propose should be placed on a continuum (Newmann, 1991). As each criterion is met, the school moves closer to Newmann's ideal of a fully restructured school. Though students with disabilities were not considered when developing these specific criteria, they do represent points of intersect between general education restructuring efforts and REI and other full-inclusion initiatives. As restructuring efforts proceed, special education administrators need to begin advocating for the use of these criteria. The four arenas of the framework are: 1) student participation in all aspects of school life; 2) professional and daily regularities in the work of teachers; 3) school decision making and governance issues; and 4) the integration and coordination of community human, health, and social resources.

Components and Criteria for
Measuring the Extent of School Restructuring

Student Experiences   Students in restructured schools experience education in very different ways than do students in more traditional schools. The questions below, which are adapted from Newmann (1991), can assist in determining the extent to which restructuring is affecting the experiences of both typical students and those with disabilities:

Is learning time more equally distributed among whole-class instruction, small-group work, and individual study, rather than being dominated by whole-class instruction?
Do students spend most of their time in heterogeneous groups?
Do learning and assessment tasks emphasize student production rather than rote demonstration of knowledge?

To complete their work, do students usually speak and write in full
sentences and continuous sequences rather than in fragments of a
few words?

Do learning tasks aim for depth of understanding rather than broad
exposure?

Do learning tasks emphasize multiple intelligences and multiple
cultures?

Are multiple academic disciplines integrated in the curriculum?

Are schedules for learning flexible, rather than divided into periods of
standard length?

Do students participate in community-based learning?

Do students interact with adult mentors—either teachers or persons
outside the school—in a long-term programmatic way?

Are students assisted by access to extensive use of computer technology in their work?

Do students serve as and have access to peer tutors?

Do students have substantial influence in the planning, conducting,
and evaluation of their work?

If these criteria are met, students in restructured schools spend most
of their time in academic, social, or community settings in heterogeneous groups. Students with disabilities can also participate in
these groups within varying time frames, depending on their own
learning goals. Teachers and staff who recognize and emphasize the
concept of multiple intelligences promoted by Howard Gardner
(1985) increase the range of tasks and activities that students with disabilities can participate in with their more typical peers. Teachers
and staff should recognize and acknowledge the cultural heritage of
members of heterogeneous groups. In these settings, students working in pairs or small cooperative learning groups can learn to appreciate the different abilities of atypical students and the frequency with
which they exceed the expectations that others set for them. As
unique partners, students with disabilities demonstrate their capacity to adjust to various learning situations in spite of their differences.
In these learning settings, typical students discuss work plans with
their teachers and student partners while engaging in self-directed activities. They evaluate their work with the help of teacher and peer
feedback. Students with disabilities likewise need their own production schedules and frequent opportunities to receive feedback on
their performance. Working in cooperative groups also gives students
with disabilities increased opportunities to develop social networks
and natural supports that can carry over to life outside of school and
into adult life.

Professional Life of Teachers The manner in which teachers carry out their work is quite unique in restructured schools. Teachers work in ad hoc or self-selected teams. They are responsible to all the members of the team, including student members. The following questions can assist in determining the extent to which the roles of teachers and staff are being addressed in restructuring efforts:

1. Do teachers function in differentiated roles such as mentoring of novices, directing curriculum development, and supervision of peers?
2. Do all staff function in extended roles with all students that involve advising and mentoring?
3. Do staff help to design on-going, on-the-job staff development based on local needs assessment?
4. Do staff participate in collegial planning, curriculum development and peer observation-reflection, with time scheduled for this during the school day?
5. Do teacher teach in teams?
6. Do teachers exercise control over curriculum and school policy?
7. Are there specific organizational incentives for teachers to experiment and to develop new programs and curriculum that respond more effectively to student diversity?
8. Do teachers work with students in flexible time periods?
9. Do teachers work with students as much in small groups and individual study as in whole class instruction?
10. Do teachers work with parents and human services professionals to meet student needs?
11. Do teachers receive financial rewards based on student outcomes or evaluation of teaching performance? (Newmann, 1991, pp. 8–9)

In restructured schools, all educators are responsible for the education of all students. Teachers teach in teams and move between integrated groups of students. All teachers work with students with disabilities and are given time during the school week to plan and reflect on their practice. Students with more extensive needs may require student support teams to provide wrap-around services in the typical classroom. In addition to weekly operational checks, reflection and evaluation sessions conducted at least once a month are necessary to support team functioning. Organizational incentives for teachers to act collaboratively and engage in new teaching practices come most frequently in the form of release time for technical assistance and training, as well as opportunities to observe others in school and in other settings and to train others in their own or neighboring school districts. From our conversations with both regular and special education teachers, in class and on the job, we have learned that professional development has increased their sense of efficacy. Having more time to work with a diversity of students and seeing marked changes in all students are two of the personal rewards that they derive from team teaching and collaboration.

Leadership, Management, and Governance   This is the topic that many writers on restructuring put first on their lists of categories to consider. Most governance and management issues have a school-site focus, and this category of activities is often referred to as school-centered decision making. Some questions on this subject that should be considered are:

1. Does the school exercise control over budget, staffing and curriculum?
2. Has the school been divided into schools within schools, divisions or houses?
3. Is the school run by a council in which teachers and/or parents have control over budget, staffing and curriculum?
4. Does the school receive financial rewards based on student outcomes?
5. Does the school make program decisions based on systematic analysis of student performance data desegregated by student subgroups (e.g. race, gender, socio-economic status, ethnicity, or disability?)
6. Does the district provide special incentives for the principal to participate in restructuring?
7. Do students enroll in the school by choice rather than residential assignment? (Newmann, 1991, p. 9)

In a restructured school, the principal seeks control over resources for all students, including students with disabilities, assigned to the school. Besides exercising control over funds received for special education and other categorical programs, principals seek the means to integrate staff and to support the application of their expertise to identified student needs. They are also finding that state or district outcome requirements can be met if they and the staff have more to say about the curriculum to be used and the instructional designs to be implemented. Principals foresee a shared responsibility between themselves and the central office on matters of outcomes, accountability systems, strategic plans, and funding. They appreciate the support of the special education administrator in dealing with advocacy groups, ensuring due process for students and their families, interpreting state and federal laws and rules, and reporting to state and federal offices. Principals look for expertise in student assessment and technical assistance with setting expectations and helping staff. When students with disabilities are assigned to local schools, principals and their staff can negotiate for supportive services in a more informed manner if they can rely on the help of the special education administrator. When students with disabilities and their teachers are included in the cohorts or block programs in the school, families can better plan how their children will proceed through the school system and how their child's education will affect his or her participation in all aspects of community life.

Coordination of Community Services This arena concerns parental involvement with community agencies serving students and families. We do not believe that this aspect of the framework goes far enough, however, since it fails to deal with issues of county, city, or state economic development that influence curricular opportunities for students and affect the availability of local resources to provide mentoring and job training. Some relevant questions on this subject are:

1. Does the school have a systematic program for parent involvement in the academic life of students that goes beyond the normal activities of PTO, parent's night, and attendance at extracurricular events?
2. Does the school have formal mechanisms for coordinating with community agencies offering services dealing with child care, drug and alcohol abuse, family disruption, homelessness, sexual abuse, teen pregnancy, crime and delinquency, economic welfare assistance and parental employment and training?
3. Does the school participate in an external mentoring program, such as "I Have a Dream," which follows students for several years?
4. Does the school have formal arrangements with local employers to place students in career-ladder jobs during the school year, summers and following high school graduation?
5. Does the school have formal arrangements with institutions of higher education to assist students in continuing their schooling?
6. Does the school have formal arrangements with institutions of higher education to assist with staff development and curriculum design?
7. Does the school offer adult education programs and recreational opportunities for the community at large? Do they include the disabled graduate? (Newmann, 1991, p. 9)

In restructured schools, parents are invited to be more than just spectators in school affairs if their child has a disability. Creating wider ownership of the schools requires outreach efforts on the part of district- and school-level leadership and staff. As restructuring progresses, parental involvement moves from the level of PTOs and bake sales to the level of shared governance and mentoring in community learning settings. There is mounting pressure for interagency mechanisms that support the full integration of community services. Collaboration among health, social, and criminal justice agencies providing services to students with special needs at the school site is occurring in many more communities. Preparation for post-school employment should also become part of the curriculum for all students. Community-based programs should be available to all students who need an alternative to traditional academic and vocational programs.

Assessing Restructuring Efforts

Newmann (1991) argues that there are certain critical outcomes that should be considered in evaluating the value or worth of any restructuring effort: 1) authentic student achievement, rather than traditional achievement measures; 2) equity issues; 3) the empowerment of students and staff; 4) the creation of learning communities; 5) reflective dialogue; and 6) accountability systems for outcomes.

Authentic Student Achievement In this area, emphasis is placed on "using the mind to produce discourse, material objects and performances that have personal, aesthetic and utilitarian value *during school, living in the school-community as well as adjusting to post school life* [italics added]" (Newmann, 1991, p. 6). This decision to emphasize new basic ends in student achievement using authentic performance measures is in direct contrast to the traditional emphasis on the memorization of facts chosen by local and state authorities. Extensive debate and discussion on what should be taught and how students should be tested leads to decisions on what kind of achievement should be most valued. Surveys of labor and management suggest that the new basics of pre-college education should focus on: 1) learning to learn; 2) creative thinking; 3) problem solving; 4) interpersonal effectiveness and leadership skills that allow one to work within and influence organizations, and teamwork skills; and 5) organizational influence leading to effectiveness and leadership skills. These five skills should be complemented by more traditional outcomes such as self-esteem, personal management, and the traditional "three Rs." Written and oral communication should emphasize listening and adapting individual communication styles to accommodate those of others inside and outside of the work organization.

Equity Equity is the moral principle that continually resurfaces in discussions of restructuring. Equal access to opportunities to participate in schools of choice means more than an admission ticket to the chosen school. It also means providing parents or guardians with full and complete information on options, which will lead to informed decision making. Information may need to be translated. Equity can also mean providing transportation, prerequisite training, or even an elevator for students with physical disabilities. Students with disabilities must be thought of as part of the pluralistic society that includes people of color; a sensitivity to and acknowledgment of gender bias must be developed; and a commitment must be made to include those students from lower-income families and those with limited English skills.

Empowerment   Releasing the power of teachers and students to create and shape their own futures is one of the goals that school leaders are seeking to attain by decentralizing decisionmaking. If teachers are going to make a difference, they will require support and coaching from top and middle management. Empowerment is an enabling factor that can be seen as an end in itself when you consider that the primary purpose of education should be to increase the student's personal ability to make a difference with their life and to take charge of themselves, their interactions with others, and the events that surround them.

Learning Communities   The creation of learning communities is an outcome that many writers emphasize as a key measure of a restructured school. As with empowerment, we see a learning community or a learning organization as both a means or process to be used in restructuring schools and as a desired outcome in itself. Changing schools from clusters of specialized, compartmentalized, isolated units into communities of people who share a commitment to a set of common goals requires diverse strategies to educate a pluralistic populace. In a learning community, each member takes responsibility for the collective life of the school. Learning communities require pursuing "a common agenda of activities through collaborative work that involves stable, personalized contact over a long term" (Newmann, 1991, p. 7). Work becomes a communal activity guided by an ethic of caring, and rewards and recognition are awarded based on the individual's contribution to the community as a whole.

Reflective Dialogue   Reflective dialogue is also a means–ends issue. As a means it is often a vehicle for creating a set of beliefs and building a foundation for new directions. It is a means to check the authenticity of interactions between school and community participants. It is a formative evaluation tool to be used to measure the quality of the ideas generated and their acceptance by the group. Reflective dialogue occurs when participants are recognized as individuals with the right to express themselves in nonthreatening settings in which individuals are stimulated and encouraged to review, critique, and question the context and culture of their schools and communities, as well as their own basic assumptions about living, learning, and teaching. As an end in itself, reflective dialogue is part of learning to learn—the most significant outcome for school personnel to consider, the ultimate goal of their work.

Accountability   This last critical outcome suggests that justification for inputs must be transformed into authentic assessment of the most valued student outcomes—active student engagement in learning, critical and creative thinking, the application of learning to life beyond school, and substantive knowledge about subjects of importance. Accountability also implies a commitment to honoring local values and community standards. It requires regular reporting on student progress and demonstrations of learning such as exhibitions, portfolios, and actual performances. For those students who are most seriously challenged, it means outcomes demonstrated in multiple settings that correspond to post-school life.

Our goal in discussing restructuring in education is to outline the current issues and to raise questions about the place of special education in that discourse. We also want to emphasize that educational restructuring is part of a paradigm shift that is affecting both private- and public-sector activities in economics, government, and the human services. Finally, we want to make the connection between these larger trends and those occurring specifically in special education. We are struck by the similarity between Newmann's criteria and those outlined by advocates involved in special education reform efforts that have, at various times, called for mainstreaming, resource-room programming, part-time integration, REI, and, presently, full inclusion. A number of works illustrate the applicability of Newmann's criteria to students with disabilities and to special education practices, from Dunn's (1968) article questioning the justification for part-time general education placement for students with disabilities, to Thomas Skrtic's (1991a) recent critical examination of evaluation and labeling practices.

Special education has been maturing within a parallel system in which little information is exchanged between those responsible for the education of students with disabilities and those involved in more general school restructuring efforts. In the summer of 1991, the leadership of International CASE, Inc., representing local administrators, and the National Association of State Directors of Special Education (NASDSE), representing state administrators, began to hold dialogues with other professional and lay associations regarding the role of special education personnel in restructuring efforts. These initial efforts must be accelerated and become the basis of a widespread dialogue on national and state policy. Few local school districts have begun to change their practices, to move beyond mere philosophical support for the ideals of inclusion to an actual unified system of education.

Restructuring is a series of multi-level organizational activities designed to increase most students' achievement. Heretofore, little of the discourse on restructuring has included discussion of issues critical to the education of students with disabilities. Likewise, the special education literature is without much discussion of restructuring, yet it is based on a series of research findings generalizable to all of education. Its success is measured on a continuum that includes authentic student performances, equity for all students and personnel, diversity, empowerment, and the creation of effective learning communities. Powerful social forces that arise out of cultural differences, professionalism, and a respect for individual autonomy build significant barriers to consensus-based restructuring initiatives. Local norms must be considered, and new ones created through extensive debate, before widespread support for restructuring can be gained.

BUILDING INCLUSIVE SCHOOL CULTURES: THE SPECIAL EDUCATION PARADIGM SHIFT

While the mandate for the education of students with disabilities in general education settings has been with us since 1975, it is not local policy in most school districts to include students with disabilities in the particular schools that they would attend if they did not have a disability. Even with inclusion policies in place, local action is not always forthcoming. Policy is at best a crude instrument that can curtail, as well as stimulate, changes in the intended direction. For example, school districts have most often interpreted the LRE requirement, not as a mandate to integrate all students into their peer group, but rather as a demand that individual needs be met, usually through professional-service arrangements based on minutes of direct services provided to the student, which are often delivered outside of the general education classroom. The LRE provision has simply been appended to the service delivery system that existed prior to the passage of PL 94-142; it has not changed the frame of reference for educational planning and placement. The existing continuum of possible placements still rests largely on individualized educational planning and segregated services.

These and other factors have been described by Lipp (1992) in the inaugural issue of the *Special Education Leadership Review* published by the CASE, Inc. Lipp's description of the perspective shift offers a summary statement of research and thought in special education and outlines the emerging paradigm. The displays below describe the points of intersect between the special education literature and that on restructuring, organized under 10 factors that Lipp discusses.

LIPP'S PERSPECTIVE SHIFT FOR SPECIAL EDUCATION

POLICY

From an emphasis on	To an emphasis on
Viewing special education exclusively	Viewing special education inclusively
Segregation	Integration
Institutionalization	Deinstitutionalization
Labeling	Functional language

Lipp's perspective shift intersects with the restructuring agenda at the policy level by viewing special and general education as a single merged or unified system rather than as two separate or parallel systems that emphasize the distinctive nature of student pathology, independent of the cultural and social circumstances of schools, their clients, and the community. Lipp suggests that special education should be viewed inclusively. Special educators should participate in the education of *all* children as they support students with disabilities; they should assist general education personnel as those teachers implement curricula and instruction for all students in the school. This perspective intersects directly with the concept that in the reconstituted mainstream, all students can and will learn, regardless of labels and differing abilities. Detracking is a large part of this policy factor and requires each staff member to assume responsibility for all students in the school.

ADMINISTRATION

From an emphasis on	To an emphasis on
Centralization	Decentralization
Teachers' responsibilities	Teachers' rights
Identifying incompetence	Developing competence
Bureaucracy	Child centeredness
Applying pressure	Applying resources
Surrendering responsibility	Participation

Lipp's perspective shift also intersects with the restructuring agenda at the school-site and governance levels. Special education administrators and principals often disagree over the centralization–decentralization issue. Central-office direction and discretion become school-site specific. The perspective shift includes a belief that, while monitoring may remain a central-office function, program development must become more site driven. Students, teachers, and principals should be the primary designers and implementors not only of restructuring efforts, but of more inclusive school cultures.

Lipp (1992) contends that a greater part of the central office leadership's function will be to apply resources to local schools to encourage the promotion of mutual responsibility and participation in order to serve all students equally well. The special education leadership role should move from providing direct services to students to providing more technical assistance to principals and their staffs in the design and implementation of student programming. The centrally based administrator becomes the district negotiator, with individual school-site authority over the resources needed to serve students within the school's attendance area and to ensure that other state and federal requirements are met.

Directing the school and its staff to external resources and services for assessment, to limited programming for select students who cannot be supported locally, and to transition services for students coming from preschool programs and those exiting to the world of work and independent or supported living should become the predominant central-office functions.

IDENTIFICATION, ASSESSMENT, AND PLACEMENT

From an emphasis on	To an emphasis on
The medical model (deviance)	The educational-needs model
Standardized assessment tools	Individualized tools, performance assessment
Reactive assessment and remediation	Proactive assessment, prevention, and intervention

Concerning identification, assessment, and placement, Lipp (1992) argues that a more educationally driven process will evolve to meet the needs of students with disabilities as a part of the unique social-cultural arrangements that students and teachers create together. Student assessment should become functional and "authentic," rather than being used only for purposes of labeling and program placement. Inducting students into special education through a protracted assessment and labeling process should be replaced with assessment designed to prevent labeling and the need for separate service arrangements. Assessment should assist the collaborative teaching team in determining the most effective way to educate the students, based on the desired outcomes. The goal of curriculum-based assessment is to determine how the student functions with his or her age-appropriate peers. If the student's need for a functional curriculum is predominant, then the instructional processes will be implemented only in part in the regular curriculum. Community-based settings outside of the classroom and the school can be used for meeting those outcomes more relevant to post-school life.

CLIENTELE

From an emphasis on	To an emphasis on
Dependence	Independence
Unilingualism (English)	Multilingualism
The dominant culture	Diverse cultures
Predictable and limited needs	Needs over the life span
Homogeneity	Diversity of clients

Demographic reports and the 1990 census emphasize that student diversity is increasing, and that the present homogeneous grouping process fails to meet students' needs equitably and effectively. In addition to the 10%–12% of the nation's children with some recognized form of disability, schools in the cities and those in some rural areas are failing another 30%–40% of their students because they do not achieve the basic competencies necessary for living independently. Viewing learning as a lifelong process filled with uncertainty requires supportive services for all students. In addition, students with disabilities in particular need supportive services beyond school. Preparing students for independent living requires other school-designed learning experiences and socialization activities that give rise to friendships and a social network that students with disabilities need to develop with their peers. Whenever possible, society needs patterns of social networks, rather than public services, to support individuals in need, to ensure productive lives, and to reduce the amount of public funds spent for social services.

CURRICULUM AND INSTRUCTION

From an emphasis on	To an emphasis on
Central design control	Flexibility and local design control
Teacher directedness	Child centeredness
Conformity in learning	Diversity of learning styles
Education only for those who could "make the grade"	Education for all (zero reject)

From an emphasis on	To an emphasis on
One curriculum for all	Individualized curricula
Monitoring of process	Monitoring of outcomes
Academic learning	Developing habits and attitudes
Access to facilities	Access to quality programs
Individual teachers taking responsibility	Collaborative teams taking responsibility for *all* students

The curriculum and instruction factors are key elements in the restructuring process. We believe the shift from offering a standard curriculum and content organized by subject matter to centering the planning process around a set of desired learning outcomes will make teaching a more exciting enterprise. Teachers and students working together can develop a number of alternatives to instruction that neither could develop alone. Locally chosen outcomes can benefit an increasingly diverse population and accommodate multiple intelligences. Gardner (1985) argues that curricula and instruction need to address the development of each intelligence. From the new perspective, special educators teach within the typical classroom and share responsibility for the education of students with disabilities with the teacher of record. Collaborative planning for all students precedes teaching, and ongoing reflection and evaluation serve as the means of self and team improvement. Our attention now shifts to quality education for all students, rather than access to segregated programs and services for students with disabilities.

SUPPORT SERVICES

From an emphasis on	To an emphasis on
Federal supports	Local supports
Minimal technology	Maximum use of technology
Student-focused resources	Trainer-focused resources

In the area of support services, we do not believe that Lipp's shift goes far enough in emphasizing locally designed and more diverse systems of choices that schools can offer in the future. Popular options include curriculum-based, rather than individually based, classroom assessment, case consultation, collaborative teaching, peer learning, and specific instructional and technologically relevant large- and small-group instructional arrangements. These staff-development enhancements must occur in an integrated context of mutual responsibility and accountability in order to ensure that each student is learning. The net effect of supportive services will be primarily the trainer-mediated and cooperatively implemented instruction of heterogeneous groups of students. Resources would change from being solely student focused to being often devoted to trainer mediation of instruction.

FUNDING

From an emphasis on	To an emphasis on
Dollars per pupil	Dollars per program
Individuals	Blocks of students
Flexible accounting	Tight accounting
Financial battles won at the national level	Battles won at the local level

Lipp's perspective on funding intersects with the restructuring agenda and the school-based change movement. We have been arguing recently within the national policy debate that school districts now have an adequate base of historical data on who has been served. These data haven't changed significantly from year to year in many districts, which should make it feasible to change from an individually based formula to a block formula and thereby reduce district administration preoccupation with head counts and assessments conducted for purposes of revenue generation. A district program administrator will negotiate resource distribution with individual schools as they take responsibility for the full spectrum of students. District leaders will engage in site-by-site negotiations for individual programs for various groups of students. Tight accountability for resources will become a shared responsibility between the district and individual schools. After a few years, stability will emerge and any further changes will be accommodated much more efficiently. District monitoring and reporting to state and federal agencies will continue to ensure equity and accountability for resources that are assigned for the purpose of achieving specific student outcomes.

TEACHER TRAINING

From an emphasis on	To an emphasis on
Specialists trained to teach the exceptional child	Training all teachers to educate the exceptional child within the reconstituted mainstream

We believe that Lipps' view of teacher training is clearly stated and accurate. Certain specialized graduate training will continue to be available in areas such as speech and hearing and visual impairment. The challenge begins with the change to an inclusive school, one where all staff share responsibility for serving all students. Therefore, special education support is primarily designed to increase the capacity of school faculty to serve a diversity of students more effectively. The specialized training might be primarily at the master's level and would focus on methods for embedding specialized instruction into the regular class context.

ADVOCACY

From an emphasis on	To an emphasis on
Locating and securing services	Monitoring services
Acceptance of tokenism	Knowledge of rights
Support during school	Support for transitions
Individual students	Individual programs

Advocacy will continue unabated, but the primary function of special education advocates in the future will be creating new methods and systems for monitoring services and helping colleagues in a merged system of education to remember their responsibilities and garner the resources needed to attend to each individual student.

INTERAGENCY LIAISON

From an emphasis on	To an emphasis on
Disassociation from education	Interagency collaboration
Surrendering students to others	Working collaboratively
Segmented services	Integrated, school-based services

Finally, the interagency issue has emerged primarily through Comer's (1980) work at Yale on the integration of community-based services at the school level. Beyond collaboration, the repositioning of human services (including health and economic assistance, in addition to education), will become a part of future service delivery models. Therefore, the family constellation and peer group, rather than just the student him- or herself, will become the focus of integrated service programs. Youth initiatives to combat poverty and crime in the suburbs, as well as the cities, require new ways of thinking about family and child development.

LEADERSHIP CHOICES AND POLICY OPTIONS

Leadership and policy choices and options are closely related, and they are the primary subject of the remainder of this book.

The rapidity of technological change and a failure to invest heavily enough in education create a large gap between what students and teachers do in schools and what awaits students in the real world of work and adult responsibility. The call for choice in public schools, changing state regulations, district- and building-level administrative and teacher-leadership shortages, limited resource growth and a limited base of school support, a labor–management bargaining mentality, and the debate surrounding organizational restructuring are some of the many factors that illustrate the extent to which schools are over-regulated and over-managed. Unfortunately, they are also under-led.

Bringing about the changes that will support inclusion in schools requires district leaders with a vision that allows them to create policy that supports a shared culture. School-based leaders who support inclusion must emphasize teamwork and encourage critical inquiry so that members of the school community work collaboratively to examine and come to understand their roles and purposes.

The primary task of the leadership team committed to inclusion is to build a joint model for the individual school, a way of seeing the patterns, relationships, and linkages between one another and between their shared values and purposes. When leaders articulate this vision, they are inductively determining a direction for the school organization. This is a very different function from planning. Planning is a management process, deductive in nature and designed to produce orderly results. The leadership in a district or a school must examine information and be continuously aware of the paradigms that influence the way that they select data, test their decisions against the beliefs articulated in their vision, and assess the results of their policies.

Leaders must set the direction for the school organization; it should be left to managers to plan and budget. Leaders inspire the people who make up the organization with a vision for the future, while managers staff and organize. Leaders motivate people and foster a community of learners, while managers implement and problem solve. Leaders create a shared culture that challenges staff and students to take responsibility for their own learning and to assist in modeling the educational practices best suited to a democracy.

A district or school vision grows out of the engagement of key constituents in a process of generating belief and reaching consensus. Visions of inclusive schools emerge from tough debate and analysis of the beliefs that school stakeholders have about human potential and about the role of education in reaching it. The vision need not be original, but it must have meaning for the stakeholders in the community. How the vision is translated into a set of competitive strategies to achieve targeted goals and objectives is closely related to the sense of ownership among staff, students, and parents in the school community. Inadequate visions fail to address the legitimate needs and rights of important constituencies.

The second key is creating local policy that supports a shared culture of inclusiveness. This culture requires a set of beliefs embedded in the shared vision. We believe that the following are key beliefs necessary to support a culture of inclusiveness and that they suggest a set of policy options to be pursued:

Everyone in the school is responsible for the education of each student residing in the school's attendance area, regardless of their learning needs.

Everyone in the school should be focused on meeting the needs of all students in a unified system of education. Labeling and segregation of students are counterproductive to educational excellence.

All educators have skills and knowledge that should be used to support the efforts of all other teachers.

All students benefit from participation in inclusive classrooms and schools. Students themselves are the best teachers and role models for individuals with significant learning needs.

The prevention of learning problems is the proper province of special education.

Assessment of students' needs is a regular part of curricular and instructional planning for all teachers and related services personnel.

Special education and related service personnel should serve as full members of teacher teams under the leadership of the school principal.

Special education and related services personnel should provide services to students within the context of the general school program.

Funding and budgeting should allow for the provision of services to students with special needs in the home school and local community.

Community-based human services for children should be coordinated at the school.
Evaluation of the effectiveness of a school's program should include
consideration of the post-school adjustment of students with special needs.

Developing teamwork is the third key leadership role necessary
to develop an integrated delivery system. The interdependence of a
restructured school requires ongoing communication and deliberation between the district leadership, the community, and individual
school members. Anyone who can block or help implement the vision for the district or the school is relevant to the process. Teamwork
is required to help individual teachers meet the needs of the increasingly challenging youngsters entering our schools today. Preparation
and support of colleagues is fundamental to the success of teaching in
the restructured school. Regular planning and preparation for teams
and individuals requires time for accomplishing the necessary integration of the curriculum and instructional grouping and delivery,
and for sharing ongoing evaluations of student progress. Cooperative
learning also requires student participation in planning. Peers are
critical participants in planning for socialization and tutoring, particularly when students with disabilities are fully integrated.

Being a contributing team member is a skill that must be
learned. Sharing expertise, knowledge, and territory are new experiences for many educators. The credibility of the team leader is crucial
to establishing teams with shared leadership. Restructuring for inclusion requires many teacher leaders to assume responsibility for assisting their colleagues to plan and participate in the management of
a more complex and interdependent school population. Shared leadership requires trust and integrity in addition to a worthy and clear
message from school leadership and the community. It also requires
leaders to "walk it like they talk it." It gives the staff license to take
risks and experiment without fear—to embrace error as a means of
learning and to accept, as Michael (1973) suggests, the inevitable conflict that comes with making choices in a pluralistic society.

The leaders in the new organization need to stress the role of informal peer exchange within and between teaching teams. The great
demands of coordinated action give rise to multiple channels of communication that accompany team planning before, during, and after
school. Multiple channels build a foundation of trust between colleagues and encourage accommodation and adaptation to changing
learner conditions and needs. When conflicts arise between generalists' and specialists' functions, relationships built on trust help to resolve them.

The final leadership task in developing restructured, inclusive schools is encouraging a culture of critical inquiry that questions the unequal access of children to the resources of society and encourages constant reflection about the practice of education. We believe that this end can be achieved by changing the rules regarding who is in charge of education and schools and the manner in which the business of teaching and learning is conducted (DeGeus, 1988). Engagement among staff and students must be geared toward satisfying basic human needs for affiliation. Members of the school community must be encouraged to develop a sense of ownership of the school and they must come to realize that by simply living up to their ideals, they will be elevated as team members and as members of the human community. These feelings of community and achievement touch individuals deeply and elicit powerful responses.

Foster (1986) has written that the nature of worker participation in school organizations has remained unchanged since the 1880s. He proposes an organizational model that he calls a community of democracy, in which teachers help administrators manage the complexity of school organization. He describes a literary metaphor for structuring and administering an educational enterprise:

> A literary model suggests that we might better understand administration of schools as texts to be written, rather than as social structures needing scientific delineation and definition. A text being written is in a continual process of transformation; it changes according to local character, circumstances, and cultures. Like a novel, whose form is universal but whose content is individual, a school represents a given purpose accomplished through many narratives. (Foster, 1986, p. 201)

Bennis and Nanus (1985) write that leadership is the ability to reach into the souls of others in a fashion that raises human consciousness, builds meanings, and inspires resolve. Organizations transform themselves through shared leadership and peer networks that derive their power from the ability to create structures that facilitate organizational learning, structures that celebrate the talent and successes that a diversity of people bring to the teaching and learning process.

The education of students with disabilities brings Bennis and Nanus's challenge to bear on the public schools. Responding to the needs of those students who are most difficult to teach gives teachers and administrators the opportunity to bring new focus, new technology, new working relationships, and a new spirit of interdependence to the process of education.

Someone once said that we had better think a lot about the future, since we are going to live the rest of our lives there. The future will require each of us to be a learner and to express our own uniqueness. Fostering a sense of purpose and belonging among students and teachers alike will require that we create new schools that support this outcome. We believe it can be done; we believe our future depends on it.

CONCLUDING COMMENTS

What, then, is the special education or specialized services leadership role in restructuring? We think that the list below serves as a summary:

Know what it means to restructure.

Know who holds what beliefs about possible changes.

Create a vision for the school that fits into the whole educational enterprise.

Design the system such that all educators take responsibility for all student learning and insist on a commitment to ensuring that all students will learn.

Develop a critical mass of specialized staff who want to change the paradigm from that of a parallel system to that of a merged system.

Allow sufficient time for the restructuring to begin to yield benefits; protect innovation from premature assessment.

Be prepared from the beginning to modify practice to fit local circumstances, and insist on regular opportunities for reflection on implementation.

Finally, remember that attitudes and behavior change only through the actual problemsolving that accompanies the implementation of inclusive school practices.

REFERENCES

Barker, J. (1986). *Discovering the future: The business of paradigms* [videotape]. Burnsville, MN: The Charthouse Corporation.

Bauwens, J., Hourcade, J., & Friend, M. (1989). Cooperative teaching: A model for general and special education integration. *Remedial and Special Education, 10,* 17–22.

Bennis, W., & Nanus, B. (1985). *Leaders.* San Francisco: Jossey-Bass.

Biklen, D. (1985). *Achieving the complete school: Strategies for effective mainstreaming.* New York: Columbia University Press.

Braaten, S.R., Kauffman, J.M., Braaten, B., Polsgrove, L., & Nelson, C.M. (1988). The regular education initiative: Patent medicine for behavioral disorders. *Exceptional Children, 55*(1), 21–27.

Branson, R. (1987). Why the schools can't improve: The upward limit hypothesis. *Journal of Instructional Development, 10*(4), 15–26.

Bryan, T., Bay, M., & Donahue, M. (1988). Implications of the learning disabilities definition for the regular education initiative. *Journal of Learning Disabilities, 21*(1), 23–28.

Burrello, L., & Gregory, T.A. (1990). Paradigm shift: School turned upside down. In K. Waldron, A. Riester, & J. Moore (Eds.), *Special education: The challenge of the future* (pp. 88–93). San Francisco: Edwin Mellen Press.

Burrello, L., & Lashley, C. (1992). On organizing the future: The destiny of special education. In K. Waldron, A. Riester, & J. Moore (Eds.), *Special education: The challenge of the future* (pp. 64–95). San Francisco: Edwin Mellen Press.

Comer, J. (1980). *School power: The implications of an invention project.* New York: Free Press.

Council for Children with Behavioral Disorders. (1989). Position statement on the regular education initiative. *Behavioral Disorders, 14,* 201–208.

DeGeus, A. (1988). Planning as learning. *Harvard Business Review, 67*(2), 70–74.

Dunn, L.M. (1968). Special education for the mildly retarded—Is much of it justifiable? *Exceptional Children, 35*(1), 5–22.

Education for All Handicapped Children Act of 1975, PL 94-142. (August 23, 1977). Title 20, U.S.C., 1401 et seq: *U.S. Statutes at Large, 89,* 773–796.

Falvey, M.A. (1989). *Community-based curriculum: Instructional strategies for students with severe handicaps* (2nd ed.). Baltimore: Paul H. Brookes Publishing Co.

Forest, M., & Lusthaus, E. (1989). Promoting educational equality for all students: Circles and maps. In W. Stainback, S. Stainback, & M. Forest (Eds.), *Educating all students in the mainstream of regular education* (pp. 43–57). Baltimore: Paul H. Brookes Publishing Co.

Foster, W. (1986). *Paradigms and promises.* Buffalo: Prometheus Books.

Gardner, H.J. (1985). *Frames of mind: The theory of multiple intelligences.* New York: Basic Books.

Gartner, A., & Lipsky, D.K. (1987). Beyond special education: Toward a quality system for all students. *Harvard Education Review, 57*(4), 367–395.

Goodlad, J.I. (1984). A place called school: *Prospects for the future.* New York: McGraw-Hill.

Gregory, T., & Smith, G. (1987). *High schools as communities: The small school reconsidered.* Bloomington, Indiana: Phi Delta Kappan.

Hamre-Nietupski, S., Nietupski, J., & Maurer, S. (1990). A comprehensive state education agency plan to promote the integration of students with moderate/severe handicaps. *Journal of The Association for Persons with Severe Handicaps, 15,* 106–113.

Johnson, S.M. (1990). *Teachers at work: Achieving success in our schools.* New York: Basic Books.

Kantor, R.M. (1989). The new managerial work. *Harvard Business Review, 68*(6), 85–92.

Kauffman, J.M., Gerber, M.M., & Semmel, M.I. (1988). Arguable assumptions underlying regular education initiative, *Journal of Learning, 21*(1), 6–11.

Kauffman, J.M. (1988). Revolution can also mean returning to the starting point: Will school psychology help special education complete the circuit? *School Psychology Review, 17,* 490–494.

Kearns, D., & Doyle, D. (1988). *Winning the brain race.* San Francisco: Jossey-Bass.

Keogh, B.K. (1988). Improving services for problem learners: Rethinking and restructuring. *Journal of Learning Disabilities, 21*(1), 19–22.

Kuhn, T. (1970). *The structure of scientific revolutions* (2nd ed.). Chicago: University of Chicago Press.

Lipp, M. (1992). An emerging perspective on special education: A development agenda for the 1990s. *The Special Education Leadership Review, 1*(1), 10–39.

Little, J.W. (1982). Norms of collegiality and experimentation: Workplace conditions of school success. *American Educational Research Journal, 19*, 325–340.

Little, J.W., & McLaughlin, M. (1993). *Teachers' work: Individuals, colleagues and context.* New York: Teachers College Press.

McNulty, B.A. (Producer). (1990). *Learning together* [videotape]. Denver: Colorado Department of Education.

Michael, D. (1973). *Learning to plan and planning to learn.* San Francisco: Jossey-Bass.

Michigan Department of Education. (1993). *Findings and recommendations: The final report of the inclusive education recommendation committee.* Lansing, MI: Author.

National Association of State Boards of Education. (1992). *Winners all: A call for inclusive schools* (Report of the NASBE study group on special education). Alexandria, Virginia: Author.

National LEADership Network study group on restructuring schools. (1993). *Total quality management: The leader's odyssey.* Washington, DC: U.S. Department of Education Office of Research and Improvement.

New Mexico State Department of Education. (1991). *Position statement on inclusion.* Albuquerque, NM: Author.

Newmann, F.M. (1991). What is a restructured school? A framework to clarify means and ends. *Issues in restructuring schools: Issue report #1*, p. 3–13, 16. Madison, WI: Center on organization and restructuring of schools.

Osborne, D., & Gabler, T. (1992). *Reinventing government.* Reading, MA: Addison Wesley.

Perelman, L. (1987). *Technology and the transformation of schools.* Washington, DC: National School Boards Association.

Peters, T. (1985). *Passion for excellence: The leadership difference.* New York: Warner Books.

Peters, T. (1987). *Thriving on chaos.* New York: Random House.

Peters, T., & Waterman, R. (1982). *In search of excellence.* New York: Harper & Row.

Porter, G., & Richler, D. (1991). *Changing Canadian schools: Perspectives on disabilities and inclusion.* Toronto, Ontario, Canada: The Roeher Institute.

Pugach, M., & Lilly, M.S. (1984). Reconceptualizing support services for classroom teachers: Implications for teacher education. *Journal of Teacher Education, 35*(5), 48–55.

Sailor, W. (1991). Special education in the restructured school. *Remedial and Special Education, 12*(6), 8–22.

Sarason, S.B. (1990). *The predictable failure of school reform.* San Francisco: Jossey-Bass.

Sarason, S.B. (1971). *The culture of the school and the problem of change.* Boston: Allyn & Bacon.

Sarason, S.B. (1982). *The culture of the school and the problem of change* (rev. ed.). Boston: Allyn & Bacon.

Sarason, S.B. (1991). *The predictable failure of school reform.* San Francisco: Jossey-Bass.

Senge, P. (1990). *The fifth discipline: The art and practice of the learning organization.* New York: Doubleday.

Skrtic, T.M. (1988). The organizational context of special education. In E.L. Meyen & T.M. Skrtic (Eds.), *Exceptional children and youth: An introduction* (pp. 479–517). Denver: Love Publishing.

Skrtic, T.M. (1991a). Behind special education: *A critical analysis of professional knowledge and school organization.* Denver: Love Publishing.

Skrtic, T.M. (1991b). The special education paradox: Equity as the way to excellence. *Harvard Educational Review, 61*(2), 148–205.

Stainback, S., & Stainback, W. (1984). A rationale for the merger of special and regular education. *Exceptional Children, 51*(2), 102–111.

Stainback, S., & Stainback, W. (1987). Integration versus cooperation: A commentary on "Educating children with learning problems: A shared responsibility." *Exceptional Children, 54*(1), 66–68.

Stainback, S., & Stainback, W., & Forest, M. (Eds.). (1989). *Educating all students in the mainstream of regular education.* Baltimore: Paul H. Brookes Publishing Co.

Stainback, W., & Stainback, S. (Eds.). (1990). *Support networks for inclusive schooling: Interdependent integrated education.* Baltimore: Paul H. Brookes Publishing Co.

Thousand, J.S., & Villa, R.A. (1989). Enhancing success in heterogeneous schools. In S. Stainback, W. Stainback, & M. Forest (Eds.), *Educating all students in the mainstream of regular education* (pp. 89–104). Baltimore: Paul H. Brookes Publishing Co.

Vandercook, T., York, J., & Forest, M. (1989). The McGill Action Planning System (MAPS): A strategy for building the vision. *Journal of The Association for Persons with Severe Handicaps, 14,* 205–215.

Wang, M.C., Reynolds, M.C., & Walberg, H.J. (1986). Rethinking special education. *Educational Leadership, 44*(1), 26–31.

Wang, M.C., Reynolds, M.C., & Walberg, H.J. (1987, October). *Repairing the second system for students with special needs.* Paper presented at the Wingspread Conference on the Education of Children with Special Needs: Growing Up To Meet the Challenges of the 1990s, Racine, Wisconsin.

Williams, W., Fox, W., Christie, L., Thousand, J., Conn-Powers, M., Carmichael, L., Vogelsberg, R.T., & Hull, M. (1986). Community integration in Vermont. *Journal of The Association for Persons with Severe Handicaps, 11,* 294–299.

2

The Scope of Special Education

Mapping the Territory

When discussing any aspect of society, the first task is to establish the subject matter's parameters and to define the relevant terms. In the case of special education, this task can be especially complex because the term itself is somewhat ambiguous and the parameters are everchanging. A variety of sources must be consulted as we arrive at these determinations, which have important consequences for all of the policy questions that follow.

FACTORS THAT DETERMINE THE SCOPE OF SPECIAL EDUCATION

The scope of special education in any given time and place is determined by at least six factors: 1) terminology, 2) philosophical beliefs, 3) history, 4) local tradition, 5) legal foundations, and 6) fiscal constraints. The ways in which these factors interact to determine the boundaries of "the territory" are discussed below.

Terminology

To most educators and informed laypersons the term *special education* seems to communicate a limited activity or domain within the general educational environment that is specifically concerned with students who have disabilities. Among such observers, long-established terminology would allow the use of *handicapped education* as a synonym for *special education.*

However, the terms *disability* and *handicapped* can communicate quite different meanings. Social psychologists have for some time emphasized that a disability is a matter of objective fact, whereas the term *handicap* implies an additional attitudinal supposition about the effect of an actual or perceived status on the individual's life as viewed by him- or herself or by others. The point has been made that a disability may become a handicap primarily as a function of how people perceive it. In discussing the concept of *handicapism*—the stereotyping, prejudice, and discrimination practiced by society against people with disabilities—Biklen and Bogdan (1977) quote one activist as saying "Our bodies make us disabled, but society makes us handicapped" (p. 4). They argue further that some of the negative loading of terminology that leads to the social phenomenon of *handicapism* can be reduced by using the term *disabled* rather than *handicapped* in referring to individuals with such conditions.

An increasing recognition of this important distinction between terms during the past decade is illustrated by the number of formal changes in the language used in legislation and by official agencies concerned with special education. In amending the Education of the Handicapped Act (EHA), PL 101-476, signed October 30, 1990, changed the original title to the Individuals with Disabilities Education Act (IDEA). In addition, the language throughout the law was modified to shift the emphasis from the disability to the child him- or herself by substituting "children with disabilities" wherever "handicapped child" had appeared. The contrast can best be observed by comparing the text dealing with the definition of the targeted clientele of special education as it was written in 1975 in PL 94-142 to the wording in 1990 in PL 101-476:

PL 94-142: (1) The term "handicapped children" means mentally retarded, hard of hearing, deaf, speech impaired, visually handicapped, seriously emotionally disturbed, orthopedically impaired, or other health impaired children, or children with specific learning disabilities, who by reason thereof require special education and related services.
PL 101-476: (1)(A) The term "children with disabilities" means children—(i) with mental retardation, hearing impairments including deafness, speech or language impairments, visual impairments including blindness, serious emotional disturbance, orthopedic impairments, autism, traumatic brain injury, other health impairments, or specific learning disabilities; and (ii) who, by reason thereof, need special education and related services.

It should be noted that in addition to the subtle semantic shift, two previously unmentioned types of conditions (autism and traumatic brain injury) are given specific attention; the significance of these additions is discussed in another section of this chapter.

Individual states, in keeping with this semantic shift, have in many cases amended laws and regulatory language accordingly. A decade prior to the changes outlined above, a change in titles that reflected a sensitivity to language could be seen in the change of the name of the *Bureau of Education for the Handicapped* to the *Office of Special Education Programs.*

The term *exceptional education* may also be used, with the conscious or unconscious connotation that the parameters include students who are at variance from the norm, or exceptional, in dimensions that would include mentally gifted and talented students as well as those with disabilities. Recognition of the additional territory that such a definition encompasses has been incorporated into law in certain jurisdictions and is discussed later in this chapter and again in Chapter 3. The phrase *student with special needs* is also sometimes substituted for *exceptional* in designating a child who requires educational services beyond the ordinary. However, in certain jurisdictions (New York State, for example), this apparently does not suffice, because a specific legal classification—*pupils with special educational needs* (PSEN)—has been established to authorize services different from those provided for *pupils with handicapping conditions* (PHC), and only the latter classification falls administratively within the realm of special education. It should also be noted that the latter term was changed by New York legislation in 1992 to *pupils with disabilities* (PD).

It is not entirely clear in some instances whether the fact that certain terms were in common usage resulted in their being written into the law, or, conversely, the terms were adopted because of the legislation. However, there is little question that the use of the term *exceptional children* has gained prominence not only because of its objective accuracy (if we do wish to encompass individual variance in dimensions other than disability) but also because the term carries more positive connotations than the term *handicapped.* However, the use of the term *handicapped* has traditionally been an important factor when the passage of supportive legislation and the receipt of funding has depended on gaining sympathy from lawmakers and their taxpaying constituents.

Another aspect of terminology comes into play when drawing a distinction between *special education* and *special services.* Although it is hard to find an objective reason for the distinction, the former term has usually been reserved for those activities that have a distinctly instructional emphasis and are provided specifically for students with disabilities, and the latter term for those supportive or ancillary functions necessary to the operation of educational programs for *all* students (including those receiving special education), such as medical, psychological, social work, and counseling services. However, the boundary between these functions has always been ambiguous, and as regulations have led to a call for more supportive services, the inclusion of such services within the domain of what had been considered special education is understandably more prevalent. The question of whether special services are a part of special education or vice versa has implications that are more than semantic. The impact of these considerations is discussed in Chapter 5.

Philosophical Beliefs

Another important factor in determining the scope of special education is simply people's propensity to classify and compartmentalize. Schools, as a reflection of the larger society, have always ranked, graded, and segregated groups of students in whatever manner best serves these organizations' objectives. The degree of segregation may vary from certain students' being placed in a particular reading group to other childrens' total exclusion from school. The decisions concerning what degree of variance warrants a particular degree of compartmentalization are based on prevailing beliefs regarding the range of differences that can be tolerated in a particular setting. This *ecological perspective* on human variance and on the identification and treatment of students has been discussed as part of a broadly encompassing and unifying theory for special education (Apter & Conoley, 1984). The parameters of special education are likely to vary as a complex function of the amount of pupil variance in a community and that community's tolerance for heterogeneity. While the degree of intercommunity variation is largely constrained by the increased universality of laws, regulations, and normative practice, it is clear from incidence reports on pupils served under traditional special education that each state and local jurisdiction has its own norms for classification and placement. Socioeconomic and other cultural factors also have an effect, despite similarities in definitional terms and categories.

At the extremes of human variance, the effect of philosophical belief is relatively stable and consistent. Children with unambiguously severe disabilities who clearly need extraordinary instructional procedures have been classified without question as belonging in special education settings. Services for children who are deaf or blind, for example, are universally perceived as being a part of the special education continuum, regardless of where the services are delivered. Students whose needs fall in the margins, however, may be classified and served quite differently from one jurisdiction to another. Students with subaverage reading skills, for example, may or may not be considered eligible for special education services, depending on prevailing attitudes concerning acceptable degrees of variance. Services for students with speech impairments also fall within this gray area.

Statistical factors must also be considered. It is generally believed that special education is concerned with a minority population. But what is the "tipping point" at which a minority condition becomes sufficiently common that it is no longer considered extraordinary? The common cold, though a significant condition calling for treatment, does not arouse particular concern in our society. Racial status, however, will be seen as a minority condition even in urban areas where African American students exceed 90% of the total school population. In the case of disabling conditions, there has been little question when the incidence of students so classified has ranged from 5% to 10% of the school population. But some proponents of services for children with learning disabilities or emotional disturbance have suggested that pupils with such conditions may exceed 20% of the total school population. Understandably, such claims raise questions as to the boundaries of the special education domain. While fiscal and organizational, as well as social and cultural issues must be considered, a single basic conceptual and philosophical question may override these: how much of the territory of the educational system can special education encompass while still remaining *special*?

History

Policies concerning the scope of special education have been products of evolution. Most scholars who have reviewed this history cite:

> massive neglect, denial, and rejection. For every Helen Keller and the other notable few who received intensive special help, tens of thousands of other exceptional children, both gifted and handicapped, were doomed to constricted lives. . . . In a sense, the development of special education can be recounted as an assault on this discriminatory attitude. (Reynolds & Birch, 1982, p. 18)

The clientele during the early history of special education included only those with obvious impairments, mental and sensory, and the organizational center of service was the residential school, whether publicly or privately supported. While this model remains prevalent in today's service system, it has been far exceeded by the many others initiated throughout the twentieth century to accommodate an increasingly wide variety of individuals. The shift during the twentieth century from a focus on residential schools to one on community-based special schools, and later to special classes within regular schools, and finally to service delivery models that permit students to remain physically present in and primarily identified with hetero-geneous classes and education, has led the field to its present con-frontation with the idea of total inclusion. The scope of special edu-cation at any point in time, then, must be viewed within the context of the accumulated history of the field as a whole, and it must be rec-ognized that the universal pressures of common attitudes and events have a broad impact.

Local Tradition

In spite of mass communication and standardization throughout so-ciety, education retains its deep roots in the doctrine of local control. While much of what constitutes the educational system reveals the force of ideas diffused throughout the culture, certain aspects of the total educational enterprise, until very recently, were optional. The shape of the particular school system's developments in special edu-cation were sometimes, therefore, the result of local idiosyncrasies. The influence of a particular family whose child demonstrated a spe-cial need, of an organization of parents with a common interest who became vigorously assertive, of a professional educator who had a par-ticular idea combined with the necessary leadership skills to put it into practice, or any of a number of other factors may have acted to create a local slant on the scope of special education. In fact, differ-ences in the status and scope of special education in a certain school system or an entire state can in some instances be traced to the efforts of a single charismatic individual.

Legal Foundations

The formalization of the parameters of special education into law is the end result of the preceding factors of definitional terminology, philosophical beliefs, history, and local traditions. Actions of the courts or legislatures are to a large degree a reflection of what society is ready to accept and stand behind. While those who make laws may sometimes lead the rest of the community to a new understanding of the common good, they must lead from a position that is not too far ahead of the majority. Legal foundations are the official codification of the approximate will of the people.

The legal foundations for day-to-day local practice, whether they have their basis in court rulings, state or federal legislative acts, or administrative regulations, are focused on delineating *who* falls within the domain of special education, *what services* are authorized or mandated, and through *what procedures* these services will be managed. In Chapter 3 we discuss in detail each of the sources of legal control. Here, it is enough to indicate that understanding the legal base is a prerequisite to mapping the territory of special education.

Fiscal Constraints

Financial considerations are always interacting with the other aspects of policy and practice, and the gap between the ideal and the actual is usually a function of perceived fiscal limitations. While the courts tend to be able to view issues in terms of what is just, irrespective of costs, legislators and executive agencies must invariably consider the financial implications of any policy. Most statutes include built-in price tags that have a major influence on their introduction and chances of passage, and even after passage, the realization of the intent of the statute and of the regulations designed to implement it is to a large extent determined by financial factors. The definition of a population to be served or the nature of the intended service will often be shaped, sometimes dramatically, by the fiscal gain or loss to be achieved by an administrative decision. Specific examples of such fiscal influences are examined in Chapter 6.

The confluence of the six factors discussed above results in the final determination of just what constitutes special education at a particular time and place. Our interpretation of the most generalizable description of special education for the United States as a whole in the last decade of this century is presented below.

MAPPING "THE TERRITORY"

Below, four significant dimensions of special education are described: 1) the clients served, 2) the services delivered, 3) the organizational units involved in that delivery, and 4) the personnel who operate within these organizational structures. This description will draw on the six determining factors discussed above, illustrating each to the greatest extent possible, but it must be acknowledged that it is sometimes very difficult to discriminate between, and separate the influence of, the various factors.

Who Are the Clients of Special Education?

The trend of the past decade or two is certainly away from describing the clientele of special education categorically. A shift in emphasis from traditional disability labels toward assessment of service needs is apparent. However, old categories are slow to fade away. Moreover, classification is an accepted means of facilitating communication, even when the risks of inaccurate communication and other negative side effects are acknowledged. In his critique of the special education knowledge tradition, Skrtic points out that the clinical model that prevails in the field derives from medicine and psychology and is based on two contrasting theories of normality versus abnormality. The *pathological theory,* from the field of medicine, is the basis for classifying children according to the presence or absence of biological conditions. The *statistical theory,* from the field of psychology, is the basis for classifying children in terms of their relative position within a normal distribution of some educationally relevant behavioral variable, such as learning style. The confounding of these two theories is further complicated by the argument of social scientists that special education's use of diagnosis, intervention, and technology based on the behavioral and biological sciences ignores the social, political, and cultural contexts of disability (Skrtic, 1991, pp. 112–114).

Those who argue that existing classification practices are of questionable validity and utility (Wang, Reynolds, & Walberg, 1988) and inflict significant harm due to the inherent stigma associated with such classification (Stainback & Stainback, 1984) are countered by the argument that guaranteeing rights necessitates the identification of those whose rights are threatened (Kauffman, 1989).

It appears that a combination of historical and legal factors make it necessary to use labels, however stigmatic, to identify clients and ensure the establishment and funding of necessary services. Despite an increasingly obvious mistrust of categories and concern regarding the questionable reliability, validity, and usefulness of labels in educating children, it is equally obvious that fears of loss of support for specific programs temper any movement to abandon categorization.

As indicated earlier, minor adjustments to specific labels, as well as major conceptual changes in classification schemes, have been introduced from time to time with the intention (at least in part) of reducing the negative side effects of the identification process. The use of the term *disabled,* as opposed to *handicapped,* is generally proposed as a designation that carries somewhat less stigma. Going beyond that level, conceptualization of the field as dealing with *exceptional* rather than only *handicapped* students changes both the image and the actual parameters of the target population.

There is no doubt that to whatever extent the classification of student clientele establishes and defines the field of special education, those students who are at variance from the norm in a disadvantageous way figure most prominently in the attention of those who deal with the field, either from the inside or the outside. In a number of states during the mid-nineteenth century, legislation affecting exceptional persons was clearly concerned primarily with the statutory establishment of state schools and institutions for the deaf, the blind, and those with mental retardation. The first public day schools and classes for students with special needs were established within some of the larger city school systems in the decades just before and after the turn of the century. Again, these educational services were targeted toward youngsters with sensory and mental disabilities and extended in some instances to children with physical disabilities and severe health conditions. One notable departure was an Oregon statute in 1923 that provided for classes for educationally exceptional children, including both the gifted and those with disabilities.

The weight of numbers and overall emphasis of special education programs clearly lean toward students with disabilities. The major consideration in what classifications of students are considered legitimate resides in state-level statutes. The state generally defines the territory as being concerned with students with *handicaps* (or more recently *disabilities*), or with *exceptional* students. Nearly half of the states use the term *exceptional* and include gifted students among the types of children served by special education. Other states define *gifted* and/or *talented* separately from *disabled*, but several states do not define giftedness in any way. Among states providing programs for gifted students, over half administer them through the department of special or exceptional education, and others administer them through a regular department of curriculum and instruction, or through one of a variety of other organizational arrangements.

The ambiguity and definitional limits described here are also evident in the federal policies that overlay all state and local provisions. The *handicapped* terminology long remained in federal initiatives, and any speculation on the possible merits of a less pejorative designation was rejected on the basis of the danger of losing a clear, sympathy-generating image deemed necessary for favorable statutory provisions and funding. Long before any federal legislation having a nationwide impact was passed, administrative units within the federal education establishment (the U.S. Office of Education) charged with overseeing special education were labeled with the *handicapped* designator. It should be noted, however, that one of the first publicly visible activities of that unit was a national study conducted during the period of 1952–1954 of the *Qualifications and Preparation of Teachers of Exceptional Children* (Mackie & Dunn, 1954), which focused on personnel of many types, including teachers of gifted children. The continuing ambiguity was evident 25 years later when difficulty arose in deciding how to assign responsibility for federal programs authorized under the 1978 Gifted and Talented Children's Education Act (PL 96-561) in relation to the similar functions carried out by the Bureau of Education for the Handicapped.

The major federal legislation has included terminology and classifications of students associated with conditions that would demonstrably interfere with ordinary educational progress. Federal laws that were enacted between 1966 and 1990 and that carried a definition of the intended clientele raised the dilemma of whether to use broad or specific definitions. While some would argue that certain terms and phrases (such as "other health impaired") are sufficiently inclusive to encompass various conditions that were intended to be covered, there was great pressure, as demonstrated in the 1990 amendments, to specifically mention *autism* and *traumatic brain injury* so as to ensure their inclusion. Athough these two disabilities were added without great controversy, a similar lobby to also include specific reference to *attention deficit disorders* (ADD), after much debate, was not successful. It was clear that the ambiguity regarding the nature and scope of the condition and the resulting uncertainty as to its potential fiscal impact influenced the decision to postpone adding it to the list of disabilities. As a compromise with the advocates of funding for ADD, the new law did provide for a major study of the condition through resource centers that focused on evaluation, research, and intervention. A policy memorandum from the Office of Special Education Programs (OSEP) in September, 1991 reassured advocates that "ADD does not need to be added [to the law] as a separate disability category. . . . Children with ADD who require special education and related services [already] can meet eligibility criteria for services . . . under the other health impaired category."

An earlier instance in which the developers of legal definitions were conscious of an inherent ambiguity in the scope of a particular classification occurred in the handling of the *specific learning disabilities* category during the development of PL 94-142. At that time it was deemed necessary to provide within the statute an extensive description of the type that ordinarily appears in administrative regulations. The definition employed, which remained unchanged 15 years later in PL 101-476, is as follows:

> (15) The term "children with specific learning disabilities" means those children who have a disorder in one or more of the basic psychological processes involved in understanding or in using language, spoken or written, which disorder may manifest itself in imperfect ability to listen, think, speak, read, write, spell, or do mathematical calculations. Such disorders include such conditions as perceptual handicaps, brain injury, minimal brain dysfunction, dyslexia, and developmental aphasia. Such term does not include children who have learning problems which are primarily the result of visual, hearing, or motor handicaps, of mental retardation, of emotional disturbance, or of environmental, cultural, or economic disadvantage.

These definitions, while not precluding a state's establishing a more inclusive one, have a great influence on state policy in that they determine the minimal level of inclusion to which a state must adhere in order to participate in programs that distribute federal funds to assist in the provision of approved services. Persons unfamiliar with the evolution of the terms included in these definitions could rightly wonder at the extensive detail with which the category of specific learning disability is elaborated, while other terms such as visual impairments appear without further explanation. While considerably more detail is provided in the administrative regulations developed later to guide the implementation of the law, the emphasis within the basic legal definition gives testimony to the general, common, historically based understanding of certain portions of the intended clientele. However, the meaning of the term and the scope of the concept of specific learning disability (and more recently ADD) are assumed to be relatively ambiguous and, therefore, subject to distortion of the legislative intent.

The ambiguity inherent in all of these definitions is illustrated by the reported figures on the numbers of students served under federal categorical definitions. Although it is possible that some localities might have a greater incidence of particular disabilities as a function of natural circumstances, with entire states as the reporting units it is difficult to believe that great differences in the actual occurrence of conditions requiring special education services would be found. It is also reasonable to expect that some differences would exist among states in services provided, regardless of incidence of need, as a function of the historical development of programs prior to the recent period of heavy federal intervention. Regardless of need or the standardizing influence of federal legislation, some states can be expected to be more progressively involved in the operation of service programs, and one could expect that this would be associated with other demographic and socioeconomic factors in the states, as well as the states' policies and positions on general educational and other social indicators.

A study of the data released by the Office of Special Education Programs in the Department of Education's *Fourteenth Annual Report to the Congress* (1992) raises some interesting questions about each of the assumptions we have just discussed. Since the earliest of these reports, wide variation among the states has been evident in the numbers of students receiving special education services as a percentage of their total school age populations. Figures for the 1990–1991 school year show that 7.05% of the resident U.S. population of children from birth to age 21 were served under the two major federally authorized programs. This is compared to 4.8% in 1976–1977, when the current federal programs (and consistent record keeping) began. Excluding the territories and the District of Columbia (where the variation was even greater), the number of children served in 1990–1991 among the 50 states ranged from 4.44% in Hawaii to 10.25% in Massachusetts. The figures were 5.49% for Georgia and 9.49% for New Jersey. Perhaps a more significant figure is that of children served by special education as a percentage of school-age children (6–17 years) in the nation as a whole—9.91%. The percentages for individual states varied from lows of 6.75% and 7.86% to highs of 14.40% and 15.65%.

Inspection of the entire set of figures reveals little in the way of a logical explanation for the variance on the basis of such possibly related characteristics as per-capita income, median years of schooling, minority enrollment, or such resource input variables as current expenditures per pupil, teacher–pupil ratio, or expenditures as a percentage of per-capita income. A study that attempted to explore such relationships (McLaughlin & Owings, 1992) examined federal data from 1976, 1980, and 1983 and correlated identification and placement data with a number of fiscal and demographic variables. The study was limited to children classified as *learning disabled* (LD), *seriously emotionally disturbed* (ED), and *multiply disabled* (ML). Since such data are only available on entire states, the differences that would be expected across individual localities and school systems were obscured. A weak but significant relationship was found that suggested a tendency of wealthier states to have higher identification rates for students with LD and ED. Wealthier states also tended to have higher cumulative placement rates in more-restrictive settings. The absence of other significant relationships could be partly attributed to methodological problems such as general inconsistencies in reporting and subjectivity in identification criteria, but the relationships that were found are at least consistent with certain expectations. It is often noted that LD identification may be a middle-class phenomenon. Furthermore, it is reasonable to expect that wealthier states may have better-developed special education systems that would permit wider identification and placement in segregated settings with more funding. The fact that in some states nearly twice as many students are identified and served as in others strongly suggests that a different standard of inclusion is being applied.

A further breakdown of similar data by categories of disability reveals an even greater discrepancy. For example, the incidences of children with mental retardation being served in Massachusetts and Alabama were 3.29% and 3.10%, respectively, of those state's total school enrollment, whereas Alaska and New Jersey reported incidences of only 0.29% and 0.37%. It is obviously quite unreasonable to think that there would be 10 times as many mentally retarded students in one state as in another. An even greater variance is evident in the *emotionally disturbed* category, in which Connecticut and Massachusetts reported 2.18% and 2.16% of their total school enrollment and Mississippi and Arkansas only about ½₀ of 1% — about a 40-fold difference.

In the reported incidence of students served under the category of *specific learning disability*, the variation among the states was not as striking. Rhode Island and New Jersey reported figures of 8.50% and 7.52%, respectively, of their total school enrollment, while Georgia and Wisconsin reported only 2.45% and 2.91% — a 3-fold difference. While it is reasonable to expect some regional differences in actual incidences of disability, and even more reasonable to expect different levels of intensity in programming as a function of state policy (not to mention simple reporting errors), these figures show that using conventional classifications, the question "who are the clients of special education?" is answered differently in each state. It should be noted that the figures presented are concerned with students who fall under the provisions of the federal programs for students with disabilities and, therefore, do not reflect any state services that may be provided for the gifted and talented, or for any other pupils who may be considered part of the special education program in a particular state, but who do not fall under the federal definitions.

The distribution of children served among the various categories of disability has undergone significant changes over the years that the federal programs have been in effect. Table 1 summarizes the data on the distribution across the reported categories of disabilties for children served in all federally overseen programs for the United States as a whole for 1980–1981 and 1990–1991.

It should be noted that the distribution reported here reflects a rather striking increase in the *learning disability* category following the implementation of PL 94-142 in the late 1970s, with a proportional decrease in certain other classifications, particularly *mental retardation*.

Demographic Variables

Another issue in defining the population to be served centers on the question of age level. The degree to which different states or local systems embrace the idea of preschool services, as well as programs for persons between the ages of 18 and 21, shows much greater variance than their approaches to programs for children 6–17. Although

Table 1. Distribution of children served, by disability, ages 6–21

Disability	Percent of total population served	
	1980–1981	1990–1991
Specific learning disability	35.1	49.1
Speech or language impairments	28.0	22.7
Mental retardation	20.2	12.7
Serious emotional disturbance	8.4	9.0
Multiple disabilities	1.7	2.2
Hearing impairments	1.9	1.4
Orthopedic impairments	1.4	1.1
Other health impairments	2.4	1.3
Visual impairments	0.8	0.5
Deaf-blindness	<.1	<.1

Source: Department of Education (1982, 1992).

federal law was concerned with persons from 3 to 21 years of age, it also included certain exceptions. In the language of PL 94-142:

> With respect to handicapped children aged three to five and aged eighteen to twenty-one, inclusive, the requirements of this clause shall not be applied in any State if the application of such requirements would be inconsistent with State law or practice, or the order of any court, respecting public education within such age groups in the State.

Given this latitude, considerable variance could be found among different states in the numbers of students at these marginal ages who had access to services during the first 10 years of the law's history. Incentives included as a part of federal law have not been sufficient to dramatically influence the extension of services to these age groups in cases in which traditional practice and financial constraints dictate otherwise. The fact that preschool or early childhood education has not been universally adopted as a part of the general education system in all states is a major barrier to providing such services specifically for children with disabilities.

PL 99-457, the Education of the Handicapped Act Amendments of 1986, placed a much greater emphasis on preschool services, both by changing the incentives for increasing services for 3- to 5-year-olds and by adding provisions for infants and toddlers (from birth to age 3). As Table 2 illustrates, the impact of these changes can be seen in the difference, between 1980 and 1990, in the numbers of individuals served, divided by age level.

Even within the school-age levels, the concentration at the elementary school years and the relatively less-advanced programming at the secondary school levels is evident in data reported in the *An-*

Table 2. Percent of total number of students served in LEA administered schools, by age level group

Age level	1980–1981	1990–1991
3–5	5.9%	8.1%
6–17	90.5%	87.4%
18–21	3.5%	4.5%

Source: Department of Education (1982, 1992).

nual Report to the Congress (1992). For example, the data for 1990–1991 show only about half as many 17-year-olds being served as 9-year-olds. The proportion of the total number of students served by special education at each age level is indicated in Table 3.

It should be noted that these data do not address the population of children from birth to age 2, who were provided for in PL 99-457, which added Part H to the EHA (now called IDEA). The data on the numbers of infants and toddlers receiving intervention services as provided for in the law are much less accurate than data on other groups, since multiple agencies are involved and there is no inter-agency data exchange system to eliminate duplications. While great

Table 3. Distribution of students, by age, enrolled in LEA administered schools, 1990–1991

Student age	Percent
3	1.3
4	2.5
5	4.3
6	6.0
7	7.5
8	8.8
9	9.1
10	9.0
11	8.5
12	7.8
13	7.5
14	6.8
15	6.3
16	5.6
17	4.6
18	2.9
19	1.0
20	0.4
21	0.2

variation among states is evident in the implementation of these services, it is estimated that in December 1990 about 1.77% of the 0–2 age cohort nation-wide had received services (Department of Education, 1992).

A long-standing concern has been the disproportionate number of males served within the special education system. Data on secondary age students, (13–21) collected as part of the National Longitudinal Transition Study of Special Education Students (NLTS) and reported in the *Fourteenth Annual Report to Congress* (Department of Education, 1992, p. 11) indicate that more than ⅔ (68.5%) of those served were male. The highest percentages of males were in the categories of specific learning disabilities (73.4%) and serious emotional disturbance (76.4%). Since males account for slightly under 50% of the general population at these ages, the reasons for this discrepancy have been of considerable interest. While there is some evidence that genetic factors may result in a greater incidence of disabilities in males, there is also evidence of gender bias in diagnosis and classification practices.

It was also noted that a disproportionate share of minority children were included in certain special education programs. As compared to the white majority, African American children were grossly overrepresented in almost all disability programs. Taking all types of special education programs combined, African Americans accounted for 24.2% of special education clientele, while constituting only about 12% of the general population. Hispanics, by contrast, appeared to be slightly underrepresented.

The NLTS study also indicated that socioeconomic characteristics are closely associated with disproportionate representation in programs for children with disabilities. Single-parent status, low family income, and low educational attainment of heads of households were all associated with placement of children in special education.

What Services Constitute Special Education?

It was indicated at the beginning of this chapter that the scope of special education, both in terms of the clientele served and the services included, was determined by a variety of factors operating in concert. The effect of legislation on actual practice at a particular time and place is largely determined by local tradition and policy. Just as we have seen considerable variation in the populations served throughout the nation, we can expect to find a certain amount of variation in what constitutes special education services.

The cataloging of special education services has historically tended to focus on physical locations—the places in which special education takes place. In citing the history of the field, we recognize that its earliest developments took place in separate, special schools, usually residential, both publicly and privately operated. This nineteenth-century practice was followed in the first half of this century by services offered within regular schools, but in separate special classes, as the primary mode of service. The activities conducted in these locations were instruction, but they were different in a number of ways from the instruction that went on in other, typical classes.

One major difference was a focus on compensatory methodology for accomplishing common instructional objectives. In the case of programs for students with visual or auditory impairments, special education has consisted primarily of devising means to bypass the sensory obstacle to normal learning and, assuming more or less average intellectual capacity, of the pursuit of scholastic objectives through the use of these alternate or compensatory channels of learning. Primary features of such programs were the use of Braille and auditory communication in educating children who were blind, and alternate-language development for those who were deaf. This description is somewhat oversimplified, since disability-related differences in adult life goals have always been recognized, as have affective and psychosocial factors that interact with the purely cognitive learning objectives. But within programs for those with sensory impairments, the major intent and approach in instruction could be defined in this manner.

Another distinction between the activities of special and general education is the difference between the educational goals and corresponding instructional objectives subscribed to in each. Based on the assumption that certain irremedial disabilities preclude the attainment of typical adult life goals, special education curriculum has, for a major part of the clientele, been adapted to suit specialized (reduced) objectives. Programs for students with mental retardation are characterized not only by instructional methods designed to accommodate the learning styles of such students, but also by the terminal goals of instruction. Especially for those with severe retardation, for whom the adaptive activities of daily living may be the ultimate goal and the cognitive development usually associated with school may be clearly infeasible, special education is oriented toward totally different purposes than general education.

Another characteristic of special education that has been consistently present is the focus on individualized instruction. While the ideal of recognizing individual differences among all children has been touted throughout education, it has been most often realized within programs for children with disabilities. This has in turn created a focus on the methodology of instruction suited to a variety of student needs, as a spinoff of the highly specialized arrangements necessitated by particular disabling conditions.

Still another differentiating aspect is seen in cases in which the clientele exhibit conditions that currently preclude regular instruction but are presumed to be remedial. In such cases, the focus of instruction is not only on accommodating the existing barrier to regular instruction, but also on measures designed to alleviate (over time) the disabling circumstances. The program of special education, in these instances, can be conceived as both compensatory and therapeutic. Programs for children with emotional disturbances, with specific learning disabilities, and with speech impairments are designed with such dual objectives in mind. Unlike the situation of those with visual impairments, for whom the aim is normal educational attainment in spite of a presumably permanent disabling condition, and unlike the situation for children who are mentally retarded, for whom the aim is the attainment of appropriately altered objectives, the design of certain programs places heavy emphasis on instructional intervention that will remediate the disability itself.

These various factors that seem to differentiate special education from general systems of instruction have allowed practitioners in the field to utilize an experimental approach rather frequently. The somewhat unique nature of both the learner and the teacher in special education can facilitate innovation and the development of techniques that would not be risked in the mainstream. In this sense, certain aspects of special education have been somewhat more experimental than has the education system as a whole.

Related Services A significantly less predominant circumstance, but one that must be acknowledged, is the situation in which a disabling condition is present, but has little or no bearing on the instructional program per se. Concerning orthopedic impairments and other health problems, a majority of the needs of those affected may be met by alterations in the physical environment or by the provision of services such as transportation and therapies of a noneducational nature. The inclusion of such programs within the domain of special education is rationalized on the basis of the disabling conditions, even though the interventions employed are not educationally specialized. The addition of the subject of *technological devices and services* in the amendments to IDEA in 1990 and its subsequent regulations has broadened the scope of what may be considered either special education or related services. This type of situation presents a complicating element in mapping the territory of special education where federal law is concerned, as is discussed later in the chapter.

Thus it can be seen that there are different bases for defining the types of services that constitute special education. The laws that have accrued over the years in each state have reflected these bases, and the combination of state law and conventional practice undoubtedly played a large part in the development of federal policy, as seen in the language of PL 101-476, in which special education is legally defined (in U.S.C. 1401) as follows:

> (16) The term "special education" means specially designed instruction, at no cost to parents or guardians, to meet the unique needs of a child with a disability including—(A) instruction conducted in the classroom, in the home, in hospitals and institutions, and in other settings; and (B) instruction in physical education.

The distinction in the language between this amended definition and that which preceded it has to do with allowing for instruction in the workplace and in training centers. Reflecting a new focus on those students nearing the chronological limits of eligibility (ages 16–21) the new law also defined *transition services* as

> (19) . . . a coordinated set of activities . . . designed within an outcome-oriented process, which promotes movement from school to post-school activities, including post-secondary education, vocational training, integrated employment (including supported employment), continuing and adult education, adult services, independent living, or community participation.

These definitions are repeated in the Code of Federal Regulations (34 C.F.R. Part 300) with elaboration on the meaning of many of the items named in the statute, such as physical education and vocational education, and on the status of speech pathology services as either special education or a related service, depending on individual state definitions. The matter of the distinction, under federal law, between special education and related services is of particular interest in mapping the territory. According to U.S.C. 1401, as amended in 1990 by PL 101-476:

> (17) The term "related services" means transportation, and such developmental, corrective, and other supportive services (including speech pathology and audiology, psychological services, physical and occupational therapy, recreation, including therapeutic recreation, social work services, counseling services, including rehabilitation counseling, and medical services except that such medical services shall be for diagnostic and evaluation purposes only) as may be required to assist a child with a disability to benefit from special education, and includes the early identification and assessment of disabling conditions in children.

Again, this latest definition includes services that reflect the emphasis on older eligible students. The regulations expand this definition, describing in great detail the types of activities included within the scope of each of the services mentioned in the law. From the standpoint of program administration at the local school district level, any or all of these services might be considered as falling within the province of a special education department. However, these services tend to be provided rather broadly across the total population of the schools and are not exclusively directed toward pupils who are disabled. Therefore, there is a rationale for viewing the administration of such services as a generic function, even though the linkage to special education, both in the terms of the activities and the clientele, is rather strong.

This is further complicated by the fact that under federal law related services can only be provided to children with disabilities, who are defined in this context as those students requiring special education. Therefore, a child who has a disability (e.g., an orthopedic impairment) that does not call for special education would not be considered eligible for related services such as transportation or physical therapy that might be appropriate to his or her condition. These situations are rare, and are usually resolved by determining that some form of special education is necessary, but according to a strict interpretation, the distinction drawn between the two aspects of the total service system illustrates the ambiguity of the territorial maps and the interaction between the legal base and traditional perspectives on service.

Instructional Services   Within the instructional realm, the emphasis on physical location has drawn attention to the evolution of service models. Reynolds, Wang, and Walberg (1987) have pointed out that even after special education moved from segregated schools and institutions and became incorporated within the regular public school systems, a "two-box" perspective continued to prevail. Schools were seen as providing two separate educational systems (regular and special), "each with its own pupils, teachers, supervisory staff, and funding system." Under such a system, a child was determined to belong in either one or the other "box," with little interchange between the two. Even though some children spent more time in regular educational settings and received their special education (or services) from itinerant specialists, as was common with resource-teacher services provided for students with visual impairments and speech therapy for students needing such service, the children were seen as part-time members of the "special box." The separateness was reinforced by the training and certification of special teachers, which usually took place in academic departments separate from those of the mainstream educators, with emphasis on the categorical nature of the competencies required.

The significant shift toward a "continuum of services" model that began in the 1960s and accelerated in the 1970s was primarily caused by the recognition that the needs of children did not fall neatly into two "boxes," that a much greater variety of options was called for. The idea of a full range of options has been expressed in a variety of ways, with the original concept of a "cascade" of services having been proposed by Deno (1970) and adapted by Reynolds and Birch (1982). The concept initially emphasized the various types of locations in which a complete continuum of services could be provided, with the assumption being that more intensive specialized service, which would be provided in facilities removed from the mainstream of education, would be required for relatively few children. The "floor" of the cascade was seen as the regular classroom, where most children would be served. The levels of increasing intensity of service, with correspondingly fewer children being served in each, were described as follows:

Regular classroom with consultative assistance: Indirect services by psychologists, resource teachers, supervisor/consultants; no direct service to child

Regular classroom with assistance by itinerant specialists: Limited direct service to child by specialists (e.g., speech therapists, mobility instructors)

Regular classroom plus part-time special class: Part-time attendance in full-time special class to meet prescribed needs

Full-time special class: Direct service provided within a self-contained group of students with similar needs

Full-time special day school: Direct service provided within a large group of students with similar needs

Full-time residential school: Direct service encompassing more than school-day instruction

Homebound, hospital instructors: Instruction provided in settings having other primary purposes

Special treatment and detention centers: Total environmental control for primary purposes other than instruction

The essential purpose behind having a complete continuum of services is that the most appropriate level, or intensity, of program can be provided and placements in programs can be guided by the general principle that no greater intensity of service than is absolutely necessary will be utilized. On the assumption that specialized services are also limiting in terms of access and participation in society, the principle of *least restrictive environment* (LRE) is employed. The value of maximum participation and minimum segregation from the mainstream gained sufficient acceptance within the culture and the professional education community to ensure its codification as a key element in the federal policy expressed in PL 94-142 and its regulations.

A manifestation of the acceptance of the LRE principle can be seen in the figures reported by the U.S. Department of Education in its *Fourteenth Annual Report to Congress* (1992). Data on the environments in which children were served during the 1989–1990 school year illustrate that for the majority of special education students, the regular class (with part-time supplemental services) constitutes the primary placement mode. Ninety-three percent of all students with disabilities of ages 3–21 were served within regular schools. The most common form of part-time supplemental support (35.5%)—defined as the provision of special education and related services during 21%–60% of the school day—was resource-room support. Almost as many students (32.5%) were classified as being primarily assigned to the general class, in that their special services constituted less than 21% of the school day. Separate classes (defined as assignments for more than 60% of the school day) accounted for 25.2% of the students. Separate schools accounted for 4.6% and other environments another 1.5%.

There is great variation in the types of environmental settings that correspond to the different classifications of disability. Table 4, which summarizes data on children ages 6–21, rather than the broader age range of 3–21 discussed above, illustrates some of this variation. Services for children with speech and language impairments are delivered in the regular class setting in over ¾ of the cases, which is a much greater proportion than for most other disabilities. Children with specific learning disabilities, who account for about half of all those served, are served primarily (over 75% of all cases) in regular classes, with, at most, resource-room support. Children with emotional disturbances are served in separate classes in 37% of all cases—almost as frequently as they are served in regular classes, and children with mental retardation were most often served in separate classes (about 61% of the cases).

Again, extreme variation between states in the use of each placement environment within certain disability categories is evident. For example, while the states of Idaho, Iowa, North Dakota, Oregon, South Dakota, Vermont, and Wyoming show almost all of their placements of children with specific learning disabilities (over 95%) in reg-

Table 4. Percentage of students, ages 6–21, served in different educational environments, by disability

Disability	Regular class	Resource room	Separate class	Separate school	Residential facility	Homebound/hospital
Specific learning disabilities	20.7%	56.1%	21.7%	1.3%	0.1%	0.1%
Speech or language impairments	76.8	17.7	3.8	1.5	0.1	0.1
Mental retardation	6.7	20.1	61.1	10.3	1.4	0.4
Serious emotional disturbance	14.9	28.5	37.1	13.9	3.6	2.0
Hearing impairments	27.0	18.2	31.7	10.6	12.3	0.2
Multiple disabilities	5.9	14.3	43.7	29.5	3.9	2.7
Orthopedic impairments	29.6	18.9	34.7	9.9	1.0	5.9
Other health impairments	31.2	22.3	24.6	7.8	1.0	13.1
Visual impairments	39.3	23.7	21.1	4.5	10.8	0.6
Deaf-blindness	8.0	16.3	29.9	16.6	28.4	1.0
All disabilities	31.5	37.6	24.9	4.6	0.9	0.6

Source: Department of Education (1992).

ular classes and/or resource rooms, the states of Illinois, Louisiana, Maryland, New Jersey, New York, and Pennsylvania placed less than 70% of such children in these types of settings. Placement in separate schools also varies greatly among states for certain categories of disability. While Maryland, Nevada, and New Jersey reported that over 30% of their children with mental retardation were placed in separate schools, the figure for 22 other states was less than 3%. Similar variations occur in the placements of those with emotional disturbance.

It should be noted that the total U.S. averages of placement environments, by disability category, as presented in Table 3, obscure the dramatic variations that exist and provide only a very rough sense of the nature of the services utilized. The six types of placement environments likewise obscure the variety of program activities that may occur in each, especially the *regular class,* within which the services may range from occasional indirect consultation with the general education teacher to intensive instruction provided by an itinerant or resource teacher for up to 20% of the child's school day. Thus, the dividing line between part-time service provided within a regular class base and assignment to a special class can be very unclear.

Also, the figures reported above are somewhat fluid for individual states. That is, data from one year's *Annual Report* to the next show variations that may reflect changes in classification and reporting, but may, at least to some extent, indicate real changes in programming practices. Aggregate data from across all states reduces these fluctuations, and the figures appear to be considerably more stable in recent years than they were a decade ago.

What Organizational Structures Provide Special Education?

The governance and operation of education in the United States is universally recognized as a state responsibility, with the preponderance of authority delegated to local school district governing boards. The participation of state government in this shared enterprise, while varying in accordance with the philosophies of individual states, as expressed in constitutions, statutes, and administrative regulations, tends to be concerned with the establishment of standards to ensure minimum student adequacy and the reduction of gross inequity in the educational programs operating at the local level. In most respects, schools belong to the local citizenry. Furthermore, education is a predominantly public enterprise, with the role of private agencies occupying a relatively small place as compared to those in many other societies.

The role of the federal government in education has traditionally been even less prominent; in fact, it could be said to have been almost inconsequential before the 1960s. Until that time, the federal role had primarily consisted of record keeping, except for the legislation of grants and other fiscal supports to stimulate educational programs focusing on specific populations and specific needs. In such instances the intervention of the federal government was usually in response to a societal need other than education, but for which an educational program could be anticipated as being a feasible part of the solution. Unemployment, economic crises, national defense, and the return of veterans of war have often been cited as the impetus for federal education initiatives. The dramatic change that has occurred in this country since 1960 will be discussed in detail at a later point, but it should be understood that, in general, education has been, and remains, a primarily local function, with assistance and supervision provided by the state.

However, special education can properly be considered an exception. Some of the earliest examples of educational services for students with disabilities were the result of legislative initiatives from the federal and state levels of government that were aimed at supporting the establishment of institutions to meet needs that were assumed to be beyond the scope of local public education. Services operated directly by these higher levels of government long preceded local school system involvement. Even after the initiation of local school programs for exceptional students, special education (along with vocational education) remained one of the particular, narrow-purpose areas in which both direct and indirect intervention from higher levels of government was deemed legitimate.

Within education in general other societal agencies also participate to some degree with the schools in the overall operation of the enterprise. Health, welfare, and justice agencies typically work with education agencies at each level of government and, depending on particular state and local policies, may play a significant role in what goes on from day to day. The interaction between these other human services agencies and the schools may be extensive in areas in which the local population includes a large proportion of students from economically deprived homes. The public health concerns of a community are often reflected in and dealt with through the clientele and personnel of the local public schools.

In the case of children with disabilities, their human services needs tend to draw more heavily on other agencies than is typical for the school population as a whole. The interaction between the families of students with disabilities and health service agencies in particular may be closely tied to the special educational issues with which the school is concerned. The boundary lines between educational, health, and social service functions, both at the point of diagnostic assessment and treatment intervention, may need to be clarified, articulated, and monitored to achieve maximum benefit and efficiency; vulnerability to gaps and overlaps in function are created by two factors. First, the expectations and practices of schools tend to be increasingly concerned with more than just instructional activities. Screening for vision, hearing, and health problems, as well as conducting more extensive assessment activities in the case of children with suspected disabilities, are generally seen as school functions. As a result of special education, a wide variety of related services, including physical therapy, occupational therapy, and parent counseling, though traditionally allied to medical services, have also become school-based functions. Second, educational programs sometimes must be offered in facilities operated by nonschool agencies. Hospitals and institutions that operate under the jurisdiction of state health, mental health, mental retardation, or welfare agencies are mandated to provide appropriate educational programs for residents of school age. Persons detained in correctional facilities under authority of state justice departments also include a large number of school-age youth whose special education needs must be met. In addition, private agencies serving school-age persons in residence with medical and psychological needs must also be responsible for the provision of appropriate educational programs. Therefore, a significant crossover of responsibility and functions between education and other human services agencies must be taken into account, and this becomes a distinguishing characteristic of special education as compared with the rest of the education enterprise. The rationale for these differences may best be understood by considering the total service system, which is a product of the nature of the population in question and the nature of the interventions called for.

Brewer and Kakalik (1979) have presented a useful means of viewing the total service system in terms of role models, functions, and rationales that drive the policy processes that affect special education. While their emphasis in this conceptualization is on the federal level, it can be shown that similar state-level applications hold equally true.

Four basic aspects of government roles are identified: 1) direct operation, 2) policy and program control, 3) revenue sharing, and 4) stimulation and innovation. These roles apply across all types of government functions, but except for the purpose of illustrative comparison, discussion here will focus on human services, particularly education.

Direct Operation   As indicated earlier, local school districts are
the primary government agencies involved in the direct operation of
educational systems. Direct operation of educational programs by the
federal government are very rare, although the overseas schools for
dependents of military personnel provided by the Department of Defense are notable exceptions. However, in the realm of services for
students with disabilities, a number of direct federal operations do
exist, such as the Social Security Disability Insurance program. In
addition, certain special education activities are operated directly by
the federal government, such as Gallaudet University and its related
elementary and secondary schools for the deaf, the National
Technical Institute for the Deaf, and St. Elizabeth's Hospital.

The rationale for such direct operation is based primarily on the
very low incidence of certain disability-related needs and the high degree of specialization called for in responding to these needs. Economy of scale is a major consideration, as is the assumption that the
benefits of knowledge and technology accrued (termed *externalities*
by economists) by both the service providers and the recipients will
be diffused far beyond the point at which the service is rendered. The
opportunity for stimulation and innovation that arises when specialized talent and equipment can be brought together is also a factor.
Operation by the broadest (federal) level of government is thereby justified in these cases (Brewer & Kakalik, 1979, pp. 62–69).

Direct operations by state education agencies (SEAs) are much
more common. Examples are the numerous residential schools for
children with visual or hearing impairments, mental retardation, and
emotional disturbance, which may operate under either the education department of the state or branches of the health or welfare departments. Aside from historical precedent, such facilities are maintained on the rationale that the low incidence of certain disabling
conditions and the sparsity of the general population mandates a
catchment area as large as an entire state or major region thereof.
Such economy-of-scale arguments are now increasingly challenged
as experience is gained with less restrictive alternatives for placement, but it is clear that for some conditions, direct state-operated
programs will probably remain in place.

Long before pressures for less restrictive environments became
commonplace, however, there was a recognition that a centralized
state-operated program was too far removed from local school disrict
services. The parents of deaf children residing outside densely populated areas, for example, would acknowledge that, although a local
program for only one or two children would not be feasible, sending a

young child away to a state residential school seemed drastic. The need for something in between these two extremes—for a program serving a larger catchment area than the local school district to operate highly specialized programs for low-incidence populations—was clear. The rationale for an intermediate unit of organization is basically an extension of that which justifies the federal and state operations, but, by being closer to the grass roots that drive education in this country, would be expected to create less dissonance with the rest of the system.

Intermediate education units (IEUs) of one sort or another have been prominently used in most states for a number of purposes. For direct operation of programs, special education, along with vocational education, has given rise to the driving need for such organizational structures. Except for those states having county-wide school districts (such as Maryland, Virginia, and Florida), in which there are no small local organizational units, some method has been employed in each state to bring together the local education agencies (LEAs) of a region to make special education programming more efficient. A variety of legal, political, and fiscal factors have influenced the exact nature of the IEU in different states. Some of these issues are discussed in later chapters, but the implications for direct operation of programs are virtually the same whether the IEU is the result of informal cooperative efforts banding together a group of LEAs to share a common need or is the product of a more formal partial decentralization of the state education agency (SEA).

The significance of the IEU as an organizational structure within the special education service system is not limited to the direct operation of programs, but the magnitude of that aspect, nationwide, is sufficient to warrant close consideration of their presence as an influence on general policy or a reactor thereto. Estimates of the prominence of IEUs are not precise, but a survey of the membership of the national Council of Administrators of Special Education in 1982 showed that out of 1,191 persons who responded, 22.7% were employed by IEUs. LEAs employed 55.9%, and the remainder were employed in a variety of other settings, including SEAs, federal offices, and private agencies (Greenberg, 1983).

Policy and Program Control   The "controllership" role, as described by Brewer and Kakalik, is applicable when the governmental agency leaves the direct operation of the program to lower-level agencies or to nonpublic agencies but retains the remaining three roles. At the federal level, such a role exists when "determinations of what to spend money on, how to spend it, and how to account for it are concentrated in one definable federal unit, as are the powers to allocate enabling resources and to create and generate new approaches to manage the underlying problems" (Brewer & Kakalik, 1979, p. 51). Examples of this kind of role are numerous throughout a variety of human service operations, particularly those in which federal grants or contracts are awarded to state or local agencies to conduct a specific program according to rather highly specified procedures. In special education, the prominent examples are: 1) the basic program of Assistance to States under PL 101-476 or Part B of IDEA, and 2) the program of Federal Assistance to State Operated and Supported Schools for the Disabled under PL 89-313. In both instances, to assist in the operation of programs, SEAs and LEAs receive considerable sums of money through a formula distribution based on the number of students served, but also must adhere to procedures designed to control that operation and to promote particular policies. The broad-scale application of these two programs mark them as having significant day-to-day policy implications for virtually every school administrator.

Of narrower scope, but still important to the full range of the service system, are other federal programs, such as Regional Resource Centers, Deaf–Blind Programs, Early Education Programs, Programs for Children with Severe Disabilities, Secondary Education and Transitional Services, and Programs for Children and Youth with Serious Emotional Disturbance—all authorized by various parts of IDEA and providing funding in the form of grants awarded on the basis of competitively submitted proposals. SEAs and/or LEAs (as well as other public and nonprofit organizations) are eligible to receive such funding to facilitate the provision of services in accordance with federally determined and monitored guidelines. The newness of this relationship between service providers and the federal government has generated much debate regarding the reasonable balance between funding and control, intensified by shifts in the general political climate with respect to the amount of government control that should be imposed on local school systems. The most pointed manifestation of this controversy was the proposed modification of federal regulations in 1982, in which support for deregulation was justified on the grounds of the imbalance between the funds provided and the controls imposed. This is a major issue that will probably remain with us as a matter of basic political philosophical debate.

The controllership role is more prominent, of course, in the relationship between state government and the local school systems, in which funding and regulation have long coexisted and the administrators and policymakers at each level have become accustomed to a relatively stable balance in their interactions. And aside from the funding issue, SEA regulation of the LEA, while varying in degree based on individual state political philosophy, is generally accepted as proper.

The rationale for such a relationship is most strongly based on the principles of *redistribution of resources* and *internalization of externalities* (Brewer & Kakalik, 1979, pp. 62–65). The elevation of responsibility for funding and control to a higher level of government is appropriate when pressing demand for high-cost services, as well as for the resources to provide them, are assumed to be unequally distributed among local jurisdictions. Concern for equality of opportunity is a driving force behind government programs that provide funds for the purchase of services. "Redress of governmental–institutional service inequities, given variations in wealth among the states and localities, is a common rationalization for formulas in grant programs characteristic of many purchase of service mechanisms" (Brewer & Kakalik, 1979, p. 63). In addition, the principle of responding to unmet needs translates to responsibility for "sensing those who are in need and then accommodating those individuals, even if they cannot effectively demand service, both by broadening the scope and improving the quality of services provided them" (Brewer & Kakalik, 1979, p. 63). Furthermore, it is assumed that the benefits of governmental programs are spread far beyond the immediate jurisdiction and that these "externalities" to the local system, if assumed by a broader political level, become "internal" to that larger base—and therefore justified—both in terms of funding and control. The principle is equally applicable among the LEA, SEA, and federal levels of government.

In discussing the controllership role, both funds and program control have been emphasized. It is clear that defining an acceptable balance between these factors is a matter of individual political philosophy, and certain programs may be viewed by one person or another as being highly regulated or very open. The distinction between this role and the next identified is, therefore, rather arbitrary.

Revenue Sharing   The major attribute of this role is the provision of funding, with relatively little control beyond the identification of the broad target group intended to be beneficiaries of the service. No specific guidelines governing the execution of the program are imposed, and little is required in the way of accounting for how resources are actually expended. Again, the magnitude of whatever accountability is required is a matter of individual interpretation. Specific examples can be cited of programs that had relatively heavy regulation at one time but became much more open due to shifts in the political climate and the gradual acceptance of the program as routine. In general, most programs emanating from a higher level of government have more controls at the time of initiation, when it is assumed that leadership is required, with gradual relaxation occurring as implementation becomes generalized. However, some exceptions have occurred when the initial rush to implement a program resulted in a distribution of funds before there was time to organize an adequate monitoring procedure. The history of the Title I program mandated by the Elementary and Secondary Education Act of 1965 illustrates how an initial lack of controls led to (apparently well-founded) fears that federal funds were being squandered in poorly conceived and operated local programs. This led to the development of more controls, which held sway for a period of years. Eventually, with a shift in the political climate toward a preference for less federal intervention and the establishment of "block grant" concepts, the Title I program came to approximate the ideal of simple revenue sharing with little regulation. By contrast, proposals by the federal administration to move federal special education programs into the block grant model were rejected (after much controversy and objection from consumers and the Congress) leaving those programs with relatively greater regulation accompanying the distribution of revenue.

The general concept of revenue sharing is always based on the idea that the lower level of government will contribute a major part of the total funding for the program and that the contribution from the higher level is reasonable and appropriate because of the effectiveness with which revenues can be collected and redistributed. It is assumed that higher levels of government have more options for collecting revenue and, through proper distribution, can facilitate the equalization of opportunity. This, of course, is the basic rationale on which all state aid to local education programs is based. Any extension of the concept, or distinction in the case of special education, would be based on the belief that the needs of disabled students constitute an extraordinary burden on the local community that should be shared by a broader base of support.

Stimulation and Innovation   A fourth role of government, which Brewer and Kakalik describe as the "catalytic" model, is best illustrated by investments in research and development projects, in which the "primary medium of currency is information rather than money" (Brewer & Kakalik, 1979, p. 54). Programs that supported research on educational problems, including the education of children with disabilities, were one of the first mechanisms by which a federal impact on the field could be registered. The model that has prevailed since the mid-1960s, through the establishment of the National Institute of Education and the specific research branches within the Bureau of Education for the Handicapped (now the Office of Special Education Programs) continues to promote the idea that a proper role of the federal government is to stimulate developments and innovations that would not arise out of local interests. Government-sponsored research affecting persons with disabilities has not been limited to educational concerns. Programs focusing on child and maternal health, neurological diseases, and mental health have also played a large part in what has occurred at the service-system level.

In addition to research and demonstration, investment in personnel development, through the provision of fellowships and traineeships, is another example of the catalytic process. Such cooperative efforts between the government and higher education result in an indirect enhancement of the service system by increasing the stock of human capital. The anticipated outcome of such investment, the dissemination of the results of research and development, occurs through both the information and knowledge created and the professional personnel produced. The rationale for investment in stimulation and innovation is "that states and locales may desire to improve the service system but (1) because of lack of start-up funds or political inertia, they have difficulty in doing so, or (2) because of lack of available knowledge about improved ways of providing services, they cannot do so" (Brewer & Kakalik, 1979, p. 67). Economy-of-scale or critical-mass principles are applicable to much of the research that is needed in the field. Direct operators of service facilities cannot be expected to mount with their own funds the kind of research efforts that are necessary to affect the field as a whole. In terms of both research and personnel development, the benefits produced are subject to broad diffusion and, therefore, become "externalities" to the local jurisdiction, which can be "internalized" only by elevating the resource responsibility to the higher level of government.

What Personnel Provide the Services?

The fourth dimension for defining the scope of special education, or "mapping the territory," is to consider the various professional roles or personnel classifications of service providers. To a large extent, the process of administration entails the handling of human resources. In heavily labor-intensive operations such as education and the related functions that support it, the qualifications of the personnel involved in large measure determine the boundaries of the system. Policy issues, therefore, may frequently include matters concerning roles and responsibilities.

Teachers, presumably, will always constitute the greatest part of the work force in any educational enterprise. However, we have seen a significant broadening of the types of personnel included within educational systems. Persons who have responsibilities that support teaching are now recognized as crucial to adequate operations. Among those usually described as *professional* support staff in education are: 1) administrators at a number of levels, 2) supervisors, 3) consultants, 4) counselors, 5) psychologists, 6) health service personnel, 7) social work personnel, and 8) therapists concerned with particular technical specialties. In addition, *nonprofessional* support staff responsible for clerical, maintenance, transportation, food service, and other such duties are also necessary to the system.

In the case of the professional roles at the top of the list above, there is little question as to their being an integral part of the general system. Administrators and supervisors, regardless of level or proximity to the instructional program, are in most circumstances seen as being essential to the operation, nearly as much so as classroom teachers. As we move down the list of support personel, however, there is less clarity and, therefore, some doubt about the centrality of the role to regular operations. These personnel may be associated with technical assistance provided directly to the pupils or to the general staff and, because of their technical specialty, may be seen as acting outside of the direct business of instruction. While curricular and instructional consultants and psychologists may be perceived as being closely related to instructional concerns, nurses, social workers, and various therapists appear to be dealing with another aspect of the child.

The presence of a special education program within the system, staffed with teachers having various technical specialties and functions that in some ways resemble the work of the support personnel, invites the question as to whether any or all of the specialists might better be considered as belonging to the special education domain. Certain personnel, such as physical and occupational therapists, are generally seen as related service staff to special education, while speech therapists are much more ambiguously viewed as either supports for general education, as special education teachers, or as related service staff to special education. How such staff are labelled and organized has a bearing on the policies that govern the operation of the service system.

In addition, special education has increased the numbers and types of nonprofessional and paraprofessional personnel who may be employed in school settings. While instructional aides are to be found in small numbers throughout general school settings, the needs of students with disabilities have resulted in a much greater use of paraprofessionals to assist teachers.

Within particular areas of disabilities, other supportive or related services personnel have become essential to programs, but they are difficult to classify in terms of their relationship to typical instructional personnel. Interpreters and interpret-tutors for children who are deaf, mobility specialists, Braillists, and readers for students with visual impairments play an important role in a comprehensive special education program. The fact that there is no comparative role within general education for many of these types of personnel can sometimes create policy puzzles when dealing with questions of personnel management.

When considering the personnel dimension as a factor in mapping the territory of special education, it is important to recognize that the variety of influences that determine the boundaries in other areas also plays a part here. History; local tradition; and philosophical, legal, and fiscal influences may all interact. The personal preferences of certain professionals may coincide or may conflict with legal or fiscal considerations as to their organizational home. This is most likely to be an issue for psychologists and speech therapists, whose connections to general versus special education are particularly ambiguous. Among personnel whose major function is the provision of technical assistance, distinctions are also difficult. For example, a resource teacher/consultant whose area of specialization is learning disabilities and who is identified with the special education program may be working in a manner indistinguishable from that of an instructional specialist who consults with regular classroom teachers on the needs of disadvantaged pupils under the rubric of federal Chapter 1 programs and is, therefore, a part of the general system.

It might be argued that, as determiners of the scope of special education, services delivered and personnel employed amount to virtually the same thing. And this would be true, to a large extent. However, since different types of personnel may be involved with the same service, and different services may be provided by the same types of personnel, it is probably useful to be aware of both dimensions and their interaction.

CONCLUDING COMMENTS

Our intent in this chapter has been to present for consideration the multiple factors that go into the determination of the scope of special education. It should be clear that some of these factors are more rational than others; some are more distinct than others. The scope of the field in some cases depends on the perspective of the individuals or groups who have a hand in defining it. No single factor can determine the boundaries, but interactions between several of them may be traced as being responsible for the accepted definition and scope of special education at a given time and place.

Mapping the territory is an essential policy matter on which many other considerations may be based. It may well be the most important policy issue, made even more significant by the rapid growth in services delivered and dollars spent in the past decade, which bring to the surface the question, "Just how big should special education be?" Knowledgeable persons, both within and outside of the field, must address this question and pursue some reasonably acceptable answers.

ILLUSTRATIVE CASE

Chris Hooker has been Principal of East High for 6 years and previously served as a middle school principal after teaching social studies for 8 years at both the middle and high school levels in another school system. Chris understands the local system but is also well aware that each community and each school organization has its own unique culture; Chris completed a sociological study of schools and communities for a doctoral dissertation in educational administration at State University.

East High, with its 1,400 students in grades 9–12, is in an older section of the city and has a sizable population of students from households with incomes below the poverty level. It also has a 30% minority population, somewhat higher than that of the city as a whole. The dropout rate at East High has been a concern to the Superintendent and the central office staff, and vocationally oriented programs have long been emphasized as a means of holding the line as the student population has gradually become less able or less inclined toward traditional scholarship. Chris has seen this as a major leadership challenge, particularly since the teaching staff at East High is inclined to accept the situation as inevitable.

Because of the school's student mix, the administration of East High has demanded (and usually received) a good share of the support services generally authorized as a matter of district policy and for which funding assistance is available under state laws and regulations. Federally funded special projects have also been introduced and have become rather standard in the school. For example, the Reading Skills Laboratory, originally established under a Title III grant many years ago, is still funded by some of East High's share of federal Chapter 1 grants. A Career Exploration Center for 9th graders, set up with a special grant from the state Vocational Education Department, was for a time a model to be envied by other schools. These programs have become so routine a part of the school that no one views them as "outside interventions" or remembers that they are made possible on a year-to-year basis by "soft money."

However, certain services and the personnel providing them are clearly identified as "special," and are viewed as appendages "tacked on" from the outside. The most notable are the three self-contained special classes for students designated "educable mentally retarded," which have operated in much the same fashion since first being established in 1962. The curriculum and the schedules in these classes seem to discourage much interaction with the rest of the school, except during lunch periods and physical education. About one-third of the kids come from across town and would attend another high school if they weren't identified as having a disability. The three special education teachers at East High depend on the Director of Special Education of the District Office or the Resource Center operated by the Intermediate Education Unit to fill most of their needs; they do not turn to Chris for much except routine supplies, health and attendance services, and assistance with emergency management situations. They are somewhat protective of their students and generally handle discipline within their classes themselves.

East High also has two vice principals (one for curriculum and instruction and the other for administration and discipline), plus several guidance counselors, a full-time nurse, a social worker, and a psychologist, all of whom provide support to the general classroom teachers.

Beginning this September, two new staff members came aboard at East High as Learning Disability Resource Teachers. Such a program had been operating at the middle school level for a few years, but it was a new concept for the staff at East High. Chris had noted that for the past year or two some of the kids coming up from the middle schools had been receiving resource services and that on arrival at East High a few had been transferred into the special education classes. Other students had to "sink or swim" in what the general curriculum offered, and too many were sinking. Therefore, Chris, with the support of the Director of Special Education, had proposed to the Central Office that this new service be extended into East High.

The added personnel slots had been approved relatively easily because, as the Budget Manager pointed out to the board, the state would reimburse the school for 70% of the funding for such personnel, and each student served would make the school eligible for additional federal funds as well. The general teaching staff at East High had acquiesced to the idea (since they felt that anything might help) but were a little unsure about how the function of these teachers would be different from that of the veteran special education teachers at East High.

Chris overheard a conversation in the teachers' lunchroom during the first week of school that illustrates this confusion:

"Exactly what are these new special ed. teachers going to be doing?" asked Bill Jones, the biology teacher.

"They're not special ed.," replied Marie, who had taught math at East High for 23 years and made it a point to be precise. "They are *resource teachers,* and that means they are supposed to be available for us to send kids to for remedial help with the work in our regular classes."

"I don't think so, Marie," Jane broke in. "Someone downtown was saying that resource teachers are mostly to come in and give us advice, like consultants, and not particularly to work with the kids."

"You gotta be kidding," Bill yelled. "That's no more help than the psychologists."

"Wait a minute, Bill," Marie cautioned. "Haven't the social workers been helpful sometimes when we have been trying to get better cooperation from parents to straighten out some problem?"

"But are they part of our school staff, or just more Central Office Special Service personnel, like the speech therapist?" said Jane.

"Well, the job title did say *Learning Disability* Resource Teacher," Marie reminded them, "and that sounds like they should be *teaching,* whether you call it special ed. or not."

"But that's what our Reading Skills Laboratory is for, since most of our kids are Chapter 1 eligible," Jane reminded them.

"Looks like I better get this sorted out," Chris thought, slipping back to the office. "The new teachers are funded with special ed. dollars, but I don't want them stigmatized like our other special ed. teachers. And besides, I would like to have more ownership of this program. In the past, the special ed. teachers have never really *belonged* to the school. I was going to emphasize the *special service* idea, but that apparently carries a negative tone for some of the staff."

"What's in a name?" Chris mused, as the door closed.

REFERENCES

An Act to Amend the Act of September 30, 1950 (PL 81-874), PL 89-313. (November 1, 1965). Title 20, U.S.C. 631 et seq: *U.S. Statutes at Large, 79,* 1158–1162.

Apter, S.J., & Conoley, J.C. (1984). *Childhood behavior disorders and emotional disturbance.* Englewood Cliffs, NJ: Prentice Hall.

Biklen D.P., & Bogdan, R. (1977). Media portrayals of disabled people: A study in stereotypes. *Interracial Books for Children Bulletin, 8,* nos. 6, 7.

Brewer, G.D., & Kakalik, J.S. (1979). *Handicapped children: Strategies for improving services.* New York: McGraw-Hill.

Deno, E.N. (1970). Special education as developmental capital. *Exceptional Children, 37,* 299–340.

Department of Education. (1982). *Fourth annual report to Congress on the implementation of Public Law 94-142: the Education for All Handicapped Children Act.* Washington, DC: U.S. Department of Education.

Department of Education. (1992). *Fourteenth annual report to Congress on the implementation of the Individuals with Disabilities Education Act.* Washington, DC: U.S. Department of Education.

Education for All Handicapped Children Act of 1975, PL 94-142. (August 23, 1977). Title 20, U.S.C. 1401 et seq: *U.S. Statutes at Large, 89,* 773–796.

Education of the Handicapped Act of 1970 (EHA), PL 91-230. (April 13, 1970). Title 20, U.S.C. 1400 et seq: *U.S. Statutes at Large; 84,* 121–195.

Education of the Handicapped Act Amendments of 1986, PL 99-457. (October 8, 1986). Title 20, U.S.C. 1400 et seq: *U.S. Statutes at Large, 100,* 1145–1177.

Gifted and Talented Children's Education Act of 1978, PL 95-561. (November 1, 1978). Title 20, U.S.C. 3061 et seq: *U.S. Statutes at Large, 92,* 2292–2296.

Greenburg, D.E. (1983). *A planning study report for the Council of Administrators of Special Education*. Indianapolis: Council of Administrators of Special Education.

Individuals with Disabilities Education Act of 1990 (IDEA), PL 101-476. (October 30, 1990). Title 20, U.S.C. 1400 et seq: *U.S. Statutes at Large, 104,* 1103–1151.

Kauffman, J.M. (1989). The regular education initiative as Reagan–Bush education policy: A trickle-down theory of education of the hard-to-teach. *Journal of Special Education, 23,* 256–278.

Mackie, R.P., & Dunn, L.N. (1954). *College and university programs for the preparation of teachers of exceptional children*. Office of Education Bulletin No. 13. Washington, DC: U.S. Government Printing Office.

McLaughlin, M.J., & Owings, M.F. (1992). Relationships among states' fiscal and demograpic data and the implementation of PL 94-142. *Exceptional Children, 59,* 247–261.

Reynolds, M.C., & Birch, J.W. (1982). *Teaching exceptional children in all America's schools*. Reston, VA: The Council for Exceptional Children.

Reynolds, M.C., Wang, M.C., & Walberg, H.J. (1987). The necessary restructuring of special and regular education. *Exceptional Children, 53,* 391–398.

Skrtic, T.M. (1991). *Behind special education*. Denver: Love Publishing Co.

Stainback, W., & Stainback, S. (1984). A rationale for the merger of special and regular education. *Exceptional Children, 51,* 102–111.

Wang, M.C., Reynolds, M.C., & Walberg, H.J. (1988). Integrating the children of the second system. *Exceptional Children, 70,* 248–251.

3

Formal Sources of Control

The Legal Structure

In Chapter 2 we identify major policy issues concerning the scope of the enterprise called special education. We now turn to the question of how that enterprise is controlled and consider the various forces that determine what goes on within the field.

Initially, two major sources of control should be recognized and differentiated: 1) formal governance and 2) informal power and influence. While these two factors often interact in day-to-day practice, they may also operate independently. Together, they constitute the major forces behind policy determination. This chapter will address the various aspects of formal governance; the nature of informal power and influence is discussed in Chapter 4.

Official authority over what occurs within special education programs arises from a combination of forces and a number of levels of government. Although the principle of local autonomy is a strong influence on education in the United States and boards of education in local school districts have the authority to set policy on much of the educational program, that authority is clearly delimited by the broader matrix of governing bodies with jurisdiction over a given district. In this country, after an initial approach to the governance of education that was almost exclusively locally based, the gradually increasing exercise of state-level authority through legislative bodies, courts, and units of the executive branch of government began to noticeably shape the practice of education. The avoidance of major involvement by the federal government in education was attributable to the clearly stated provision of the Tenth Amendment to the U.S. Constitution that reserves for the states those powers not specifically mentioned in the Constitution.

Because of the degree to which the federal government has become the central authority over special education, and because constitutional issues have come into play, to fully appreciate the controlling forces behind special education one must understand the whole governance system. The system is based on organizational structures among which certain orderly relationships exist. These structures and the relationships between them are outlined below, along with discussion illustrating their relevance to education in general, and to special education in particular.

We have indicated that three levels of government—federal, state, and local—operate in most of the public activities affecting our society, and bodies at each of these levels have the appropriate legal powers and strategies to carry out their duties. While certain functions of government are concentrated at the federal level (e.g., national defense), others are relatively concentrated at the local level (e.g., education). While responsibility for a number of different functions may fall under the jurisdiction of a single unit of government at the local level (e.g., health, social services, police, and fire departments within a municipal administration), the function of education is almost universally governed by a separate local agency, the school district. The degree of independence of local school districts varies among the states and among certain large cities, and this factor is significant in comparing the intergovernmental relations across functions within the legal structures.

In a discussion of intergovernmental policy influences on education in America, Mosher (1977) has pointed out that "the question of locus of effective power—who dominates in the partnerships or cooperative arrangements—is a matter of considerable dispute" (p. 119). She elaborates on a view of American education proposed by Thompson (1976) that places the local school system at the vortex of many interacting systems. As a "special" unit of government, a local school district is acted upon not only by the upper levels of the education system, but also by agencies of other governmental units, as well as nonpublic agencies, each of which has a locus of identity and sources of influence at the local, state, regional, and national levels.

Across all levels of government, the legal structure is based on four sources of authority: 1) constitutions (usually called charters at the local level), 2) court decisions, 3) statutes (usually called ordinances at the local level), and 4) administrative regulations. In accordance with the U.S. Constitution, in the case of a conflict, federal statutes (or regulations or court decisions) take precedence over state and local provisions. Similarly, state provisions take precedence when they conflict with local ones.

CONSTITUTIONAL LAW

At each level of government, the U.S. Constitution establishes the primary legal basis to which all other sources of control must adhere. The federal constitution and those of individual states can only be amended through complicated processes; therefore, they are written in broad, general principles that will remain appropriate through changing times and conditions. All statutes and regulations must stand the test of compliance with constitutional law. The breadth of constitutional provisions necessarily contributes to their ambiguity, frequently making the test of constitutionality of statutes dependent upon judicial interpretation in the courts.

Since the U.S. Constitution does not address education as a federal concern, appeals based on constitutional concepts as justification for educational practices have been based on fundamental civil rights that are clearly articulated, particularly those addressed in the Fifth and Fourteenth Amendments. The U.S. Constitution has been invoked in the context of education over such issues as freedom of religion, speech, and assembly. With increasing frequency in recent years, arguments based on civil rights and liberties have focused on protection against governmental violation of such rights without "due process of law" and against any state's "deny[ing] to any person within its jurisdiction the equal protection of the laws." It is within this context that much of the force of law has been brought to bear concerning educational and human services practices affecting individuals with disabilities.

Constitutional precedent concerning special education is not, however, isolated from that which is applicable in more general settings as well. The determination of whether special education services will be provided to meet the needs of all children (including the particular needs of certain students who are disabled, disadvantaged, or otherwise exceptional depends in part on an extension of the basic legal principles upon which all public education is authorized. These basic principles include such concepts as: 1) equal protection under the law, 2) equal access to publicly provided services, 3) impartial due process, and 4) protection from discrimination on the basis of classification. Judicial interpretation of the Constitution and related statutes concerning these concepts in cases centering on broad-based educational questions have also been used as precedents in special education cases. While these instances will be elaborated on later, in discussing the role of the courts in this chapter it is important to recognize that the U.S. Supreme Court has ruled that education is *not* a fundamental right guaranteed by the Constitution. Education is not, therefore, protected in the manner that voting is, for example, but rather must be secured, if possible, under the equal protection or due process clauses.

State constitutions, however, include educational provisions and provide a more consistent basis for the development of related statutes and for the rulings of state-level courts. Constitutional pronouncements pertaining to the inclusion of all children, without exception, become key to the statutory basis for special education programs.

COURT DECISIONS

The court system usually serves as the intermediary in the application of constitutional principles to daily practice. In such cases, educational practices and their "fit" with constitutional intent are carefully scrutinized before judicial opinion is issued. The most directly applicable precedent for the many judicial rulings affecting special education in the 1970s and 1980s was the landmark Supreme Court decision in *Brown v. Board of Education of Topeka* (1954). Touching on a number of civil rights issues concerning race (nondiscrimination, access to nonsegregated educational programs, equal protection, etc.), the principles established in the decision have been found to be equally applicable in addressing other discriminatory classifications, most notably disabling conditions. The notion set forth in the *Brown* decision—that education is the means by which all other constitutional rights are secured and that education is necessary for individuals to function in a democratic society—has provided a foundation for arguing that no one may be excluded from educational programs, regardless of special or disadvantageous status. Furthermore, the notion that segregation inherently constitutes nonequality, as established in *Brown*, provides a rationale for the inclusion of a variety of classifications of students, including those with disabilities, within the mainstream of education. The *Brown* case stands as a landmark in this respect.

To fully appreciate the importance of the application of the court opinion on race to the area of disability, one should be aware that earlier court rulings had stood in sharp contrast to *Brown*. In the case of *Watson v. City of Cambridge* (1893), for example, a state court supported the school committee in expelling children who persisted in disorderly conduct "either voluntarily or by reason of imbecility." Also frequently cited is the case of *Beattie v. Board of Education*

(1919) in which a Wisconsin superior court ruled that although a child with a physical disability constituted no threat, and was academically capable, his presence produced a "depressing and nauseating effect on the teachers and school children" and took up an undue portion of the teacher's time, and that "the rights of a child of school age to attend the public schools of the state cannot be insisted upon, when its presence therein is harmful to the best interests of the school." A dramatic shift is evident in the attitude expressed in these cases compared to that in the 1970s, when the principle enunciated in *Brown* was applied to a number of decisions on rights to education for students with disabilities. Basing decisions on the equal protection and due process guarantees of the Fifth and Fourteenth Amendments, courts have invoked the language of *Brown*:

> In these days it is doubtful that any child may reasonably be expected to succeed in life if he is denied the opportunity of an education. Such an opportunity, where the state has undertaken to provide it, is a right which must be made available to all on equal terms.

The litigation over special education that began in the early 1970s and has become more frequent since that time has covered a wide range of topics, but can be classified into a few basic categories, which are described below.

The Right to Treatment

Some of the earliest cases concerning special education dealt with the right to treatment and were initiated by the case of *Wyatt v. Stickney* (1972). These cases are concerned with the rights of institutionalized persons with retardation to habilitation, care, and education within the least restrictive environment, with due regard for privacy and other basic attributes of human living. While these issues go well beyond the concerns of school policy makers or administrators, the cases illustrate many of the principles involved and the means by which the judicial system may intervene in the responsibilities of the executive branches of government. Similar examples include the Willowbrook case (*New York State Association for Retarded Children v. Carey*, 1975) which was resolved through a consent agreement specifying a number of remedies based on equal protection principles, including the deinstitutionalization of the majority of the residents in the case. The case of *Halderman v. Pennhurst State School and Hospital* (1977) also resulted in a ruling that institutionalization was inconsistent with an individual's rights to habilitation in the least restrictive environment.

The Right to Education

A second group of cases that more directly involved access to public school education was initiated by the suit brought by the Pennsylvania Association for Retarded Children against the Commonwealth of Pennsylvania (*PARC v. Pennsylvania*, 1972). Resolved by consent agreement, this case established that every child with retardation is capable of benefiting from education and set forth specific stipulations regarding the manner in which the delivery of services and procedural safeguards would be handled. The principles underlying these stipulations were to be cited repeatedly in succeeding cases and used as justification for legislation drafted in the years that followed. While the *PARC* case dealt only with children with mental retardation, it was closely followed by more comprehensive litigation in *Mills v. Board of Education of District of Columbia* (1972). The court stated in 1972 that the system had failed to provide appropriate services for all types of children with disabilities and ordered that hearing procedures be established to guard against indiscriminate suspension, exclusion, and placement of pupils in special education programs. It established that children with disabilities could not be excluded from schools unless alternative programs and services suited to their needs were provided. It provided procedures for correcting official records in the case of previous expulsions that might have occurred in violation of such due process requirements. The school district was ordered to provide suitable educational programs within specified time limits, to advertise the availability of free public education, and to identify previously excluded children and inform them of their rights. Furthermore, this case directly addressed funding, which is often raised as a barrier to implementing programs:

> If sufficient funds are not available to finance all of the services and programs that are needed in the system then the available funds must be expended equitably in such a manner that no child is entirely excluded from a publicly supported education consistent with his needs and ability to benefit therefrom. (*Mills v. Board*, 1972)

The *Mills* case appears to have opened the door to a number of succeeding rulings that have established that children with disabilities have the right to an education and that it is unconstitutional to deny that right, that public funds must be provided for educational opportunities for all children, and that legal redress in the courts is available if these rights are denied. While these cases, decided at the level of the U.S. District Courts, gave considerable strength to the principle of a right to education for *all* children, it remained for the higher courts to rule that the coverage extends to those with the most severe disabilities, in cases in which the definition of *education* was tested to its limits.

The concept of "zero reject" was brought into focus by the case of *Timothy W. v. Rochester, New Hampshire, School District* (1989), in which the local school district argued that extremely severe disabilities rendered the child incapable of benefiting from instruction. The complexity of this issue is evident in the differing opinions expressed as the case made its way through the court system. The first (hearing officer) level ruled that the child was eligible for special education, despite the fact that he was affected by severe spasticity, brain damage, joint contractures, and seizure disorder; made virtually no sounds; and was nonambulatory, quadriplegic, and cortically blind. The federal district court's opinion, however, was that since (on the basis of expert testimony) the child appeared to be incapable of cognitive learning, and since the intent of special education was to provide educational benefit, the school was not obligated to provide services. On appeal, the First Circuit Court of Appeals reversed this decision, relying on the wording of the federal Education of the Handicapped Act, concluding that under this legislation, "ability to benefit" is not a prerequisite to the provision of services. The school district's request for review by the U.S. Supreme Court was refused, without explanation or recorded dissent, leaving intact the appellate court's ruling that a school district must provide a program for all children, regardless of their ability to benefit from it. The decision in this case was undoubtedly influenced by the disagreement among experts testifying as to what constituted *education* and *benefit*. Although the ruling is only officially binding in the First Circuit (Maine, Massachusetts, New Hampshire, Rhode Island, and Puerto Rico), such cases have considerable influence in all other jurisdictions.

Related Services

A central issue in cases involving children with extensive needs (as in the *Timothy W.* case) is the definition of education itself and the dividing lines between special education, related services, and medical treatment. Although the laws and regulations have attempted to delineate these services, individual instances are frequently fraught with ambiguity. The questions are usually exacerbated by the high costs associated with the type of services likely to be called for. In the past, the courts have been called upon to intervene in these cases, a pivotal landmark being *Irving Independent School District v. Tatro* (1984), in Texas. The child in this case clearly required a particular service, clean intermittent catheterization (CIC), in order to be able to remain in school and receive the special education program to which she was determined to have been entitled. The only issue was whether such service constituted medical treatment, and was therefore not the school system's responsibility, or a related service, and thus covered by provisions of the law. The case was taken all the way to the U.S. Supreme Court, where it was ruled that since CIC was a simple process that could be easily learned by any adult and administered as needed without the presence of a physician or nurse, it was in fact a related service and must be provided by the school as part of the child's program. In this case the expense of the service was modest, but in a number of other cases that followed it, on which further definitional rulings were required, the complexity of the child's needs (and the attendant costs) were great enough to warrant different findings. A good example of this difference is the case of *Detsel v. Board of Education of the Auburn Enlarged City School District* (1987) in New York. The Second Circuit Court of Appeals in this instance ruled that although Melissa Detsel could be readily provided with appropriate educational services in a regular classroom, her need for a full-time nurse in the classroom to care for her trachiostomy was beyond the intended scope of *related services*. This particular case is of interest since, although the necessary services were ruled to be *medical*, and therefore not the obligation of the school system's special education program, it led to a subsequent action that dramatically changed the policy of the federal Health and Human Services Department. Prior to this time, services covered under Medicaid could be provided only in the home or hospital. In *Detsel v. Sullivan* (1990) it was argued that Melissa was entitled to Medicaid, and that she should not have to be home- or hospital-bound, since a more appropriate educational program could be delivered in a regular classroom, but only with ongoing medical intervention. The ruling of the court in Detsel's favor resulted in the broadening of the federal policy regarding physical settings in which Medicaid services can be provided.

Discriminatory Classification

Another line of litigation focused on the crucial issue of standards and practices used in classifying children. It should be recalled that the primary issue in the *Brown* case was one of discriminatory classification on the basis of race. The classification of children as disabled is not as direct or automatic, but rather involves a deliberate process. *Diana v. State Board of Education* (1970) in California was the first case to challenge classification procedures, followed by *Ruiz v. State Board of Education* (1972) and *Larry P. v. Riles* (1972). While the cases cited in the Related Services section above centered on securing a desired and presumably appropriate special educational service, this line of litigation attacked practices of placing children into special education programs when they did not belong there. In each of these cases, the state school system in California was charged with using procedures that resulted in a disproportionate number of children who were members of minority groups being classified as having disabilities and placed in programs that were of questionable value and carried a negative stigma.

In the *Diana* case, it was pointed out that classes for those labelled educable mentally retarded contained approximately twice the number of Chicano pupils as should have been expected based on the proportion of such children in the general school population. It was clear that school personnel had been faced with children whose language and cultural background were significantly different from that of the typical Anglo child, and that they had used the special education program as the most readily available alternative to the regular classroom. It was charged that the plaintiffs had been certified as eligible for such placement on the basis of intelligence tests, in English, which, as the court found obvious, were totally inappropriate for this purpose. The universality of such practice wherever populations of non–English-speaking persons were found led California to mandate the development of test instruments and testing procedures that would be appropriate for children from other cultures and with first languages other than English.

In the *Ruiz* case, group testing was a major issue because it was charged that the results from such tests tended to result in a self-fulfilling prophecy when given to teachers. The demonstrated bias in such tests when used to classify pupils for special programs for the gifted led to constraints on the use of group intelligence testing. Additional strength to arguments regarding that there was inherent bias in assessment and classification procedures came from the widely disseminated findings of Jane Mercer, who conducted an 8-year study of public school and agency classification of minority children in California. Her data demonstrated that, of all agencies, the public school system was the primary labeler of individuals as having mental retardation. In elaborating on her conclusions regarding the classification of black and Chicano children, Mercer (1974) stated:

> We believe that psychological assessment procedures have become a civil rights issue because present assessment and educational practices violate at least five rights of children: a) their right to be evaluated within a culturally appropriate normative framework; b) their right to be assessed as multi-dimensional, many faceted human beings; c) their

right to be fully educated; d) their right to be free of stigmatizing labels; and e) their right to cultural identity and respect. (p. 132)

An extensive analysis of courts' rulings on student classification has been conducted by Kirp (1974). He points out that while many courts have been assertive in dealing with broad issues of school policy, they have been reluctant to intervene in matters concerning minute details within the individual school or classroom unit, which are legally less manageable. However, in the domain of student classification, the courts have found it feasible to intervene, since such cases can be argued on clear constitutional grounds from any of three approaches:

1. The educational harm attributable to either exclusion or assignment to remedial groups, or special education programs that are not only inferior, but can cause psychic injury in addition to deprivation
2. The disproportionate assignment of minority children, which leads to racially or ethnically based isolation
3. The possible unfairness of schools' procedures for determining how a particular student or class of students should be treated, irrespective of the legitimacy of the classifications themselves

The *Larry P.* case focused specifically on black students who were placed in classes for the educable mentally retarded (EMR) in the San Francisco Unified School District at a rate three times their incidence in the general school population. It was argued in this class action suit that the students did not have mental retardation, but rather were the victims of a testing procedure that failed to take into account their cultural background. The relief sought was a moratorium on the use of individual intelligence tests for the placement of black children and a ceiling on the placement of black children based on the percentage of Anglos out of the total school population who were placed in such special classes. A temporary injunction in 1972 stopped the use of IQ tests as the main criterion for placing black students and ordered yearly reevaluation of children in such classes.

After much deliberation, Judge Robert F. Peckham's ruling in 1979 prohibited California school districts from using IQ tests in this fashion, on the grounds that the tests were culturally biased. The case had been, by this time, expanded to include all black children in the state. This decision was affirmed in 1983 by a three-judge panel of the U.S. Court of Appeals for the Ninth Circuit, which held that the state did not take reasonable steps to ensure that nondiscriminatory methods were used to identify and place black students and did not make a reasonable attempt to alleviate existing disproportionate enrollment. Defendants had argued that the low IQ scores of black students were the result of lower socioeconomic status and that their placement was not based solely on the use of standardized test results. The court found, however, that students' school records did not contain sufficient evidence to support the contention that school personnel had considered other factors beyond the test results in making placement decisions. Judge Peckham had noted that there is "less than a one-in-a-million chance that the over-enrollment of black children and the under-enrollment of nonblack children in the EMR classes in 1976–1977 would have resulted under a color-blind system" (*Larry P. v. Riles,* 1979).

It should be noted that during the time between the initial filing of *Larry P.* and the decision in 1979, legislation in California had brought about a different "Master Plan" for special education and a moratorium on the use of IQ tests for EMR placement of any child, regardless of race. These major changes were certainly influenced by the impending judicial action. However, the court concluded that these changes had been insufficient to rectify the imbalances in enrollment and that the state had failed to gather data to support the validity of the tests used and had "revealed a complacent acceptance" of discriminatory practices. Further remedies that were stipulated were: 1) constraint in the use of IQ tests unless data could be supplied pertaining to the validity of proposed tests for both blacks and whites, 2) mandatory monitoring and adoption of procedures to correct existing racial imbalances, and 3) required reevaluation (without IQ tests) of all black children currently enrolled in EMR classes (Smith & Barresi, 1982).

During the time that the case was on appeal, between 1979 and 1983, continued implementation of the Master Plan in California had resulted in the elimination of EMR as a placement classification, but state officials expressed continued concern that the prohibition of certain tests creates a "practical dilemma" in that professionals may be denied the use of a valuable tool. A reflection of this legitimate concern can be seen in another case dealing with alleged discrimination in testing in the Chicago public schools. In *Parents in Action on Special Education (PASE) v. Hannon et al.* (1980) the court focused on the test items within the instruments, rather than the results of the testing, and ruled that although a few items were culturally biased, this did not invalidate the tests as a whole. Questions regarding racial bias and discriminatory assessment have continued, but courts have tended to be less likely to accept disproportionate enrollment as evidence of discrimination per se. In *Georgia State Conference of*

Branches of NAACP v. Georgia (1985) the Circuit Court ruled that although misclassification had undoubtedly occurred as a function of errors in measurement, there was no evidence of *intentional* bias and the court's actions were limited to admonishing the state to sharpen its classification procedures as much as possible. As in many other cases of this nature, conflicting expert testimony forced the courts into decision making on matters that involved professional standards rather than legal questions (Smith & Barresi, 1982, p. 77).

Procedural Versus Substantive Issues

The courts have, in many instances, taken pains to avoid ruling on issues on which professional judgment was at the center of the dispute, preferring to focus on questions that more clearly involved a legal right. For example, the question of access to *some* education (or exclusion therefrom) is more readily dealt with as a legal issue than the more difficult question of establishing what is *appropriate* education. In dealing with the definition of *appropriate*, the concept of *functional exclusion* must be considered. In *Brown*, the argument was that blacks should be given equal access to the same resources as whites. In *Mills*, it was that all students with disabilities should have equal access to the same resources as all other students. In more recent cases, the issue has changed to the call for *different* resources for *different* objectives. This concept was established as being especially relevant in a case concerned not with children with disabilities, but with bilingual education. In *Lau v. Nichols* (1974) the plaintiffs argued that Chinese students had been "functionally excluded" since they had to attend public schools in which all instruction was in English. This case, followed by others concerned with the education of children with disabilities, raised the issue of exclusion from *meaningful* equal educational opportunity. While the rulings in some of these cases have tended toward establishing means for ensuring appropriate education through timely and sufficient evaluations, individually planned programs, and periodic reviews, it is clear that the courts have been reluctant to go beyond such procedural mechanisms and to make a substantive judgment about what constitutes appropriate educational opportunities. This was particularly evident in the first case heard by the U.S. Supreme Court to test the limits of the concept of appropriate education for children with disabilities.

It should be noted that most of the cases (concerning the education of persons with disabilities) discussed above were argued in federal district or appellate courts. The first case of this type to reach the U.S. Supreme Court was an appeal by a school district regarding the educational program for Amy Rowley. In this case the lower courts had established that a sign language interpreter must be provided by the school district for the deaf child to participate fully and profit from the educational program. There was no argument over access or the provision of various special supportive services. The contention was over *how much* service was required and *how far* Amy was to progress. The lower courts had ruled that the child must be provided all the services that the parents had requested in developing Amy's individualized education program (IEP), and the school system had appealed the ruling.

The decision of the Supreme Court in *Board of Education of Hendrick Hudson Central School District v. Rowley* (1982) stated that the system was already providing "sufficient support services to permit the handicapped child to benefit educationally from . . . instruction." Since the services provided were apparently allowing the child to achieve passing marks and to advance with her peers, no additional services were required by law. The parents contended that Amy's intelligence was above average and that with a sign language interpreter her greater potential could be more fully realized. The court noted that the legal requirement had been satisfied by the fact that *normal* progress was occurring and it is the prerogative of the state and local agencies (not the courts) to determine the best methods for providing the required services. This is consistent with a number of other cases in which the courts have refrained from dictating educational methods or judging the merits of particular instructional approaches.

Least Restrictive Environment

Issues involving educational settings, which are usually concerned with the accepted desirability of providing the least restrictive environment (LRE), have been more readily tackled by the courts. A number of such cases were brought to federal district courts during the 1980s, and some advanced to the circuit level. The issue seems to be particularly controversial in cases in which children with severe hearing impairments are concerned, and there are strong differences of opinion regarding the relative merits of more highly specialized (separate) schools versus more integrated local schools. Cases involving children with mental retardation have also been argued on a similar basis. A ruling that makes a strong statement in favor of "full inclusion" was made in federal district court in California in March 1992. In *Sacramento City Unified School District v. Holland* (1992) the district was ordered to place a child with moderate mental retardation (IQ 44) in a regular second grade classroom with supplemental services. This is a striking contrast from the Fifth Circuit's 1989 decision in *Daniel R.R. v. El Paso Independent School District* (1989), in which a more restrictive separate special setting was mandated. In reaching the decision for Rachel Holland, the court took into consideration: 1) the relative educational benefits in regular versus special education classrooms, 2) the nonacademic benefits of interacting with peers, 3) the child's effect on the teacher and other students in the general classroom, and 4) the relative costs of the services. The decision in this case, in contrast with that reached in *Daniel R.R.,* was apparently based on real differences in individual circumstances, that is, on observations regarding the four factors noted above. It is noted that courts are looking beyond traditional academic factors, and that

> Today, courts are also likely to consider the benefit of integration to the child, the child's effect on the rest of the class, the cost of placing the child in regular education, and—perhaps, most importantly—the district's attempts to try regular education placements with supplementary aids and services before rejecting full inclusion. . . . The argument that a regular education placement "just won't work," if unsupported by the facts, is likely to ring hollow in the ears of a federal judge. (*The Last Word on Full Inclusion?* 1992, p. 260)

The accuracy of this observation was demonstrated in the ruling of the U.S. Third Circuit Court of Appeals on May 28, 1993, in the case of *Oberti v. Board of Education of the Borough of Clementon School District.* Supporting the findings of the lower court, it was held that the New Jersey school district had failed to demonstrate that the child's needs could be met only in a special class. The decision was based on the interpretation that the school was obligated to fully explore the use of supplementary aids and services to meet the child's needs in a regular class before resorting to placement elsewhere. The language of the lower court's decision, that "Inclusion is a right, not a privilege of the select few," was noted in the circuit court ruling.

Given the growing interest in this issue, and the increasing rate of appeals in such cases, it is likely that an appeal to the U.S. Supreme Court will be forthcoming. While the school district in Oberti elected to forego an appeal, a defendant in a similar case might pursue such a test.

Other Issues

The length of the school year has become another issue in which courts have intervened. It is clear that if a school district provides extended-year programs for its students without disabilities, it must not deny such services to children with disabilities. In addition, it has been ruled that any school law or policy that limits the school year to 180 days (or any similar cap) is in violation of the provisions of PL 94-142, since the law requires that schools retain sufficient flexibility to provide extra services for those who need them. *Yaris v. Special School District of St. Louis County* (1983) followed a number of similar cases that emphasized the fact that if a child with a disability will regress over the summer months, an appropriate program would include provisions for an extended school year, and the school system must be free to elect such a program for such individuals. That is not to say that the courts have mandated summer programs, but that states and local school districts *must not preclude* such programs as an option.

The courts have also been asked to rule on what constitutes an educational *placement*. In a case involving the New York City Board of Education, the Second U.S. Circuit Court of Appeals held that "the term educational placement refers only to the general type of educational program in which the child is placed." The issue in this case was whether the movement of a group of children from one school to another was in fact a change in placement if essentially the same program of activity was being provided in both locations. It was pointed out that to consider any alteration in a child's educational program as a placement change would impair the ability of teachers to make appropriate modifications or improvements (*Concerned Parents and Citizens for the Continuing Education at Malcolm X (P.S. 79) v. New York City Board of Education*, 1980).

However, change of program (or placement) was a central issue in the case of *Honig v. Doe* (1988), which involved exclusion from school as a disciplinary procedure in California. A number of previous cases (such as *S-1 v. Turlington*, 1981) had dealt with similar issues at the federal district and appellate court levels, and the courts had attempted to make a distinction between behavior that occurs as a *result* of disability and behavior that is unrelated to a student's disability. The lower courts had been unanimous in regarding the expulsion of a student with disabilities as a change in placement and in ruling that for this reason, the IEP committee, rather than the school administrator, should make such a decision. It was recognized that in some such cases there is a potential danger to other students, and *Honig* was appealed to the U.S. Supreme Court, asking for exceptions in cases in which safety was an issue. The Court stated in 1988 that Congress had intended to strip schools of their unilateral authority to remove students, and ruled that beyond a limit of 10 days of suspension within a school year, change-of-placement procedures must be employed. A "stay-put" principle is to be employed—the child must

remain in the current setting while the new placement is being negotiated. It is noted that in cases that involve an extreme danger to self
or others, a school could obtain a court order to remove the student,
but it would be necessary to have persuasive evidence that the behavior was persistent and not an isolated incident. Furthermore, the ruling reinforced the notion that even when expulsion was properly executed, the school could not simply terminate educational services,
but must provide services in some other setting.

It is interesting to note that although the U.S. Supreme Court has
agreed to become involved in special education issues only a few
times, the particular content of these issues has varied widely. The
common denominator has been the potential for far-reaching consequences in relationships between individuals and the agencies of
government at the local, state, and national levels. The next relevant
case (after *Honig*) to be heard by the highest court involved the issue
of *sovereign immunity*, which in accordance with the Eleventh
Amendment renders the states immune from suits in federal courts
by individuals for monetary relief. In the case of *Dellmuth v. Muth*
(1989), which involved the state of Pennsylvania, the Supreme Court
ruled that while immunity did apply to the states, it did not exempt
local school districts. It was also quickly recognized that a legislative
amendment to the Education of the Handicapped Act could explicitly
abrogate Eleventh Amendment immunity in cases brought under the
EHA. Since the general view in the Congress was that the intent was
to ensure a right to meaningful relief in cases in which a state had
failed to provide a free, appropriate, public education, an amendment
to the statute was readily passed, and the relevance of the Supreme
Court's action was quite short-lived.

The U.S. Supreme Court again became involved in special education in 1992, in agreeing to hear a case involving a possible violation
of the Establishment Clause of the First Amendment. In *Zobrist v.
Catalina Foothills School District* (1992) the Ninth Circuit Court
had ruled that the provision of a sign language interpreter to a parochial school student at his Catholic high school would be a violation
of the principle of separation of church and state, which holds that an
action of the government must not have the primary effect of advancing religion. In this instance it was held that religious and secular education were inextricably intertwined within the school's program.
However, the Supreme Court, on June 18, 1993, ruled to the contrary,
finding that the provision of the sign language interpreter was not
only an appropriate service for the disabled student, but also did not
violate the constitution when delivered within the religious school.

It can be seen that the judicial system has paved the way in establishing connections between constitutional rights and day-to-day practice in the delivery of public services for students with disabilities. To decide every service issue in the courts, however, would be extremely impractical. Statutory provisions have always been the major control mechanism over practice, and legislative initiatives arising from court decisions have become the major force for change at both the state and federal levels.

STATUTORY CODE

In contrast to the policies dictated by the rulings of single judges or judicial panels, laws passed by a legislative body presumably reflect the intent of a large group of individuals, as the members of such bodies are elected to officially represent the will of the people. The legislative process involves the writing of proposed laws, or statutes, in the form of bills that become the subjects of study, debate, testimony from interested parties, and revision before finally being voted on by the elected representatives. In addition, the required endorsement of the proposed legislation by the chief executive further broadens the presumed base of acceptance of the policy before it becomes law. This process of statutory development operates in basically the same manner in each state and in the U.S. Congress. This broad, representative input on legislative acts is the justification for expecting statutes to be implemented in accordance with the intent of those initiating and approving them. Being more focused and specific to a particular purpose than constitutional provisions, statutes authorize certain policies; however, they are usually not sufficiently detailed to be totally explanatory or self-enforcing. Statutes generally set forth broad principles permitting, authorizing, or mandating activities in the jurisdiction concerned, but leave to the executive branch of the government the responsibility for determining exactly how to carry out the understood intent. The degree of detailed specificity included within a statute is often an issue of controversy, and the achievement of an optimal level of detail is a significant factor in the chances of a bill becoming a law and, if it does pass, of being implemented. These factors are particularly apparent in some of the statutes recently passed in the area of special education.

State Initiatives

At the state level, the 1970s were marked by a rapid upsurge in legislative changes. While almost every state legislature had periodically added and modified existing statutes with some degree of regularity during the 1940s, 1950s, and 1960s, the focus of that period's legislation tended to be on incremental expansion and addition of services, the securing of somewhat more favorable fiscal provisions, and the development of standards for the delivery of quality instruction to children with disabilities. There was encouragement and, in many cases, incentive for local school systems to improve their service offerings. However, strongly worded mandates for comprehensive service for students with all conditions and degrees of disability were rare. But legislative activity in the early 1970s was so pronounced that by 1975, most states had passed such legislation. It was recognized, however, that exemption provisions and loopholes allowed for considerable slippage in the realization of full services.

The legislation of the 1970s tended to focus on guaranteeing service for *all*, with no child excluded from services or education for any reason whatsoever. Due process protections, growing out of the upsurge in court actions at the time, were also frequently included in the legislative changes. The laws of this period also reflect increasing attention to the principles of LRE and maximum feasible normalization, which had not been evident before this time. Fiscal modifications, including increases in funding, occurred in virtually every state. Legislation concerning state-wide planning was passed, and advisory councils were authorized. Provision for preschool services, very rare before 1970, were also introduced in nearly half of the states. In summarizing the effects of this upsurge in state legislation, it should be noted that by the time federal legislation was passed in 1975, many individual states had already taken action of a similar nature.

In accordance with the Tenth Amendment, education is basically a concern of the states, and federal intervention has been limited to cases in which equal protection principles have been at issue. Exceptions have been noted where, to address certain other social concerns, federal initiatives have been taken to promote and facilitate particular educational objectives.

Federal Initiatives

Discussing the federal role in a historical context, Kaestle and Smith (1982) mention the popular notion that federal aid to education has tended to occur in connection with incidents of national crises, many of which have been war related. They cite the Morrill Act, providing aid to higher education, passed during the Civil War, and the Smith-Hughes Act for vocational education (directly affecting elementary and secondary schools) passed during World War I. The Lanham Act, which introduced the concept of federal impact aid to areas under federal control (such as military bases and manufacturing centers of private defense contractors), was passed at the beginning of World War II and expanded during the Korean conflict. The Cold War is credited with influencing the National Defense Education Act in 1958. These federal programs have tended to be limited in scope, enabling rather than mandatory, and always supplemental to the major state and local roles in providing education. Combination federal–state programs in vocational education had long been a source of support to local schools, but these had been highly categorical and were not accompanied by significant federal intervention. Departure from this stance dates only from 1965.

It should be noted that certain pieces of federal legislation concerned with the education of children with disabilities predated this point. However, these initiatives offered only indirect support, in that they dealt with the funding of research on the problem, the training of personnel to work with children with disabilities, and the development of instructional materials, specifically for children who were deaf or blind. This earlier legislation, dating from 1954 to 1964, contained no provision for funding of or intervention in local school system special education programming. While aspects of these earlier federal programs have been retained as parts of more expansive provisions in recent years, they have been largely overshadowed since the early 1970s in both the amounts of funding involved and the impact of the federal government on the education community and the general public.

The Breakthrough   The Elementary and Secondary Education Act of 1965 (ESEA, PL 89-10) was again a response to a social concern, with its major focus on problems associated with poverty and its mechanisms designed to supplement local practice. Consistent with the trend of federal interventions in education being associated with war and other national crises, this initiative, introduced during the Vietnam involvement, was a major part of what Lyndon Johnson called the country's "war on poverty." The scope of ESEA, the magnitude of federal funds distributed, and the extent to which its mechanisms intervened in state and local educational practices clearly constituted a breakthrough in legislative history. ESEA broke the logjam on federal involvement in local education. Certain principles set forth in the law have become a part of standard interaction between different levels of government in the delivery of education services. Many of those principles have since been reflected in policies and procedures in special education as well. Some of the parallels between ESEA and the later federal legislation concerning persons with disabilities are quite obvious. The focus of both pieces of legislated policy includes: 1) disadvantaged populations; 2) individual needs; 3) systematic planning; 4) consumer participation; 5) personnel development; 6) public/nonpublic cooperation; 7) supplementing, rather than supplanting, regular school services; and 8) evaluation and accountability.

These aspects of ESEA have been carried forward into much of the legislation concerning federal involvement in education. Title VI, which was added to the original ESEA by amendment in 1967, extended certain provisions of the Act to cover services for students with disabilities and thereby became the forerunner of three major federal civil rights initiatives—the Rehabilitation Act of 1973 (PL 93-112) and the Education for All Handicapped Children Act of 1975 (PL 94-142), and the Americans with Disabilities Act of 1990 (ADA) (PL 101-336).

Concern for Persons with Disabilities The prohibition of discrimination on the basis of disability is the major focus of PL 93-112; Section 504, though constituting a very broad umbrella, was unusually brief in its statement that

> No otherwise qualified handicapped individual in the United States, as defined in section 7(6), shall, solely by reason of his/her handicap, be excluded from the participation in, be denied the benefits of, or be subject to discrimination under any program or activity receiving federal financial assistance.

The programs referred to include education, and since virtually all education agencies receive some form of federal assistance, this policy has direct application to the education of persons with disabilities as well as to the full range of other public services (such as health, welfare, and employment) and to participants of all ages. The implications of this statute will be discussed more fully under the topic of Administrative Regulations.

The concepts addressed in Section 504 were broadened by the ADA, which extended prohibitions against discrimination to apply to entities throughout both the private and public sector, without regard to the receipt of federal funds. The ADA's four titles deal with: 1) employment, 2) public services (e.g., transportation), 3) public accommodations (e.g., barrier-free access to commercial establishments), and 4) telecommunications (e.g., relay services for individuals with hearing and speech impairments). The law provides for implementation over a period of time, but will eventually affect an extremely broad sweep of society. While the ADA does not affect educational institutions more than any other segment of society, schools will certainly have to make some adjustments to comply with its provisions.

A more narrow target was addressed in PL 94-142, which dealt only with education, and only with individuals from 3 to 21 years of age. PL 94-142 reflects the intent of Congress to ensure that a free and appropriate education and related services be provided to all disabled children. Its major provisions, which remain intact after many subsequent amendments and are now a part of the broader Individuals with Disabilities Education Act (IDEA), include:

1. Grants to assist states in providing mandated programs
2. The requirement of state plans and local applications to receive allocated funds
3. State and local procedural safeguards for students and their parents
4. Education within the least restrictive environment, to the maximum extent appropriate
5. Procedures for nondiscriminatory evaluation and assessment of students
6. The development, implementation, and periodic review of an individualized education program (IEP) for every student
7. A comprehensive system of personnel development for each state
8. Cooperation between state and local education agencies and those other public and private agencies concerned with children with disabilities
9. Involvement of parents in the approval of assessment procedures and in determining how and where children will be served

Within these broad parameters of statutory control, the articulation of federal, state, and local policies and procedures are carried out. The details that affect day-to-day practice must be provided in administrative rules and regulations. It has been noted, however, that as compared with many federal statutes, and certainly as compared with the degree of intervention from the federal level to which state and local school administrators were accustomed, IDEA is rather highly prescriptive. Although the Bill passed the Congress by a comfortable margin, in retrospect it should be recognized that such specificity, entailing such intrusion on previous autonomy, was a significant change in intergovernmental relations in the educational domain. The reactions from the education community in the years since the Act's passage demonstrate the effect of that change. Proposals to modify the statute have come from a number of quarters, but the complexity of the political process, together with the significant advocacy forces that remain intact, have very effectively forstalled attacks on the statute.

The Nature of Federal Intervention   The criticisms of PL 94-142 as being intrusive were not unique to the issue of special education, but were consistent with long-standing attitudes of the education community regarding its status as a "special" entity. Mosher (1977) points out the tendency of educators to adhere to isolationist politics, with a "hostility to general governmental controls and competition for resources with other public services" (p. 101). Furthermore, she cites the observations of political scientists on the effects of cooperative federalism that were evident in the general government programs of earlier decades. Some such features that are particularly applicable to special education are: 1) the tendency to bypass traditional political jurisdictions; 2) the slanting of local programs to pursue what is supported federally, regardless of local need; 3) the tendency in grant-supported programs to develop specialized roles and personnel without accountability to mainline organizational units; and 4) the development of programs outside of existing functional networks that compete with established programs from grass-roots support.

These tendencies and others of a similar nature have been cited by analysts of the impact of ESEA on local education, from which many parallels may be drawn to special education. Some frequently cited problems are: 1) the insensitivity of the federal policymakers to the diverse capabilities of local recipient agencies; 2) disappointment over shortfalls in funding; 3) invasions of local turf through mandates regarding targeted beneficiaries and other operational matters; 4) lack of trust among branches and levels of government; 5) a tendency to resort to narrow, special-purpose projects as a means of maintaining control when trust is lacking; and 6) an increase in vested interests at the local and state levels to keep federal funds flowing.

Given these recognized limitations, there is every reason to expect that the impact of legislation, particularly from the federal level, would be felt rather gradually. Sarason and Doris (1979) have discussed the expectations that may be held for legislated reform, pointing out that "when we endeavor to make a change in our schools, we fail to recognize that the *structure* of the schools was developed in relation to earlier societal problems, and that these structural characteristics will be effective obstacles to our efforts at change" (p. 156). Despite these obstacles, it is apparent that those who are interested in improving and expanding services have not lost faith in the legislative process as a means of pursuing their goals. The amendments over the years have maintained consistency with the original intentions, have extended the provisions in response to recognized shortcomings, and have demonstrated determination to resist any significant dilution of these goals.

The Goals   PL 94-142, as well as its precursors and the numerous amendments that followed, clearly show that legislators were convinced that help from the federal level was necessary to allow the states and local school systems to extend services to children not being served and to improve the quality of existing services. However, they were also quite conscious of the need for constraint, both in terms of financial demands and undue interference in local practice. The balancing of these objectives is not easy. The members of Congress were very much aware of the interests of parents and advocates who saw the law as fulfilling their expectations of a more accepting philosophy and an end to the segregation that had characterized special education in the past. But, as Sarason and Doris (1978) have reminded us:

> Change in societal attitudes and social policy was spearheaded by a dedicated minority relying on political pressure and the courts; but at every step of the way, this minority encountered opposition, especially from personnel in schools, institutions, and state agencies who saw how drastic the proposed changes would be for them. (p. 7)

One major aspect of these changes would be that general educators would need to become knowledgeable about the characteristics of children with disabilities and less prone to send such children elsewhere for instruction and related services. For both general and special educators, it would be necessary to learn to relate better to each other and to become more responsive to parents, while being more aware of the rights of both children and their parents. The bottom line for all educators is that they can no longer be so arbitrary in making decisions about the classification and placement of students with disabilities.

Some Problems   While the passage of the laws described above can correctly be hailed as a major victory in setting the stage for comprehensive quality services, their actual implementation is generally recognized as falling far short of the anticipated ideal. Some of the shortcomings are quite concrete, such as the failure to appropriate anywhere near the level of federal funding that has been authorized. Others are more ambiguous, such as the question as to whether the significant increase in the numbers of children being identified and served is really an indication of an improved system or is only a demonstration of the schools' capacity to shift boundary lines between regular and special education in order to focus on the least expensive alternative. It is clear that the data showing an increasing proportion of students being served in or near the mainstream is to a large extent a function of the increasing numbers of students with very mild disabilities being identified, while those with more complex needs remain in environments as restrictive as ever. The tenacity of categorical thinking, and particularly the pressure to add still more categories, is regarded as a problem by many observers. It is also evident that the focus on compliance with procedural safeguards and processes has reduced attention to substantive program quality.

Outcomes   However, it is possible to point to positive outcomes. A great number of studies have been conducted in the years since the passage of PL 94-142. The federal government itself has sponsored many studies as part of the mandate within the law to evaluate its own effects. These studies provide the data for the *Annual Reports to the Congress.* Individual states have also conducted numerous studies to assess the combined impact of the federal law and statutes at the state level. Interpretations of these data, though containing some ambiguities, exhibit a good number of fairly consistent findings:

1. Increasing numbers of children are being identified, assessed, and placed for service.
2. Numbers of students found to be in need of service have not reached anticipated levels.
3. The greatest increases in identification have been in the various categories of students with mild disabilities, who, in the past, might not have been regarded as having a disability at all.
4. Increasing varieties of service options are found, with the greatest growth in the number of students placed in regular settings with supplemental instruction and related services.
5. Increasing numbers of students with more significant disabilities are being served in private placements with public support.
6. Procedural safeguards in student assessment and program decision processes have become technically sophisticated, complex, and time consuming, but are accepted as valuable and necessary by most participants.
7. Participation by most parents and general education teachers in the processes is passive, if it occurs at all.
8. School personnel are increasingly conscious of the parents' role (though still largely symbolic) and make an effort to observe relevant appropriate procedures.
9. Effective use of due process by parents is predominantly an upper–middle-class phenomenon.
10. Alternatives to expensive due process hearings are being explored and used more frequently.
11. The majority of due process hearings have dealt with parent requests for more-restrictive (usually private) placements than

those proposed by school personnel; parents (particularly the well informed and relatively affluent) tend to win such cases.

12. The greatest hesitancy by school systems has been in the area of the provision of related services, in which high cost and ambiguity concerning eligibility is most pronounced.

13. Interagency relationships between schools and other health and human services programs, particularly when funding responsibility is an issue, has been addressed, but still remains a complex problem.

14. The availability of personnel with the necessary technical competency is a problem in many less-attractive localities.

15. Support for inservice training of personnel in both general and special education has been given increasing attention, but remains a challenge that will require more than money to overcome.

16. The demand for thorough, individualized evaluation of pupil needs is constrained by the realistic organizational demand for efficient management of labor-intensive procedures; this is particularly problematic in large systems with great numbers of eligible students.

17. The IEP process, originally viewed quite negatively, has become recognized and accepted as valuable, even though it is often no more than a "paper exercise" with only modest instructional utility.

18. Communication among all parties in the service system has increased, as has record keeping to document it and all other procedural matters.

Most observers conclude that given the sweeping scope of the federal law, its implementation has progressed reasonably well, with many of the most fearfully anticipated problems being solved or accommodated. The major amendments that were made in 1983, 1986, and 1990 each extended the scope of entitlements and refined the focus of services. The emphasis on preschool children (infants and toddlers) brought about by the addition of Part H by PL 99-457 in 1986, although meeting with major implementation obstacles, has clearly established a foothold. The focus on transition from school to adult living in the Education of the Handicapped Act Amendments of 1990 (PL 101-476) has already been noted. While the dollar amounts actually appropriated have been far less than those authorized and funding has not kept up with inflation, compared to other federal education programs, special education has done fairly well.

ADMINISTRATIVE REGULATIONS

As we indicate above, statutes are usually designed for broad authorization of desired policies, with the expectation that the necessary details will be taken care of in regulations developed by the executive branch of the (state or federal) government. In the case of education, responsibility for regulation development and implementation rests with the office of the chief executive for education, presently the Secretary of the U.S. Department of Education. In each state a similar responsibility rests with the chief state school officer as representative of a state board of education or other policy-making body (the exact designation of this group again varying from state to state).

The process of regulation development typically begins with an expression by the professional staff of the executive agency of what rules, regulations, or guidelines are necessary to permit reasonable execution of the intent of the law. Advice may be sought from informed sources outside of the government, and technical guidance by legal experts within the agency must always be part of the process. Publicizing proposed regulations in order to gain additional advice and gauge potential reaction to and acceptability of the proposal is a standard procedure in most jurisdictions. This may be done through a public notice (e.g., in the *Federal Register*) with an invitation for written comment or testimony at public hearings scheduled at times and places that presumably will allow adequate input. This procedure then leads to revision and adjustment before final adoption by the official policy body or chief executive.

The interval between the passage of a new statute and the adoption of administrative regulations, in cases in which policies and practices of operating systems are likely to undergo extensive change, may extend over a considerable period of time and be filled with controversy. The smaller scope of the impact of regulations at the state level, as compared with the federal, usually allows the necessary negotiations and compromises to be accomplished with reasonable dispatch, but in some instances it becomes necessary to introduce a mandatory time frame for phase-in of the new regulations in order to secure initial agreement and set the stage for future implementation. Some of the policy changes covered by state-level regulatory developments in the late 1980s and early 1990s, like the federal developments, have been of major interest to a variety of constituents, thereby sparking time-consuming controversies.

Two Examples

At the federal level, two typical cases illustrate the nature of the process described above. The Rehabilitation Act of 1973 was signed on

September 26, 1973, and contained a number of provisions pertaining to vocational rehabilitation. The part of the Act dealing with non-discrimination, Section 504, was only a brief paragraph, but it emphasized a civil rights issue, which went beyond the social welfare provisions of the rest of the Act. The development of regulations in this case included the participation of the staff of the Office of Civil Rights. The forthcoming regulations would cover a wide variety of life needs, including access to education and all other public services, as well as employment and the removal of architectural barriers.

Since Section 504 was rather "open ended," the development of associated regulations required the consideration of a vast number of issues. Defining the population covered by the law was a problem only partially addressed by language included in the Rehabilitation Act Amendments of 1974 that mandated the inclusion of "any person who (A) has a physical or mental impairment which substantially limits one or more of such person's major life activities, (B) has a record of such an impairment, or (C) is regarded as having such an impairment."

This definition led to consideration as to whether certain individuals such as alcoholics, drug addicts, or homosexuals were to be included as "handicapped" under the law. Decisions on these questions were based on different opinions as to logic, precedent, and public perception. The decision to include alcoholism and drug addiction, but not homosexuality, represents a "best compromise" among various advocacy groups. There was no question that many conditions become a disability primarily because one is "regarded as having such an impairment" rather than because the condition constitutes an objective physical or mental limitation. It was recognized that homosexuals experience this status from the perspective of much, but certainly not all, of society. However, there is much more agreement within the medical field and among those who actually have the conditions, as to the diseased status of alcoholics and drug addicts.

Other major questions addressed in the Section 504 Regulations concerned the relationship of its provisions to other federal initiatives that were also in the process of being interpreted. The right to treatment for individuals in institutions was covered by PL 94-103, the Developmental Disabilities Assistance and Bill of Rights Act, and while Section 504 included guarantees of equal rights of those with disabilities to whatever is provided to other persons, it was not intended to establish substantive rights to treatment. Similarly, the parallel intent of PL 94-142, the Education for All Handicapped Children Act, to guarantee educational access created areas of overlap, particularly concerning definitions and procedures, necessitating coordination between the Bureau of Education for the Handicapped (responsible for administering PL 94-142) and the Office of Civil Rights (responsible for Section 504). These considerations, the complexities of attaining consistency in definitions and procedures among the relevant laws and their regulations, not to mention uncertainty about the potential costs of implementation, greatly inhibited progress on the writing of regulations for Section 504. Proposed rules were published in the *Federal Register* on July 16, 1976, leading to over 700 written comments from members of the field and testimony at 22 public hearings conducted around the country. The controversial nature of the provisions and their potential impact again delayed final action until political pressure and demonstrations (including wheelchair sit-ins at government buildings) by consumers and advocates forced adoption by the administration. Final regulations were published in the *Federal Register* on May 4, 1977, nearly 4 years after the passage of the original law. In this case, regulations to administer a section of a law only one paragraph in length covers over 40 pages (including appendices of comments and explanatory content) of the Code of Federal Regulations.

A comparison can be drawn to the link between the statute and its administrative regulations in the instance of PL 101-476, which amended the Individuals with Disabilities Education Act (IDEA) on October 30, 1990. The original law and its regulations had been long and prescriptive, and had undergone a number of amendments in the years after 1975. A notice of proposed rulemaking (NPRM) was published in the *Federal Register* on August 19, 1991, and after receipt and consideration of responses to the invitation for comments, the final regulations were published on September 29, 1992. Although described as "final," this publication also invited comments, and left the date of enactment for certain portions to be determined later. The text of these regulations required almost 60 pages in the *Federal Register*.

Format

In view of the impressive volume of at least the two examples of regulations, it may be useful to examine the format of such publications. Federal and state regulations tend to follow a similar structure, the nature of which may be illustrated by the table of contents of the final regulations generated from PL 101-476, dealing with Assistance to States for the Education of Children with Disabilities Program and Preschool Grants for Children with Disabilities. These regulations, when put into effect, became the current version of Title 34 of the Code of Federal Regulations, Parts 300 and 301.

In accordance with typical format, an initial statement (Subpart A—General) sets forth the purpose, applicability, and general provisions of the regulations and includes definitions of terms used throughout the rest of the document. Such definitions frequently constitute a major portion of regulations in which it is anticipated that obscure and specialized language must be used to establish the scope of the provisions in question. In this instance, 15 terms are defined, including such possibly obscure or ambiguous ones as *assistive technology device*, *free appropriate public education*, and *related services*, as well as presumably well-established concepts such as *parent*, *native language*, and *state*. Within some of these 15 definitions, such as that for *children with disabilities*, there are as many as 13 other definitions, from *autism* to *visual impairment including blindness*.

The remaining parts of the regulations spell out the substantive requirements:

Subpart B. State Plans and Local Educational Agency Applications
These sections deal with the required content of the plans that states must submit annually in order to be a participant and thereby receive available federal funds, as well as the content of local educational agency applications (again for funds) and the procedural requirements controlling local participation, including public participation in the adoption of such plans.

Subpart C. Services These sections detail the ingredients of a free, appropriate, public education; set forth priorities in the use of funds; establish the process and content of individualized educational programs; outline procedures for the provision of direct service by state agencies in cases in which local agency services are precluded; and establish the state's responsibility for instituting a comprehensive system of personnel development.

Subpart D. Private Schools These sections cover procedures for children in private schools, distinguishing between situations in which such children are placed or referred by public agencies and those in which children are enrolled without public agency involvement but are still eligible for agency services.

Subpart E. Procedural Safeguards These sections outline the due process procedures for parents and children, including protection in evaluation, confidentiality of information, and hearings; the use of least restrictive environment in placement considerations; and accountability for such procedures at the local, state, and federal levels.

Subpart F. State Administration These sections cover the state agency's responsibility for program monitoring, adoption of a complaint procedure, use of federal funds for state administration, and operation of an advisory panel.

Subpart G. Allocation of Funds, Reports These sections detail the formulas and procedures for the allocation and distribution of federal funds to agencies within the state and outline the required contents of various mandatory reports to the federal government.

The volume of detail as well as the extensive scope of regulations of this type have been cited in many quarters as an extreme example of overly intrusive federal activity. Although directly concerned consumers and their advocates, as well as most professional special educators, have seen the regulatory process as a necessity, the general educational administrative establishment quickly recognized that the degree of prescription, when weighed against the level of support, was somewhat unusual. Individuals and groups such as the Council of Chief State School Officers, perennially conscious of the balance of power and funding among the federal, state, and local levels in many areas of the education system, have been prone to point to special education as the prime example of creeping (or perhaps galloping) federalism. Congressional support for the underlying principles of the regulations has remained consistently strong, however, and unlike some other policies in which regulation had included much more prescriptive detail than the original statute, supporters of PL 94-142 and its subsequent amendments have been able to attest accurately that the law itself contained most of the detail, which represented the intent of Congress and had broad grass-roots support.

The Regulatory Burden

Aside from the particular case of this federal initiative, however, scholars of social reform and intergovernmental relations have frequently cited the problem of "regulatory unreasonableness," in which either federal or state government gets involved in program operation at the "street level." Kagan (1981) points out that standards promulgated by the government to control schools often require the investment of local resources as well, and "thus shift responsibility for deciding the precise trade-off among conflicting claims on scarce resources away from local administrators to government officials in Washington or state capitals" (p. 29). Since school systems are highly diverse, regulations that may be appropriate to ensure service adequacy in one place may be unnecessary in another. In contrasting educational regulation to that imposed on business (e.g., by the Environmental Protection Act or the Occupational Safety and Health Act), Kagan argues that more discretion is granted to "the regulated" in education. To an extent, schools are able to plan their own programs and execute them in accordance with broad procedural guidelines. In addition, sanctions for violations are more limited and less automatic. That is, school officials may face a threatened cut-off of federal funds, but are not subject to personal criminal prosecution for violations, and withholding of funds is seldom used, since in most cases it would only make the situation worse for the students involved. Furthermore, regulatory failures are less dramatic in education than in business and, therefore, regulators are more likely to recognize that given the uncertain technology of education, there is room for reasonable differences of opinion as to the proper means to each end.

However, this open endedness of standards also permits clients and advocates to take public agencies to court for failure to pursue statutory goals and provides "more discretion for ideologically minded enforcement officials and judges to read their own substantive views into the law, even to the point of unreasonableness" (p. 34). The lack of a fixed standard of "appropriate" education has certainly allowed educators to make decisions that have led to appeals, litigation, and an overabundance of legislation concerning special education. Furthermore, there is a general assumption that because the emphasis in regulation is on procedural rather than substantive standards, accountability is problematic. Since tangible outcomes are illusive, we must compensate by overloading on process, with documentation and reports to assure regulators that the process has occurred. The development of the IEP and other due process steps illustrates this.

Another major problem in special education is the balancing of regulatory intensity to monitor those systems in which minority needs might be neglected if left unsupervised, without stifling the conscientious activity in others through overbearing surveillance. To the extent that such regulation is overemphasized, an undue focus on literal compliance is found, with less attention to substance and quality considerations. If it were believed that school systems were uniformly bad in their execution of programs that fall under the intent of the law, then intense accounting for regulatory detail would be appropriate. However, this is probably not the case. School systems vary widely in this dimension, and there is good reason for fear that regulatory zeal may yield diminishing returns when the focus on details of compliance intrudes upon time that could be better spent on substantive matters. In reporting on the implementation of laws and regulations in suburban districts of the state of Massachusetts, which were similar to, but preceded the federal initiatives, Weatherley and Lipsky (1977) indicate that despite the fact that monitoring efforts by the state were only moderate, school personnel focused in an all-consuming fashion on the bureaucratic details required to process routine cases, in order to have some time left to deal with those cases that were sufficiently problematic to warrant their professional attention.

While it is generally observed that school system personnel, particularly special educators, have responded to the heavy burden of regulation with valiant effort and only mild resentment, the presence of even this moderate level of reaction runs the risk of stimulating a backlash when added to a general political thrust toward decentralization and a reduced federal role in education. Given such risks, the argument for flexible regulation (or flexible enforcement of regulation) becomes very persuasive. In the relatively technologically uncertain field of education, in which differences of opinion regarding "most appropriate" are the rule and cost–benefit analysis is virtually impossible, Kagan suggests that such flexibility, though fraught with many risks, is a goal worthy of serious pursuit:

> Constructing criteria for such nonuniform treatment and developing a legally defensible rationale for a flexible mode of implementing regulations and broadly stated student rights are important goals for the regulation of schools and businesses alike. The alternative, as suggested earlier, may be continuing political backlash and wholesale "deregulation" that throws out the baby of progress with the bathwater of regulatory unreasonableness. (Kagan, 1981, p. 56)

Deregulation

The conditions described above were prevalent with respect to federal regulatory activity in general, and to PL 94-142 in particular, during the early years of the Reagan administration. The movement to collapse a large number of federal education programs into many fewer "block grants" under the provisions of the Education Consolidation and Improvement Act of 1981 was a strong signal of the federal government's intent to allow greater discretion at the local level in the use of federal funds for the administration of programs authorized to pursue a variety of national priorities. Discussing the place of categorical grants when rethinking the federal role in education, Levin (1981) cites the nature of complaints and contradictions that accompanied the dramatic expansion of federal financial involvement from 1965 to 1980. He points out the doubts regarding the efficacy of certain categorical programs; the concerns that, in spite of rules to the contrary, federal grants were being used to supplant local and state funding; and perhaps of greatest influence, the fact that administrative regulations connected to each categorical grant program resulted in a duplication of paperwork. The potential for wasted resources under existing procedures and the promise of savings in administrative costs (however exaggerated) provided a potent argument for consolidation, as did the presumed opportunity for decisions about the use of funds to be made closer to those who were actually affected by them.

Opposing arguments focused on the fact that federal categorical grants were initially established because state and local education agencies were not providing for special educational needs. Turning decisions over to locals would create a risk of federal block grants being used to replace state and local funding, possibly at the expense of the needs of the poor, minorities, and those with disabilities. The strength of these opposing arguments and the lobbying power of special education interests were apparently responsible for modifying the original intent of the Reagan administration to include all categorical education programs within the block grant package.

As a result, the final form of the Education Consolidation and Improvement Act included two chapters, with Chapter II comprising more than 30 existing programs consolidated into a single block, and the major intent of financial assistance being to meet the special educational needs of disadvantaged children (replacing the former Title I program). All programs encompassed by the Education of the Handicapped Act, including the major PL 94-142 Part B Assistance to States for Education of Handicapped Children, were excluded from the consolidation and permitted to retain their independent categorical status, with all existing regulatory provisions left intact.

Subsequent attempts to introduce deregulating initiatives by Executive Order from the President were unsuccessful, despite support from state-level organizations. The federal Office of Special Education and Rehabilitative Services (OSERS) proposed 16 "targets of opportunity for deregulation," based on problems that had been brought to light by state and local agency administrators. However, when an actual notice of proposed rulemaking was published in the *Federal Register*, August 4, 1982, the reaction from the field of consumers and advocacy organizations was so strong, with over 23,000 communications being received, that the Secretary of Education saw no choice but to postpone and finally withdraw all attempts at deregulation.

This scenario rather clearly demonstrates the balance of forces that act upon public policy. The trade-offs in the case of an obviously intensive and extensive degree of official governmental regulation of local education practice, in which two branches of government were on opposite sides of a political and philosophic issue, were in the final analysis determined by the action of informal sources of influence. The following chapter discusses in greater detail the nature and impact of such informal sources of control of public policy in special education.

ILLUSTRATIVE CASE

As Director of Special Education in Metropolis, Dale Walker is recognized as one of the leaders among administrators in the state of LaFayette. During 10 years in this position, Dale has frequently been active in affairs of the governance of special education in the state, serving as legislative committee chairperson for the LaFayette Council of Administrators of Special Education before being elected to the presidency of that organization. Therefore, it was not unexpected when Dr. Walker was offered a membership on the Advisory Committee to the State Education Department convened by the Assistant Commissioner for Special Education.

This is a critical time to be on such a committee, as new legislation was passed last year in Dale's state that promises to have major implications for both regular and special educators. Dale had spoken in support of the bill and there had been surprisingly little opposition, perhaps because it had been seen primarily as encouraging experimentation with new models, and not actually *mandating* any change. Since there appeared to be only routine budgetary implications, the Governor had signed the bill into law with no hesitation.

One aspect of the law, however, now appears to be destined to cause greater controversy than had been anticipated. Generally overlooked at the time of the bill's discussion was authorization for the State Education Department to study means of organizing instruction so that students with disabilities, as well as those with limited English proficiency (LEP) or any other special needs, could be instructed in regular classes. This was seen by the bill's authors as a natural extension of a previously accepted change that permitted the mixing of children with various categories of disabilities. The obvious intent behind both pieces of legislation was to emphasize the functional needs of pupils rather than any particular disability, and to promote the ideal of least restrictive environment. Furthermore, the Department was authorized to create and promulgate regulations that would encourage school districts to develop pilot programs to test such models of instruction.

Thus, the State Education Department has charged its Assistant Commissioner for Special Education with developing such regulations, with appropriate participation and advice from the field, which includes the Advisory Committee in particular. Initial meetings of the Committee revealed considerable interest in the concept of functional needs, with some members focusing on the corresponding deemphasis on disability classifications. As Professor Jones, a Committee member from State University, put it, "We now have a mandate to move to merge special and regular education and really get rid of the dysfunctional, stigmatizing labels!" Other more conservative members were insistant in their warnings "not to throw out any babies with the bathwater of clinical categories." After all, special education has enjoyed rather favorable support in the state as a separate, technical field.

As usual, Dale was found in the middle, arbitrating between these two positions, not because of any special skills as a mediator, but because of honest uncertainty regarding the trade-offs. Dale could hear a variety of arguments with open mindedness. The special education system had been based on the assumption that the special needs of children should be met by highly specialized professionals who knew the technology of instruction for particular disabilities. The state standards for program organization (grouping, teacher certification, supervision, instructional materials, etc.) reflected this and had served the state quite well. However, there is no disputing the charge that the system sometimes appears to suffer from "hardening of the categories." With the growth of the resource room and consultant teacher models, as opposed to self-contained special classes, and with the increased emphasis on learning disabilities and the correspondingly lower incidence of students identified as having mental retardation, it certainly made sense to focus on functional needs rather than categories for purposes of instructional grouping (as well as all other aspects of state standards).

Against this backdrop of competing considerations, the development of proposed regulations has proceeded and a first draft circulated among all school district superintendents, special education administrators, teacher organizations, and consumer advocate organizations. In essence, the draft allows (but does not require) school districts to group students for instruction, regardless of whether or not they are disabled, as long as "due consideration is given to the similarity of needs in terms of (1) scholastic performance, (2) social development, and (3) physical development." It further specifies that in cases in which students with disabilities are substantially served in general classes, there must be contact with that class by a certified special education teacher, the amount of such contact to be determined by the needs of the students enrolled, but to be at least 1 hour per week. In short, Dale observed, the proposal does not *force* any change in practice but emphasizes flexibility and encourages local administrators and educators to try new organizational arrangements.

Reaction has been mixed, but swift. The local superintendents (especially those from smaller districts) favor the increased flexibility, noting that the new regulation would permit much more logical and efficient organization for instruction. Some special education administrators and consumers are in agreement that this flexibility would facilitate serving children in a less restrictive environment and permit the assignment of teachers in accordance with subtle interests and capabilities not always reflected in certification classifications. Perhaps the strongest reaction has come from the few large school systems in the state, most notably Dale's own city's system. Metropolis is the state's major urban center, and the LaFayette United Teachers are well represented there. A subcommittee for special education includes teachers on Dale's staff. The LUT position, as articulated in the press by the spokesperson for the special education subcommittee, is as follows:

1. Mixed grouping of students with and without disabilities will require teachers to cope with intolerably varying types of problems.
2. The amount of support to regular teachers by specialists is too discretionary, providing no assurance of adequate help for either students or teachers.
3. School districts will be permitted to dump all kinds of kids together as an administrative means of cost cutting, without assurance of quality instruction for those who need it most.
4. Supervision and technical assistance to teachers will be ineffective because pupils with particular disabling conditions will be scattered across many classrooms and buildings.

After this initial reaction, the first draft of the proposed regulations is to be studied, redrawn (if this is deemed appropriate), and resubmitted for public comment at hearings around the state. While the staff of the State Education Department has the major responsibility for the process, the members of the Advisory Committee (including Dale) will be expected to play a key role in recommending revisions, explaining the finished product, and presumably defending it. Dale believes that the thrust of the new regulations is in the right direction. But resistance will be strong—especially right at home.

Is LaFayette ready for this much innovation? Can local school systems be trusted with this much flexibility? How can the quality of programs be ensured? How much regulation is desirable? How much is possible?

REFERENCES

Americans with Disabilities Act of 1990 (ADA), PL 101-336. (July 26, 1990). Title 42, U.S.C. 12101 et seq: *U.S. Statutes at Large, 104,* 327–378.
Beattie v. Board of Education, 169 Wisc. 231, 232, 172 N.W. 153, 154 (1919).
Board of Education of Hendrick Hudson Central School District v. Rowley, 50 U.S.L.W. 4925, 4932 (U.S. June 28, 1982).
Brown v. Board of Education, 347 U.S. 483, 493 (1954).
Concerned Parents and Citizens for the Continuing Education at Malcolm X (P.S. 79) v. New York City Board of Education, 629 F. 2d 751 (2d. Cir. 1980).
Daniel R.R. v. El Paso Independent School District (5th Cir. 1989).
Dellmuth v. Muth, 109 S.Ct. 2397 (U.S. 1989).
Detsel v. Board of Education of the Auburn Enlarged City School District, 820 F.2d 587 (2d Cir. 1987), cert. denied, 484 U.S. 981 (1987).
Detsel v. Sullivan, 895 F.2d 58 (2d Cir. 1990).
Developmental Disabilities Assistance and Bill of Rights Act of 1975, PL 94-103. (October 4, 1975). Title 42, U.S.C. 4000 et seq: *U.S. Statutes at Large, 89,* 486–507.
Diana v. State Board of Education, C-70, 37 RFP (N.D. Calif. 1970).
Education for All Handicapped Children Act of 1975, PL 94-142. (August 23, 1977). Title 20, U.S.C. 1401 et seq: *U.S. Statutes at Large, 89,* 773–796.

Education of the Handicapped Act Amendments of 1986, PL 99-457. (October 8, 1986). Title 20, U.S.C. 1400 et seq: *U.S. Statutes at Large, 100,* 1145–1177.

Elementary and Secondary Education Act of 1965, PL 89-10. (April 11, 1965). Title 20, U.S.C. 3801 et seq: *U.S. Statutes at Large, 79,* 27–58.

Georgia State Conference of Branches of NAACP v. Georgia, 775 F.2d 1403, (11th Cir. 1985).

Halderman v. Pennhurst State School and Hospital, 446 F. Supp. 1295 (E.D. Pa. 1977).

Honig v. Doe, 108 S.Ct. 592 (1988).

Individuals with Disabilities Education Act of 1990 (IDEA), PL 101-476. (October 30, 1990). Title 20, U.S.C. 1400 et seq: *U.S. Statutes at Large, 104,* 1103–1151.

Irving Independent School District v. Tatro, 468 U.S. 883 (1984).

Kaestle, C.F., & Smith, M.S. (1982). The federal role in elementary and secondary education, 1940–1980. *Harvard Educational Review, 52,* 390–392.

Kagan, R.A. (1981). *Regulating business, regulating schools: The problem of regulatory unreasonableness.* Project Report No. 81-A14. Stanford, CA: Institute for Research.

Kirp, D.L. (1974). Student classification, public policy and the courts. *Harvard Educational Review, 44,* 7–52.

Larry P. v. Riles, 343 F. Supp. 1306 (N.D. Calif. 1972).

Larry P. v. Riles, 343 F. Supp. 1306, 502 F. 2d 963 (N.D. Calif. 1979).

Lau v. Nichols, 414 U.S. 563, 94 S.Ct. 786 (1974).

Levin, H.M. (1981, Spring). Categorical grants in education: Rethinking the federal role. In *IFG policy perspectives.* Stanford, CA: Institute for Research on Educational Finance and Governance.

Mercer, J.R. (1974). A policy statement on assessment procedures and the rights of children. *Harvard Educational Review, 44,* 125.

Mills v. Board of Education of District of Columbia, 348 F.Supp. 866 (D.D.C. 1972).

Mosher, E.K. (1977). Education and American federalism: Intergovernmental and national policy influences. In *The politics of education: Seventy-sixth yearbook of the National Society for the Study of Education* (pp. 94–123). Chicago: National Society for the Study of Education.

National Defense Education Act of 1958, PL 85-864, (September 2, 1958). Title 20, U.S.C. 401 et seq: *U.S. Statutes at Large, 72,* 1580–1605.

New York State Association for Retarded Children v. Carey, 393 F. Supp. 715 (E.D. N.Y. 1975).

PARC v. Pennsylvania, 343 F. Supp. 279, 302 (E.D. Pa. 1972).

Parents in Action on Special Education (PASE) v. Hannon, et al., C.A. No. 74 C 3586 (1980).

Rehabilitation Act of 1973, PL 93-112. (September 26, 1973). Title 29, U.S.C. 701 et seq: *U.S. Statutes at Large, 87,* 355–394.

Ruiz v. State Board of Education, C.A. No. 218294 (Super. Ct. Sacramento, Calif. 1972).

S-1 v. Turlington, 635 F. 2d (CA 5, 1981).

Sacramento City Unified School District v. Holland (E.D. Cal. 1992).

Sarason, S.B., & Doris, J. (1978). Mainstreaming: Dilemmas, opposition, opportunities. In M.C. Reynolds (Ed.), *Futures of education for exceptional students: Emerging structures.* Reston, VA; The Council for Exceptional Children.

Sarason, S.B., & Doris, J. (1979). *Educational handicap, public policy, and social history: A broadened perspective an mental retardation.* New York: Free Press.

Smith, B.J., & Barrresi, J.G. (1982). Interpreting the rights of exceptional citizens through judicial actions. In J. Ballard, B.A. Ramires, & F.J. Weintraub (Eds.), *Special education in America: Its legal and governmental foundations* (pp. 65–81). Reston, VA: The Council for Exceptional Children.

The last word on full inclusion? (1992, May 12). *The Special Educator,* pp. 255–260.

Thompson, J.T. (1976). *Policy making in American public education.* Englewood Cliffs, NJ: Prentice Hall.

Timothy W. v. Rochester (NH) School District (CA-1 1989).

Weatherley, R., & Lipsky, M. (1977). Street level bureaucrats and institutional innovation: Implementing special education reform. *Harvard Educational Review, 47,* 171–197.

Watson v. City of Cambridge, 157 Mass. 561, 32 N.E. 864, 865 (1893).

Wyatt v. Stickney, 344 F. Supp. 387, 392 (M.D. Ala. 1972).

Yaris v. Special School District of St. Louis County, 558 F. Supp. 545 (E.D. Mo. 1983).

4

Informal Power and Influence

Control over special education is not limited to the legal entities responsible for formal governance. As in any organizational system, the influence of informal forces is also significant. Special interests typically play an important part in the determination of what educational administrators experience in their day-to-day work. Within the field of special education, the nature of these forces may be somewhat unusual and of surprising potency. Such interests, sometimes bolstered by a coalition of groups or by an established advocacy posture, have become quite common. And these influences (both internal and external to the educational system) often compete with and sometimes overwhelm the legal determinants of practice.

Attention to and utilization of special interest groups may be a key factor in personal and organizational goal attainment. Developing a sensitivity to some of the particular interests of individuals and groups who identify with certain exceptional populations, as well as those whose interests are more general, is a concern relevant to both special and general administrators. These groups may be classified on a number of dimensions and viewed from a variety of perspectives.

A TAXONOMY OF CONSTITUENCY GROUPS

Public social service agencies (including education) certainly have a set of constituencies that are different from those of other organizations, and special education service agencies in particular can be characterized as having especially varied and potent constituencies. A taxonomy of relevant constituency groups may be useful to the administrator in analyzing their nature and needs and planning for effectively accommodating them.

One could begin from almost any point in classifying the different types of these constituencies, but certain distinct differentiating attributes stand out clearly. One such dimension is the insider–outsider attribute. Whether an individual or group is inside or outside of the organization makes a significant difference in the manner in which influence is exercised, which, in turn, determines the appropriate leadership behavior for the administrator. In a similar way, the generalist–specialist dimension, lay–professional, teacher–administrator, instruction–related service, and consumer–provider dimensions can each be identified and analyzed with regard to their implications for constituency management. It would be impossible to capture all of the details of such a multidimensional model on the printed page, but Table 1 may be helpful in illustrating the variables most relevant to the educational administrator.

It should be noted that any choice as to how to classify certain individuals or groups might be contested. We have considered the local school district, as a legal entity complete with staff and policymakers, as constituting the organization. The groups inside the organization include professionals, paraprofessionals, and laypersons. They include both specialists (those with technical expertise and/or interest in the special needs of children with disabilities) and generalists (who work with all school children). Furthermore, these groups can be broken down into those who are primarily concerned with instruction and those who are associated with supportive or related services.

Those outside the organization also include professionals and laypersons who act in a variety of capacities more or less directly concerned with the special education program. Examples of significant constituency relationships are cited below, with particular attention to the very different roles that the administrator must play with different groups.

Consumer Groups

Parents are generally seen as being the consumers of special education, standing in proxy for their child. Parent organizations have tended to be organized around specific classifications of disability and have promoted their interests on the basis of rather narrowly defined needs and populations. Born of a perception of themselves as an oppressed minority, groups of parents of children with disabilities who successfully organize to gain strength in numbers often perceive their power as depending on maintaining a specific and concrete identity rather than risking becoming diluted through affiliation with more broadly defined groups. This "circle the wagons" attitude was probably more common during the early history of such organizations, when few battles had been won, than it is in the 1990s. No trust in coalition could be developed until a group had achieved some

Table 1. A taxonomy of constituency groups affecting special education administration

ORGANIZATIONAL INSIDERS

	Laypersons/ paraprofessionals	Professionals	
	Personnel	Generalist	Specialist
Instructional services	Teacher aides	General class-room teachers	Special education teachers
		Library-media specialists	Chapter 1 teachers
			Bilingual teachers
Related services	Therapy aides	Nurses	Psychologists
		Social workers	Physical therapists
		Physicians	Occupational therapists
			Speech therapists
Support services	Bus drivers	Principals	Special education supervisors
	Custodians	Curricular supervisors	Special education consultants
	Food service personnel	Business managers	
	Secretaries		
Policy-making bodies	School board members	Central administrators	

ORGANIZATIONAL OUTSIDERS

	Laypersons	Professionals	
		Generalist	Specialist
Service providers	Concerned taxpayers	Health agency personnel	Psychological/ educational clinicians
	Citizens advisory committees	Social agency personnel	Private school personnel
		Private practitioners	University personnel
			State-operated program personnel
			State education agency personnel
			Regional service agency personnel

(continued)

Table 1.   (*continued*)

	Laypersons	Professionals	
		Generalist	Specialist
Service consumers	Special education parents General education parents		
Special interest groups	Parent advocacy organizations	Health professions Teachers' associations Administrators' associations	Special education associations
Policy-making bodies	Legislators State boards Courts	State education agency administrators	State advisory committees

success. While a large number of groups representing those with a specific disability may be identified, three examples will be presented here to illustrate the typical attributes of consumer organizations. Each of these organizations has a national headquarters office and affiliated state and local chapters in many locations. The strength of affiliation varies among the different national organizations, and within each group, the degree of identification with the central office varies from one locality to another.

The Arc   Established in 1952 as the National Association for Retarded Children (NARC) and made up largely of parents of persons with mental retardation, with minimum participation by professionals, this organization continues to exert a significant influence on legal progress at both the state and federal levels, but has also been a consistent force in the development and operation of local direct service programs. Advocacy at the local level has sometimes resulted in the establishment of private service programs, but has frequently been used to exert the necessary pressure within the local political structure to cause public services to be initiated, regardless of whether they were mandated by law. Reflecting the increasing number of services provided to adults as well as children, the organization's name was changed to the National Association for Retarded *Citizens* in 1974. Because of the increased sensitivities of self-advocates, young parents, and others who objected to the term *retarded*, the name was changed again in 1991 to *The Arc*, with a tag line describing it as a "national organization on mental retardation."

With 140,000 members and 1200 state and local chapters, The Arc is not a monolithic group, and its posture varies significantly from state to state and among localities. In the main, however, its membership has tended to adhere to the assumption that their cause would not be well represented by any other more broadly based group. At one time it was not uncommon, in cases in which local chapters of The Arc had established and were operating their own private service programs, for there to be competition among the various private and public services, with a clearly felt threat to the association-sponsored service when other options became available. This was probably due in part to a concern about loss of control, but it also clearly showed a concern for the protection and safety of the children. More recently the organization has come out very strongly for a policy of inclusion. A *Report Card to the Nation on Inclusion in Education of Students with Mental Retardation* (The Arc, 1992) cites the dramatic variance among the states in the degree to which special education programs for students with mental retardation include participation in general education. In general, the document argues that only a handful of states are demonstrating a satisfactory "inclusion rating." The organization's focus on advocacy for adults is also reflected in concern over services to facilitate the transition from school to independent living.

The Association for Children with Learning Disabilities   The ACLD was established in 1963 and followed much the same course of political activity as NARC had earlier, influencing state and federal legislation and subsequent regulations governing publicly mandated and supported service programs. The ACLD was much less inclined to establish its own direct service facilities (although this was done in some locations) than to focus on the influence of public policy. This difference is in part attributable to the fact that children with learning disabilities tend to have less extensive needs than those represented by The Arc, but it is also probably due to the ACLD's having been established later, at a time when there was a greater promise of public provision and the need for privately sponsored service was subsequently less critical.

The interest of the ACLD in maintaining an earmarked status for its population in laws and regulations was quite clear. As a group with a more newly established and somewhat ambiguous identity, there was a need for the organization to sharply distinguish the nature of learning disabilities and the prescribed interventions from those of the other, more familiar classifications of disability. It is clear that the element of perceived stigma also plays a part in this case as a function of the social desirability of certain "labels." Thus, the differences between the ACLD and The Arc are probably less due to the clinically observable status of the students than to social-psychological factors in the adult community. Concern regarding the overuse of the learning disability classification has been expressed in many quarters. The very rapid growth in the number of school children identified as having specific learning disabilities, which is reflected in the *Annual Reports to the Congress*, has been attributed both to the strength of the ACLD as an advocacy organization and to the preference of the classification over more stigmatizing labels.

The Autism Society of America   This organization was initially established in 1965 as the National Society for Autistic Children and later added *adults* to its title (NSACA). Its membership and the population it represents are smaller than those of the groups discussed above, but in 1992 the Society had 186 chapters around the nation, with all but four states represented, and over 11,000 members. As with specific learning disabilities, autism is a condition that is only recently coming to be understood by laypersons and professionals. Its definition and classification in state and federal laws and regulations required much complicated argument. An amendment to existing federal regulations was published in January 1981, officially deleting autism from the *emotionally disturbed* category and adding it to the category of *other health impaired* under the definition of *handicapped children*. In 1990 autism was added to the list of disabilities in the federal law, giving it specific separate status from other disabilities. The individuals represented differ from those represented by the other organizations discussed above in that the condition is exclusively a severe one with which most schools would deal only in a restrictive fashion until very recent times.

For these reasons, the Society had a major challenge both in establishing an identity and in ensuring its appropriate inclusion within existing special education program provisions. Furthermore, ambiguities of etiology created social-psychological complications; it was initially widely believed that autism was caused by parents who rejected their children and that both parents and children required treatment as persons with mental illness. Recent research has invalidated that hypothesis as more constitutional and chemical factors have been identified. Much of the Society's current effort is focused on overcoming inaccurate beliefs about its parent membership and their children as viewed both from within and without the group.

Children with Attention Deficit Disorder   One of the more recently established, but rapidly growing organizations of this type, Children and Adults with Attention Deficit Disorder (CH.A.D.D.), was formed in 1987 as a group of parents, educators, researchers, and physicians. By the time of their fourth annual convention in the fall of 1992, the CH.A.D.D. membership had grown to 20,000 and represented over 400 chapters nationwide. The organization pressed very vigorously for specific mention of ADD in the list of disabilities in the federal law at the time of its reauthorization in 1990, when autism and traumatic brain injury were added. However, they expressed satisfaction with the compromise that was negotiated by the federal Office of Special Education Programs, which authorized four centers to analyze and synthesize research on ADD and to explore effective ways to identify, assess, and provide interventions for children with the disability. A major point in the official government response to the proposed inclusion of ADD in IDEA was that responsibility for serving these children belonged, to a major extent, to the regular education establishment. Thus, the advocacy focus of CH.A.D.D. is much broader than those of the other groups with which special educators have traditionally been associated.

  Other Consumer Organizations   Other organizations of a similar nature, representing the interests of individuals with specific disabilities, and with a particular focus on children, include:

Epilepsy Foundation of America
International Association of Parents of the Deaf
National Association for Visually Handicapped
National Easter Seal Society
United Cerebral Palsy Associations, Inc.

Each of these organizations maintains a national office as well as affiliated chapters at the local and state levels. They vary widely in the degree to which they concentrate on the operation of services at the local level as opposed to focusing on political and social advocacy. Information on these and other organizations concerned with persons with disabilities, including addresses and telephone numbers of their offices, is published in the *Directory of National Information Sources on Disabilities* (U.S. Department of Education, 1991). The directory provides a cross-referencing of organizations according to their functions and the particular disabilities with which they are concerned.

  An issue for each of the consumer organizations discussed above, and probably for most of those involved with persons with disabilities, is the dilemma regarding minority status. The groups exist because their members have previously had a problem—unmet needs. As such a group becomes successful, some of these needs may be satisfied as a result of unified effort, hard work, and sacrifice. In this case, although the factors that created the unmet need have been reduced, and the minority status has been ameliorated by acceptance and inclusion, there is still a concern about equal status and the adequacy of the group's achievements. Therefore, while it might be appropriate to abandon the minority identity, it is not always quite safe to do so. This ambivalence is sometimes seen by representatives of the majority establishment as inconsistent or erratic behavior on the part of consumer groups.

There is no question regarding the power that such groups have been able to bring to bear in both individual cases in which advocacy was needed to bring about a resolution and in larger-scale political actions aimed at modifying the formal governance structure. The role of consumer organizations in allowing the individual citizen (usually a parent) to grow from an advocate of a single child with particular needs, however critical, into a leader of a social movement has been repeatedly documented.

The Consumer–Professional Conflict

One theme running throughout the accounts of consumers (parents) who are also professionals is that of internal conflict, particularly among those whose professional roles are in a field directly or closely related to the provision of services for children with disabilities. This would be most pronounced in the case of the special education teacher, pediatrician, psychologist, social worker, or child development researcher who becomes a parent of a child with disabilities. To a lesser degree, general educators, attorneys interested in civil rights issues, the clergy, and other human services professionals also find themselves behaving in accordance with their role as a professional at one point and as a parent and consumer of social services at another. The issue of professional legitimacy comes into play here in these cases, as well.

In discussing the problem of leadership in community organization, Biklen (1983) points out that consumer groups depend on voluntary participation by individuals of all sorts, including professionals whose field of expertise may or may not be related to the issues in which the consumers are interested. There are two sides to the problem. In cases in which the professional is not acting "in his field," the public (and especially the establishment against which the consumer organization is fighting) tends to discount that person's legitimacy, as compared with that of experts in the field. In our society, with its emphasis on credentials, people are expected to stay within their own domain of expertise. However, when the professional is acting "within his field," it may be difficult for the individual to place the substance of the issue ahead of the inclination to be cooperative and loyal to the "guild" or system in which professional colleagues conduct their affairs. The obstacles to a professional educator functioning as a member of an advocacy-oriented consumer organization are extremely pronounced when that organization is challenging existing educational services.

Another aspect of the consumer organization as an influence on the service system is the differentiation between the various groups who are in the business of "doing good." Biklen describes the place of charitable organizations as the primary leaders in social reforms, followed by professionals, and finally community organizations. In pointing out how the charity model went wrong, he indicates that while the general concept and practice of being charitable and helping one's neighbor remains valid, the institutionalization of charity has unexpected results. Members of charitable organizations have always tended to see themselves as being responsible for differentiating between the worthy and unworthy. "Charity, with its characteristic moral imperialism, assumed that people suffered as a result of their own failings or by fate (old age, disability, abandonment, and neglect) and not of social injustice (economic exploitation, class origin)" (Biklen, 1983, p.67). The dramatic dollar growth in the "charity business" in this country over recent decades has not been accompanied by any major change in the attitudinal factors that drive its success, or in its tendency to treat symptoms rather than the possible causes of social problems. Charities generally depend for their fundraising success on appealing to the public's feelings of guilt and pity:

> On balance, charity, both in its historic and present-day form, has failed to achieve the ends espoused in its noblest ideals—relief with dignity, greater independence, and equality. While no one would deny that charity has relieved immediate human suffering, few would contend that it has altered the structural social conditions which cause human suffering. (p. 74)

Professionalism, as a means of influencing social reform, has gone beyond charity in improving the quality of life of those represented. However, it has also sometimes had unexpected results. In reviewing the classic attributes of professionalism (pursuits that are essentially intellectual in character, autonomy and responsibility, specialized knowledge, practical application of that knowledge, transmission of knowledge and skills through an organized brotherhood, and altruism in serving the public interest) Biklen points out the increasing skepticism regarding their universal validity. The conflict between public interest and self-interest that may be manifested in the tendency to inflate the image of intellectual pursuit, exaggerate the specialized knowledge, restrict its communication, and demand autonomy without risk can be seen in the tendency of professional societies to seize and maintain control of institutions that purport to serve the public. The basic conflict between the professionals' pecuniary interest and their altruism results in an emphasis on attending to paying clients rather than the reform of social systems (pp. 75–83).

The conflict in the consumer–professional role is further demonstrated when one attempts to identify organizations that are devoted to the special interests of certain populations. It is noted above that those organizations listed and described here (NARC, ACLD, NSACA, CH.A.D.D., and others) are made up primarily of consumers. However, they do not exclude from membership those individuals who have only a professional or general interest in the welfare of the target population. These organizations could be classified as charitable groups and would certainly qualify as such legally. However, to the extent that they have taken an activist stance in the influence of public social policy, they have gone far beyond the classic charity.

There are actually many more organizations that could be listed and described as having an interest in the provision and improvement of services for children and/or adults with various types of disabilities, but whose membership is more heavily weighted toward professionals. Such organizations may legitimately describe their purpose as advocating for better conditions for the clients they represent through the promotion of more and better services. However, to the extent that they include a mixture of consumers and professionals, their basic goals and activities must be interpreted differently. While we do not mean to suggest that professional altruism toward the public (or client) interest is not an important commodity, the presence of a professional interest also positively influences the nature of an otherwise consumer-oriented organization.

Professional Groups

The professional groups that can be expected to have an impact on special education policy are of two general types, those representing all teachers and administrators and those made up of professionals specifically responsible for the education of children with disabilities. There are relevant subdivisions within each of these groups that must also be considered. It must be recognized that professional organizations almost always have a dual purpose. While a primary purpose is always to ensure the welfare of the client population, a secondary and possibly conflicting purpose is to secure the welfare of the individual professional. It is also obvious that the overall interests of the various groups may result in some intergroup conflict. The nature of these intragroup and intergroup conflicts and their effect on special education policy should be taken into account.

Teachers' Organizations Whether officially designated as unions or not, teachers' organizations have been quick to respond to changes in public policy concerning the education of students with disabilities. A major issue has been whether the inclusion of such children in less restrictive settings would constitute an unreasonable expectation for general education teachers. In the early days of discussion regarding mainstreaming, the pronouncements of teachers' unions frequently expressed the skeptical opinion that mainstreaming was a thinly disguised ploy by school boards to save money at the expense of teachers. As they became better informed, unions have pointed out that unless proper training could be provided for regular teachers, along with appropriate supportive services to aid such teachers in working with students with disabilities, the union must consistently resist the efforts of school systems to implement the inclusion of such children.

Teachers' unions in certain locations have defended this position as a means of guaranteeing the welfare of all children, protecting them against the possibly pecuniary interests of taxpayers and school boards. The increasing press for accountability, usually expressed in calls for measures of average performance by classroom groups, constitutes a threat to teachers when the inclusion of children with disabilities is proposed. But they have also argued strongly for the teacher input in decisions about pupil placements, which is consistent with the ideal of restructured schools in which teacher participation at the school site level is a key element. The membership of special education teachers in local unions has in some instances placed such teachers in the middle of the fray in cases in which the interests of children with disabilities and those of teachers in general seemed to be in conflict. On the state and national levels, unions have exercised a strong voice in reaction to legal and regulatory proposals.

Special Educator Organizations Associations comprising only special education personnel have experienced some of the same dilemmas as consumer groups in regard to the relative benefits of broad versus narrow identity. The issue has been whether there is more in common among the concerns of teachers of students with varying exceptionalities, or more that is uniquely associated with each particular condition. The Council for Exceptional Children (CEC), as an umbrella organization established in 1922 and attempting to represent professionals across a wide spectrum (including those who work with the gifted and talented), has been able to partially resolve this issue through the use of divisions within the organization that are focused on particular interests. These interests are both disability related (e.g., Division for Physically Handicapped, Division on Mental Retardation) and functionally oriented (Council of Administrators of Special Education, Teacher Education Division). However, there have been recurring conflicts over degree of affiliation, with occasional proposals by subdivisions to secede from the larger group and the establishment of new divisions as previously unrecognized interests are identified. The status of a division representing the interests of personnel concerned with learning disabilities has been a most notable point of conflict as that group has mushroomed numerically and evolved conceptually in recent years.

Within some states and localities, completely separate professional organizations have maintained some prominence, usually in cases in which the group has concluded that their specific interests were not well represented by the existing organization or that participation was stifled by the magnitude of the larger group's membership. Special education teachers have often charged that their primary professional organization (CEC) fails to represent their interests due to its domination by university professors and administrators. At the same time, special education administrators have in some instances demonstrated their parochial orientation through disaffiliation from the major organization (CASE) and the establishment of independent alternative groups that presumably better satisfy their purposes. The growth of The Association for Persons with Severe Handicaps (TASH), which was founded in 1974 and in 1992 had a membership over 9,000, has been attributed to the beliefs of some professionals that the more established groups (such as CEC) were too prone to compromise at a time when radical change was called for in order to bring about the full inclusion of persons with disabilities in schools and society.

Much of the dissension regarding professional organizations can be attributed to differences in the degree to which individuals view their role as being an integral part of some larger scheme of educational practice, as opposed to a relatively isolated and unique activity. Social status may also play a part in the choice of primary identity. Among persons who are involved with services to special populations, there are those who view their role as being more closely associated with the medical, psychological, or social work fields than with education. These views tend to be reflected in choice of organizational membership.

The importance of the various consumer and professional groups lies primarily in the power and tendency of such organizations to advocate for particular interests. Special interests may weigh heavily in policy decisions and everyday practice. An understanding of the most prominent perspective of each group may be of crucial importance to administrators in negotiating decisions and managing practice. Central to such understanding is a sensitivity to the conflicts among interest groups as well as to the ambivalence that often exists within the membership of a single group.

Administrator Organizations   CASE, as a division of CEC, can be seen as a specialists' group in two different respects. While the organization is certainly concerned with the particular issues surrounding the instruction of children with disabilities, it is also concerned with issues of delivery of services, which tends to involve more general administrative matters. CASE has recently moved into the policy-influencing arena, producing position papers dealing with inclusion, attention deficit disorders, Section 504 interpretations, and definitions of severe emotional disturbance. CASE is somewhat role specific in its membership, but probably not as specific as certain similar groups such as the National Association of Elementary School Principals or the National Association of Secondary School Principals. These organizations represent a membership having a major interest and powerful voice in the exercise of day-to-day practice in special education. Similarly, the American Association of School Administrators (AASA), primarily representing local school district superintendents, is in a position of great influence in the implementation of policy on special education. The Association for Supervision and Curriculum Development (ASCD) represents a considerably less role-specific group of educators, including teachers and administrators having a variety of interests in both policy and practice. Each of these organizations have national headquarters offices in or around Washington and exert influence on national education policy. The degree to which they have focused on special education issues has grown noticeably during the past decade. It should be noted that in 1992 the ASCD endorsed the concept of inclusion in a strongly worded policy resolution. Noting that "A nonlabeling approach to special program regulations can result in the elimination of tracking and segregated services for children with unique needs," the resolution urged its members "to work with federal and state agencies, as well as congressional and legislative delegations, [and to] provide special programs that offer an enriched instructional environment—one that addresses learning needs without assigning labels, minimizes restrictive regulations, and supports flexible use of funds" (ASCD, 1992).

Policy Maker Organizations   Another type of organization that may be best classified as professional, based on the nature of its membership, but having a somewhat different purpose and function, are those representing governmental units or persons in their status as officers of such units, rather than the individual professionals themselves. A number of such organizations are of relevance to school administrators in general and to special education administrators in particular, in that they have often taken strong stands on matters of policy in special education.

Especially during the first decade of major federal activity in special education, when the relationship between federal, state, and local agency operation was being negotiated and uncertainty was common, general and special education interests were sometimes perceived as being in conflict. At the state agency level, the Council of Chief State School Officers and the National Association of State Directors of Special Education, each having headquarters offices in the nation's capital, represented somewhat different perspectives on the nature of optimal federal and state relationships. In both of these organizations the focus is not on individual membership, but on the interests of the governmental units that the officeholders represent.

The National Association of State Boards of Education is a similar group, representing a membership whose policy-making authority over the executive branch of state governance of education gives the organization major significance. This organization's strong endorsement of the concept of "full inclusion" of children with disabilities in a report entitled *Winners All: A Call for Inclusive Schools*, presented at their fall, 1992 convention, called for a major shift in the delivery of education for children with disabilities (National Association of State Boards of Education, 1992).

Advocacy Groups

The preceding discussion has covered three types of organizations. These include: 1) consumer groups, usually made up of nonprofessional members (generally parents) and devoted to securing necessary services for their own children; 2) those made up largely of professionals, whose mission is often a mix of defending the interests of their clients and their own membership; and 3) those whose central interest is broad social policy. Yet another type of organization has appeared in recent decades, one devoted exclusively to advocacy for individuals or groups who are in apparent need. On the assumption that there are classes of persons with similar needs who are unable to speak effectively for themselves, agencies have been established, many with assistance grants from branches of the federal government, to provide guidance and training to individuals or groups in securing their civil rights. Such agencies have generally displayed an activist posture, going beyond the goal of attaining specific necessary services and focusing on longer-range change in the system. A major part of the Developmental Disabilities Assistance and Bill of Rights Act, originally passed in 1975, but with periodic amendments, including those in PL 101-496 in 1990, has provided for the establishment of Protection and Advocacy Offices at the state level. Such offices are required to be independent of the service system and are intended to intercede for parents in securing services for their children and, at the same time, to help to educate both the consumer and the service providers on issues related to dealing fairly with each other. The Developmental Disabilities Act also funded a number of national projects designed to provide for research and the training of personnel specifically responsible for advocacy for persons with disabilities.

The list of organizations serving an advocacy function is very long; The *Directory of National Information Sources on Disabilities* (U.S. Department of Education, 1991) lists a total of 150 such agencies. While many of these focus on adults, rather than school-age children, and most are associated with one particular disability, the number and variety of such organizations is impressive. Examples of those established primarily for the purpose of advocating across many disability categories and having played an important civil rights role in influencing policy concerning children with disabilities include the following:

Center on Human Policy
Syracuse University
Syracuse, NY 13244

Children's Defense Fund
1520 New Hampshire Ave., NW
Washington, D.C. 20036

Mental Health Law Project
1101 15th St. NW, Suite 1212
Washington, D.C. 20005

National Information Center for Children and Youth with Disabilities
P.O. Box 1492
Washington, D.C. 20013

Certain other organizations maintain a much broader program, defending the interests of any group that appears to need assistance in obtaining fair treatment in society. An example of the latter is the

Center for Law and Education, located at Harvard University, which over the years has dealt with such concerns as the education of Native Americans, vocational and career education, migrant education, compensatory education for the disadvantaged, desegregation, tracking, sex discrimination, student records, and corporal punishment, as well as education for children with disabilities. Most advocacy centers feature a strong legal component, though few maintain an attorney on full-time staff. The focus of a particular organization may be suggested by its title, but this is by no means consistent. The organizations listed here maintain a nation-wide scope, but may in practice tend to also engage more intensively in events near their geographic base. Other groups are organized exclusively for a regionally constrained thrust. A rather dramatic example of a focused but major activity of this sort occurred in 1989 when two groups, Parents for Integrated School and Community Education Services (PISCES) and the Maryland Coalition for Integrated Education (MCIE) joined forces and requested that the federal Department of Education withhold special education funds from Maryland until certain state regulations were changed. The groups charged that existing state practices violated federal law and fostered the segregation of children in special education programs. While state officials defended their placement practices and maintained that their regulations were in compliance with all federal policies, it is clear that the action of the advocacy organizations brought to attention a philosophical issue regarding programming that existing relationships between official local, state, and federal agencies had not adequately addressed.

Many variations on this theme, both in terms of the motivating force behind advocacy and the programs of action carried out by organized advocacy groups, can be found throughout the country, and these actions are often successful in influencing the service system at the local level, as well as public policy. One possible limitation on the potential impact of these activities has been the difficulty of mounting a consistently coordinated attack.

Coalitions

As mentioned above, consumer organizations have frequently hesitated to affiliate with other persons or groups who do not share the particular interest with which their primary identity is associated. There are many factors that contribute to this resistance, including such rational concerns as strategic maximization of impact by maintaining a target that is clearly identifiable and understood in the public mind. However, mistrust of broader affiliation is undoubtedly also due to less defensible concerns over image and turf, not to mention the egos of individual organization leaders.

Advocacy organizations have also experienced this problem, but general interest in advocacy has sometimes permitted a somewhat more coordinated effort, especially when generally recognized crises have occurred. One successful instance of coalition on a national scale occurred in 1980 when a group of 13 separate advocacy organizations (with both national and local orientation) combined to form the Education Advocates Coalition. The focus of concern was the perceived lack of progress in implementing the Education for All Handicapped Children Act (PL 94-142). The Coalition gathered data on local practices throughout 11 states, and evaluated the activity of the federal Bureau of Education for the Handicapped. The report published by the Coalition listed 10 major problem areas in which the federal agency's failure to develop policies and compliance procedures had led to confusion and delays in parents' efforts to obtain mandated services (Education Advocates Coalition, 1980).

The impact of this report, along with other sources of criticism regarding the administration of PL 94-142, stimulated a response from the federal agency, resulting in the establishment of a task force that studied the charges of the Coalition, in addition to a report prepared for the Civil Rights Transition Task Force for the new Department of Education and a draft report by the Council of Chief State School Officers. This task force then developed a set of policy recommendations that included a Memorandum of Understanding between the Office of Civil Rights and the Office of Special Education Programs regarding the responsibilities of each agency for implementing both PL 94-142 and Section 504 (Office of Special Education and Rehabilitative Services, 1980). The Memorandum specifies procedures covering enforcement, data collection, policy development, and technical assistance activities. It was stated that these procedures would permit better targeting of compliance-review activities on the basis of priority problems identified by parents and advocates, and that through joint planning efforts and better coordination in the handling of complaints, necessary data could be obtained while reducing the burden on state and local agencies and providing better technical assistance to the agencies involved in the resolution of implementation problems.

The success of the federal offices in subsequently realizing such worthy objectives is arguable, but there is no doubt that the plan and the efforts were in direct response to the pressure from the field, from the informal sources of influence. It would appear that the consumer-advocate group, in this instance strengthened through an identified coalition, was the primary force behind the changes.

It should also be noted that 2 years later, when the federal Department of Education attempted to modify significantly the regulations governing PL 94-142 (discussed in the previous chapter), the storm of protest that resulted in withdrawal of the proposed changes came largely from consumer-advocate groups. While professional special educators (teachers, administrators, and higher education personnel) joined in support of consumer interests, the message from other educator groups was more ambiguous. General administrators at both the state and local levels were understandably attracted to the idea of less oppressive federal intervention. This created some interesting interplay between certain organizations. The membership of CASE, for example, while supporting better programs and procedures from much the same perspective as consumers and also maintaining a strong professional affiliation with the rest of the special education community, could scarcely avoid being influenced in their official stance by their alignment with the membership of the American Association of School Administrators. Similarly, members of the National Association of State Directors of Special Education (NASDSE) (presumably special educators at heart) are employed directly by the individuals who make up the Council of Chief State School Officers, who tended to have a strong interest in state, rather than federal, prerogatives in the regulatory process. The public positions taken by some of the special education organizations were understandably the product of philosophical and political compromises. Thus, the balance of forces among professionals concerning the issue of federal deregulation was somewhat equivocal. It was, therefore, the voice of the organized consumer that tipped the scales and convinced the educational establishment as a whole that the principles set forth in the litigation, legislation, and regulation of the past decade should remain solidly in place.

An example of a coalition among consumer and a variety of professional groups, but focused on a particular interest, can be seen in the controversy over the education of deaf students. The Education of the Deaf Act of 1986, in addition to reauthorizing funding for Gallaudet University and the National Technical Institute for the Deaf and other projects, created a national Commission on Education of the Deaf (COED). The Commission was to study the quality of the education of deaf students and make recommendations to the Congress and President. COED's 1988 report cited a long list of inadequacies and made 52 recommendations. In 1992, a Council of Organizational Representatives (COR), which consisted of 17 member organizations having a common interest in improving education for deaf persons and persons with hearing impairments, testified before the House Select Subcommittee on Education regarding the shortcomings of existing programs of services. One of the most controversial questions had to do with whether the emphasis on least restrictive environment (LRE) in federal policy had helped or hindered professionals in the education of deaf students. The testimony argued that since a workable interpretation of LRE had not been achieved, a more practical concept might be *most appropriate service*. The obvious perspective of some of the members of this coalition was that education in a general school setting was not adequate for *some* deaf students, and that a segregated setting was more appropriate in these cases. It was suggested that "LRE is being used as a justification for placing children who are deaf in local programs or other similar programs even when [such programs] do not meet educational needs of those students" (NASDSE, 1992, p. 6).

The two professional organizations centrally involved in the development of the testimony were the National Association of State Directors of Special Education (NASDSE) and the Conference of Educational Administrators Serving the Deaf (CEASD). However, these two organizations also extended an invitation to participate in a *Deaf Initiatives* project to other professional and consumer groups who were known to have knowledge and a vested interest in educational programs. These include the National Association of the Deaf (NAD) (the major consumer group in this area), the Alexander Graham Bell Association of the Deaf (AGBAD), Convention of American Instructors of the Deaf (CAID), the American Society for Deaf Children (ASDC), the Association of College Educators of the Hearing Impaired (ACEHI), Council on Education of the Deaf (CED), and the American Deafness and Rehabilitation Association (ADARA), as well as the much more generic CEC. The very fact that such a large number of different groups took an interest in a seemingly singular area of disability provides a clue as to the complexity of the issues involved and the variety of perspectives and philosophies around which individuals may organize. While it would be very difficult for a general school administrator (e.g., a principal) or even a special education administrator to be totally conversant in all of the nuances of the interests that precipitate the formation and actions of so many groups, the simple realization that such differences of interest exist may serve to sensitize the administrator to the need for a pluralistic outlook.

CONCLUDING COMMENTS

In this chapter we present a description of three identifiable types of interest groups that from time to time play a large part in the determination of social policy through their interaction with the official, legal, and governance structures of our public institutions. The need to work with such multiple forces is a fact of organizational life.

Attempts to change public policy are inescapably complex ventures. Such attempts take place in economic, political, and social environments that virtually ensure that tensions will be present at the time of policy implementation. Since the policy process involves interactions among individuals and groups, we can expect these interactions to reflect all the idiosyncrasies of human behavior. As indicated at the beginning of this chapter, a sensitivity to the goals and influence of such interest groups may be an important key to program administration.

ILLUSTRATIVE CASE

Green Meadow Central School District has maintained a vigorous program of cooperative school–community partnerships, enhanced recently by the public's attention to school quality brought about by reports from various national task force groups and commissions. Reading some of the "success stories" in the education-related publications, such as *Kappan* and *Educational Leadership,* Superintendent Lee Brown had vowed to make Green Meadow a model in working with the business community to improve the school system.

Descriptions of some of the projects in other states showed that business leaders could be very successful in promoting a statewide educational agenda. It was the type of thing that could also work locally. Attention was being focused on minimum graduation standards, beefed-up state testing, curriculum guidelines, stronger attendance and disciplinary laws, a longer school day and year, deregulation of state restrictions on teacher dismissals and layoffs, and new concepts in teacher training. And, in response to the opportunity to exert such influence, business leaders had apparently been instrumental in getting significantly larger school finance appropriations passed.

While Lee could hardly be expected to cause the whole state to embrace a standard model, the local initiative that had been developed seemed to be off to a good start. The Chamber of Commerce had convinced some of its most dynamic leaders to work with Lee in setting up a Partnership for School Improvement, and the primary thrust of this PSI had been to examine graduation standards. As Partnership Chairman Bradley Strong had stated in a recent news release, "Business firms who employ Green Meadow graduates in the future will know what a high school diploma means—that the youngster has attained a reasonable standard of literacy." Moreover, the teacher and building administrator representatives on the PSI seemed to be getting along famously with the business people. So far, everything on the agenda had been well received by the Teachers' Organization. The mutual interest in improved standards provided a sound basis for cooperative problem solving. The feedback from the general public had never been more favorable.

Lee's euphoria was therefore jarred by a letter received from the president of the local chapter of The Arc, which read, in part, as follows:

> Our membership has been duly appreciative of the progressive stance of the Green Meadow Central Schools, under your leadership, in seeing that high school diplomas have always been awarded to the members of special education classes. We are keenly aware that such recognition of their accomplishment of the objectives set forth in each student's Individualized Educational Program, as opposed to some "second class" symbol, goes a very long way in enhancing the self-esteem of our children.
>
> We are, therefore, quite concerned about a bill being proposed in the state legislature which, as presently drafted, would prohibit the award of diplomas to any students who have not passed the state minimum competency tests. We understand that one version of the bill mentions the awarding of a "Certificate of Attendance," while another version makes no mention of any symbol of completion. Our local chapter, as well as the State Federation of The Arc, finds all such proposals unacceptable. It is apparent that the courts have been inconsistent in rulings on this type of issue, and we cannot depend on that avenue to protect our children's rights. We are therefore launching an attack on this most damaging proposal. We have considerable strength among our statewide affiliations, but we will also need the support of forward looking professional groups and individuals as well. We are aware that not every school district had been as enlightened as Green Meadow on this issue, and therefore we look to school administrations such as yours to stand beside us in protecting what can and must be maintained. We are sure that we have your private, personal goodwill on this, but we expect to also need your public testimony.
>
> We anticipate a legislative hearing on this bill during the next month, and we intend to send a delegation from our local chapter to join the state officers in testifying at the Capital. Could you accompany us? We know of no better spokesperson from the professional side of this issue.

Superintendent Brown recalled having some nagging thoughts about inconsistency that had been troubling from time to time, but dismissing them, since the two issues seemed to be completely separate. But were they? How many special education "graduates" applied for jobs in the community? But shouldn't they be able to? Would more in the future? The school had been placing some special education students in work–study situations that sometimes led to supported employment, and eventually real jobs. Was this going to be a problem? How could the interests of two very different but equally legitimate constituencies be protected? Lee didn't really know.

REFERENCES

The Arc. (1992). *Report card to the nation on inclusion in education of students with mental retardation.* Arlington, TX: Author.

Association for Supervision and Curriculum Development. (1992). *Resolutions*. Alexandria, VA: Author.

Biklen, D.P. (1983). *Community organizing: Theory and practice*. Englewood Cliffs, NJ: Prentice Hall.

Developmental Disabilities Assistance and Bill of Rights Act of 1975, PL 94-103. (October 4, 1975). Title 42, U.S.C. 6000 et seq: *U.S. Statutes at Large, 89*, 486–507.

Education Advocates Coalition. (April 16, 1980). *Report on federal compliance activities to implement the Education for All Handicapped Children Act (PL 94-142)*. Washington, DC: Children's Defense Fund and Mental Health Law Project.

Education for All Handicapped Children Act of 1975, PL 94-142. (August 23, 1977). Title 20, U.S.C. 1401 et seq: *U.S. States at Large, 89*, 773–796.

Education of the Deaf Act, PL 99-371. (August 4, 1986), Title 20, U.S.C. 4301 et seq: *U.S. Statutes at Large, 100*, 781–795.

Individuals with Disabilities Education Act of 1990 (IDEA), PL 101-476. (October 30, 1990). Title 20, U.S.C. 1400 et seq: *U.S. Statutes at Large, 104*, 1103–1151.

NASBE Study Group on Special Education. (1992). *Winners all: A call for inclusive schools*. Alexandria, VA: The National Association of State Boards of Education.

National Association of State Directors of Special Education. (1992, September). Decade holds promise of continued progress in education of deaf students. *Liaison Bulletin, 18, No. 7*, 1–15

Office of Special Education and Rehabilitative Services. (October 15, 1980). *Final report to the secretary of the task force on equal educational opportunity for handicapped children*. Washington, DC: Author.

Rehabilitation Act of 1973, PL 93-112. (September 26, 1973). Title 29, U.S.C. 701 et seq: *U.S. Statutes at Large, 87*, 355–394.

U.S. Department of Education. (1991). *Directory of national information sources on disabilities* (5th ed.). Washington, DC: U.S. Department of Education, Office of Special Education and Rehabilitative Services, National Institute on Disability and Rehabilitation Research.

5

Organizational Structures

Within any enterprise, the issue of organizational structure can have a significant effect on how the system operates in carrying out its mission. The design of the structure is of considerable importance to the administrative process, since it affects the manner in which major administrative tasks may be executed. The structure may be established as a product of careful planning, during which a clear purpose or mission guides its creation, or it may merely be a reflection of traditional patterns, following the lines of least resistance. In either case, persons concerned with the policies that guide organizational goals and the management of the activities carried out in pursuit of those goals have a stake in the administrative structure of the organization.

In discussing the general purpose of organizations, with a particular focus on the administration of schools, Morphet, Johns, and Reller (1982) emphasize that organizations must make provisions for decision making concerning which goals, purposes, objectives, policies, and programs will be accepted by the organization as legitimate. They point out that the primacy of decision-making processes as the central core of administration has been fully elaborated by Griffiths (1959), who set forth the assumption that the specific function of administration is to develop and regulate the decision-making process in the most effective manner possible. Griffiths posited that the structure of an organization is determined by the nature of its decision-making process and that maximum achievement is dependent on the congruency of the formal and informal aspects of the organization. Furthermore, the proper role of the administrator is controlling the decision-making *process*, rather than actually making decisions.

The process of decision making is inherent in the pursuit of the purpose of any organization, which is, in general, to provide the procedures by which its members can achieve their common goal. As noted by Morphet et al. (1982), these include, at minimum, procedures for:

1. Selecting a leader or leaders
2. Determining the roles to be played by each member of the group
3. Determining the goals of the group
4. Achieving the goals of the group

The question of how the enterprise of special education should be organized has caused certain long-standing dilemmas and has been subject to some rapidly changing legal and philosophic trends. As discussed in Chapter 2, the perennial ambiguities concerning the scope of special education—that is, the boundaries between special education, general education, and other human services functions—are manifest in the search for optimal organizational structures to administer the enterprise. A fundamental question is the degree to which special education should be seen as unique and therefore differentiated from other human services or as only a minor variant within the broad scope of education and related social services. A secondary question to be addressed, irrespective of the answer to the first, is whether the enterprise is primarily focused on instruction (and variations within that function) or on a variety of support services covering a broad range of habilitation, of which instruction is only one (though a very important) part. Both questions bear heavily on how special education is organized at various times and places.

Furthermore, the question of organizational structure is of interest at various levels of the societal system as a whole. At the grassroots level, where direct service providers come face to face with clients (we are not limiting the consideration solely to teachers and children), the manner in which these personnel relate to others in the immediate system is a matter of organizational concern. Among the various units that a local service system comprises—for example, a school district or combination of local agencies—the structure has a major influence on how planning, communication, and all other administrative functions are executed. The issue remains relevant at higher levels of government—for example, among the state agencies responsible for education and certain other social services, as well as at the federal level. Whether we are considering the supervision of a speech therapist employed in a typical elementary school or the organization of cabinet-level departments of the federal government, there are similar structural issues that are important to effective operation.

While there have always been ambiguities regarding the scope and purpose of special education, leaving the issue of optimal organization variously and often poorly resolved, the area of special education, no matter how it was conceived, was at one time too small to be of much concern to anyone. Only since the 1970s has the field grown large enough to warrant serious thinking about its structural design. In addition to rapid growth in the numbers of clients, service providers, and organizational units, significant trends in philosophic perspectives, buttressed by legal developments, as well as increased pressures to educate all students more effectively, have created a need to justify the way that the system is put together.

CONSIDERATIONS FOR ORGANIZING

The primary consideration in any organizational structure is whether the existing design facilitates, permits, or hinders getting the job done. However, "the job" may be multifaceted and it may not always be clear what the highest priorities of the organization are. Within special education, one may reasonably argue over the relative merits of technical skill attainment versus those of the social assimilation of the students involved. The argument for students is easily extended to include the question of whether these two differing goals are in fact compatible and of what effect administrative structures may tend to have in enhancing either of them. One could ask, for example, if the special education student's growth is affected by a teacher's being supervised by a building principal rather than by a central office special education supervisor. Or is the growth of the individual student at a particular time and place of less consequence than the impact that the supervision of the teacher might have on the way special education is perceived in the educational establishment and the community? While it may exaggerate the possible influences, this example represents one of many dimensions on which basic questions of optimal structure should be considered.

Given the primary consideration of getting the job done, a host of secondary issues becomes evident. It may be assumed that organizational structures should be calculated to facilitate at least the following:

1. Systematic program planning (comprehensive, groups, and individuals)
2. Efficient ongoing operation (day to day management)
3. Fiscal accountability (budgeting, managing, monitoring)
4. Influence on staff personnel (selection, supervision, evaluation, development, retention)

5. Effective communication among all relevant parties (professionals, clients, and the public)
6. Consistent evaluation of program quality (based on measurement of individual student outcomes)

Beyond those elements necessary for general organizational effectiveness, some particular considerations for a special education service system would probably also include the following:

7. Thorough assessment of group and individual needs
8. Procedural safeguards in assessment and programming decisions
9. Least restrictive appropriate environment among program alternatives
10. Reduction of the stigmatizing consequences of special classification
11. Consumer participation in all aspects of the service delivery process
12. Acceptance of human variance within school and society

Given this variety of legitimate objectives that should influence the planning of the service system, the development of an optimal structure is understandably complex, and it is not surprising that the structures are determined more often by default than by design.

Special educators can credit themselves with having led the way in the development of ideas that later became standard practice throughout education as a whole. The concepts of individualized instruction, certain technologies for delivering instruction in spite of unusual obstacles, and the whole philosophy of students' rights, which affects the entire educational establishment, have largely been the product of the efforts of the professionals, advocates, and clients involved in special education.

In contrast, special educators have not been particularly creative in meeting the challenge of developing organizational structures for administering programs. Considering the demand for innovative structures that the wide variety of service needs in special education imposes, the administrative organization within most systems remains (with a few exceptions) surprisingly routine. In most cases, existing organizational structures have been the product of reactive circumstances rather than proactive planning. Especially in moderate-to-large–size school systems, in which special education in some form has long been established, the structure for its administration has tended to reflect the accidental presence of individual personalities to fill specialists' roles and the idiosyncratic perspectives of key general-organization leaders.

Creative development in organizational structure has occurred, however, in cases in which it has been necessary to set up entirely new organizations. The driving force in such instances has been the need to create a viable unit within the array of a total service system. For example, the problems presented by rural, sparsely populated regions, where the issue has been the aggregation of a sufficient population base to justify the provision of services, have resulted in the development of cooperative systems organized under joint agreements between school districts or intermediate education units that have at least questioned the traditional concept of rational administrative structure. In other isolated instances, such as a major shake-up in the administration of an established system, a reaction to a significant legal problem, or unusually progressive policy leadership, systems have undergone careful study and improved structures have been created.

Unit Magnitude

In considering what should go into appropriate organizational structures, the size of the unit, generally determined by the state government as well as by population density factors, should have a significant influence. For example, the governance unit of Hawaii, in which the entire state comprises a single school district, removes from consideration certain issues of revenue collection and resource distribution but forces administrative policy groups to deal with other questions concerning the best methods for managing the system. School districts in a number of states (e.g., Florida, Maryland, Nevada) are coterminous with the county, which has the general effect of creating fewer, but larger, administrative units. Other states in which local "town" governance is a major part of the cultural heritage (e.g., California, Illinois, Texas) tend to have significantly more districts (in each of these examples, over 1,000 in 1990), with many of them being very small. The geographic expanse of each state, of course, also plays a part in determining the number of governance units. As one would expect, Rhode Island and Delaware have relatively few districts, 38 and 22 respectively, whereas Nevada's 17 districts and Alaska's 55, when compared with Texas's 1,087, must be viewed in light of the population density factor. The country's urban centers will have large school systems (in terms of enrollment) regardless of the state's school governance system, simply because of population density.

General school consolidation has reduced the number of local school districts in the United States from about 120,000 in 1940 to under 15,367 in 1990. Data from the National Center for Educational

Statistics (1991) shows that in 1990 the 179 "large" (over 25,000 students enrolled) districts, constituting only 1.2% of the total number of districts in the country, served 28% of all the country's children. Conversely, 6,511 districts (42.4% of the total) served fewer than 600 children each, thereby accounting for only 3.8% of the country's total enrollment. It should be clear that when considering questions of organizational structure, we must recognize that a relatively few school systems are responsible for a large proportion of the nation's students. If we are to focus on the school system when thinking about viable organizational structures, we must remember that over half of these are responsible for less than 1,000 students each. However, if we wish to focus on where the children are, it should be recognized that nearly half of them attend school systems of at least moderate (over 10,000) enrollment.

Organizational unit size becomes an especially important factor as we consider the viability of systems for the delivery of special education services. What constitutes a "critical mass" for a special education organization? It has long been assumed that to provide for every imaginable contingency, even very large systems may need to go outside to secure appropriate services. However, it has been recognized that those systems with over 25,000 students enrolled should be able to provide for virtually every child's needs within the system. The degree to which smaller systems must secure services from outside of their own organization depends upon a number of factors, and a major challenge to traditional assumptions concerning unit magnitude has come about as a function of changing attitudes regarding inclusion and the doctrine of least restrictive environment.

As pointed out in Chapter 2, educators have long recognized a need for some type of mechanism to pool the needs of many smaller school districts. While this need extends to vocational education and certain other support activities (e.g., pupil personnel services, research, data processing, and instructional resources and materials) that can be provided more effectively and efficiently to a larger student population base, special education has tended to be the major reason for multidistrict organization. Historically, interdistrict contracts, wherein larger districts agreed to serve children with disabilities from smaller neighboring districts, led the way to informal cooperatives in many states, in which a modest amount of systematic planning among a collection of small districts permitted the establishment of a much more complete array of services than would have occurred through any single district's initiative. Although interdistrict contracting and informal cooperatives are still used, the more formalized cooperative, legally established as an intermediate education unit (IEU) between the local districts and the state education agency (SEA), has become the major means of organizing for service delivery in small districts. The driving force behind the formation of such units, whether stated openly or not, has been the implicit goal of achieving capacity programming in a manner ordinarily possible only in large systems, while still retaining the benefits of the smaller local education agency (LEA).

The Status of Intermediate Education Units

IEUs vary among states on a number of dimensions, such as scope of program involvement, governance, fiscal base, and organizational structure. U.S. Department of Education data covering the 1989–1990 school year listed a total of 1297 units under the title of "Education Service Agencies" (ESAs) and "Supervisory Union Administrative Centers." These were found in 31 states, which ranged from 179 such units in Ohio to only 1 in Missouri. A study by Stephens Associates (1979) identified three basic ESA patterns:

Special district A legally constituted unit of school government between the SEA and a collection of LEAs, usually established by the state, or by the state and client LEAs together to provide services to both the SEA and the LEAs. Eleven states were reported to employ this model.

Regionalized agencies ESAs established as a regional branch of the SEA to deliver services to LEAs. Four states were reported to use this model.

Cooperative agencies Two or more LEAs sponsoring an ESA to provide one or more common services exclusively for the member schools. This model was used to some degree in 13 states.

The same publication noted a variety of official names for regional education service agencies in various states, including such titles as Cooperative Educational Service Agency (CESA), Area Education Agency (AEA), Educational Service Unit (ESU), Intermediate Unit (IU), Educational Service Center (ESC), Intermediate School District (ISD), Regional Educational Service Agency (RESA), Board of Cooperative Educational Services (BOCES), and Intermediate Education District (IED).

It should be noted that some states have more than one type of ESA and that classification is rather difficult. Organizational and financial characteristics differ widely among the states that have such agencies, with some being mandated by state law while others operate under permissive legislation. A high degree of variation is noted in most characteristics, with similarities found only in the method of selection of the chief administrator, the eligibility to receive federal grants, and the authority to enter into service contracts with constituent LEAs. It is obvious that the function of an ESA in a relatively small state with a large number of units (e.g., Massachusetts, with 84) would be quite different from that in a large state with only a few units (e.g., Texas, with 20). Much of the variance may be attributable to the initial purposes for which intermediate agencies were established in each state. In New York, for example, the Board of Cooperative Educational Services (BOCES) originally placed great emphasis on direct instructional services in special and vocational education for LEAs believed to be too small to provide their own such services efficiently. The provision of increasing varieties of administrative and support services came later. By contrast, the Texas Regional Educational Service Centers have always emphasized support services, with little involvement in the direct operation of instructional programs. Differences in functions obviously influence the numbers and types of staff employed by an IEU. A reflection of the emphasis on direct program operation can be seen in the fact that in 1975, 67% of all personnel employed in ESA/IEU type organizations in the nation were in three states: New York, Michigan, and Pennsylvania.

Regardless of the programmatic scope of IEUs, they have certain inherent organizational problems. The IEU is always perceived as a limited-purpose structure when compared with the regular LEA. The development of an IEU tends to be in response to an unmet need, usually centered on a particular service. As a result, the IEU, in focusing on that service, cannot become an integral part of the entire educational system, which places IEU personnel in a role that is tangential to the major business of the regular school system. Personnel employed by the IEU may be identified only with the special-purpose program and may suffer the same "second-class citizenship" status as the students for whom services are provided.

The legal governance structure of the IEU varies from state to state. In cases in which the agency is an integral part of the state-to-local chain of command—serving as an extension of the SEA into the field, rather than merely a cooperative group of LEAs—the capacity of the administrator to affect the direct service field is enhanced. However, this "official" status also carries the disadvantage of setting the IEU apart from, and somewhat superordinate to, the mainstream system. The governance structure will certainly influence the degree to which regular educators and consumers feel that the special education program operated by the IEU is accessible, integral, and relevant.

The ultimate in separate governance, and a unique model for dealing with the problems of population base and "critical mass," is the St. Louis County (Missouri) Special District. Mandated by special state legislation in 1957, the district has legal, fiscal, and governance structures similar to all other school districts in the state, but geographically, it overlays all the regular school districts in the county. Its ability to operate programs independently of local district constraints earned the system praise for 2 decades as the ultimate solution to the programming problems of small school districts. However, the separation from mainstream educational programs was recognized as a barrier to interaction, constraining the flow of special services among different levels of the continuum and exerting a negative influence on decisions regarding least restrictive alternatives in programming. With the philosophic shift at the beginning of the 1980s, this perceived barrier became the basis for litigation against the state of Missouri (*St. Louis Developmental Disabilities Treatment Center Parents' Association v. Mallory*, 1985) that was expected to have implications for all organizational structures similar to the Special District. Although the federal district court (and subsequently the court of appeals) upheld the state's contention that the separate facilities were not a violation of any law, the issues surrounding the case generated considerable interest.

The "special purpose" status of the IEU is also reflected in its fiscal base, which in most states sets it apart from the mainstream of state-to-local revenue collection and expenditure and renders it dependent upon tuition payments for contracted services. This difference in basic funding structure may have both positive and negative implications, but the fact that the system and its funding are specialized constitutes an articulation problem with the educational system as a whole.

The one thing that appears quite clear is the steady growth of IEUs, both in their numbers and their assigned responsibilities. Forecasts regarding their roles point to still broader functions in the future—in research, the development of technology, staff development, and similar administrative services, with somewhat less emphasis on the direct operation of programs of instruction. These trends are a reflection of changes in the rationale for cooperative organization as local school districts come to recognize their responsibility for the inclusion of all students. A problem is sometimes created by differences among the component districts' degrees of usage of the cooperative's services. When districts share equally in the administration costs of the cooperative, yet some make much less use of its services, the fairness of the arrangement can be questioned. Furthermore, in some localities the economic pressure that at one time was a stimulus for the increased use of intermediate districts is now bringing into focus the problem of administrative redundancy, and the question of how many overlapping structures the education system can afford. Both idealism and pecuniary considerations can be the driving force behind the examination of existing organizations and the functions that they perform. In some regions the IEU may continue to be used to "closet" populations of students that are, at best, problematic. In others, as an inclusionary philosophy has become established in component districts, concerted efforts have been made to change the functions of the IEU and to collapse existing organizations into one another to reduce administrative overhead.

Notable movement in this direction has been evident in the Southern Cook County region of suburban Chicago (Committee on Educational Delivery System, 1993). In that setting, a new administrative structure for the IEU and its functional relationships with the individual local districts that are components of the cooperative have been proposed. Figure 1 illustrates those functions and the personnel who execute them. However, in states in which numerous small school districts are an embedded part of the culture, the role of some type of ESA/IEU as the service provider for students with low-incidence disabilities appears to be long enduring. It should be noted, however, that in some states, such as Vermont, and in certain districts of others, dependence on such structures is far less pronounced.

The question of optimal enrollment and organizational unit structure for special education service delivery is not limited to the small district or to the use of service agencies or other intermediate units. In larger school systems as well, one must consider how to organize administrative units to attain the most effective and efficient management and operation.

Emphasis on Form

One approach to the organization of a program is based on some form of client or service classification, delineated either in terms of statistical incidence, clinical disability, or type of service delivered. Students with very low-incidence disabilities (e.g., in much less than 1% of the general school population), have traditionally been assigned, for administrative purposes, to the broadest-based centralized service delivery unit. Incidence-based organization assumes that a client population receiving similar types of services should consist of some minimum number of individuals (e.g., at least 100 pupils, ages 3–21) in order to constitute a viable planning and service unit.

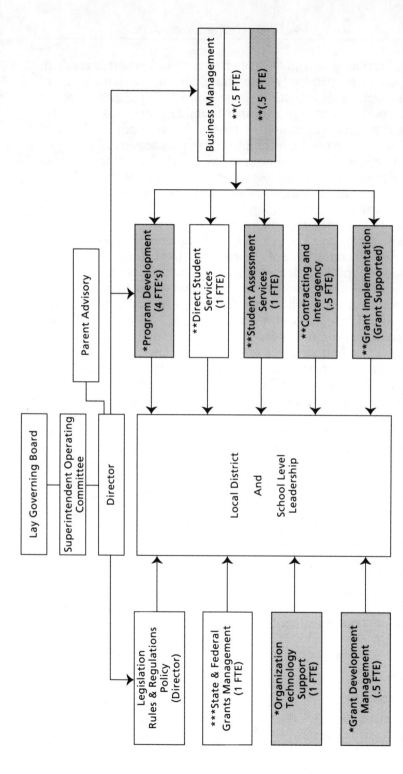

Figure 1. Administrative structure intermediate/cooperative unit functions. Shaded areas indicate ad hoc functions that are formed and reformed based on the needs of the local district. *Indicates financing to all member districts, based on general assessment. **Indicates financing based on district use. ***Indicates financing by federal and state grants. (From the Administrative and Governance Committee, Chicago South Metropolitan Association. [1993]. Report of the Administrative and Governance Committee, South Metropolitan School Association, Chicago, IL: Author; reprinted by permission.)

Application of this incidence criteria would probably result in centralized (or cooperative) administration for programs for groups of students such as those with orthopedic disabilities, some types of mental retardation, autism, multiple disabilities, or visual and severe hearing impairments, as well as those who are home or hospital bound. Service systems covering decentralized regions of large systems (or independent smaller systems) would be viable for those groups of students requiring less-extensive services. It should be evident, however, that classification difficulties will occur because incidence rates will fluctuate depending on where the cut-off lines are drawn on the severity continuum.

Those taking another approach might ignore incidence rates and organize solely on the basis of clinical disability classifications. Such a plan would permit the deployment of instructional and supervisory expertise to the units at which the population was served. While this would result in much the same divisions between organizational units as would the statistical approach, it could realize a benefit based on the presumed common need of a disability group, regardless of degree of severity. This approach tends to break down in practice, however, as there tend to be many more children with mild forms of disability than with severe disability in any school unit of a given size, and those responsible for programmatic organization invariably take into account the number of children who need a particular service.

A third approach places emphasis on the type of instructional service, ignoring both incidence rates and clinical disability categories. Such an approach is most viable within systems that can provide a full continuum of services. Under this plan, all services that are delivered in an essentially self-contained mode, isolated from the mainstream, are provided by the centralized unit. Services that are most articulated with the mainstream, such as those provided by resource teachers, itinerant teachers, and consultants, are administered by decentralized units, through which proximity to general education teachers and administrators can be optimized.

In each of these three approaches, it is assumed that persons responsible for special education will be employed at both the centralized (or cooperative) unit level and at the localized (or independent district) level and that the assignment of responsibility can be organized according to programs of services and/or classifications of children.

Emphasis on Function

A different approach to organization may focus on the processes that constitute the leadership role. A simple division into administrative and supervisory processes has often been used to identify two levels of organizational hierarchy and may provide a basis for distinguishing between those functions that can best be executed by a broad, centralized unit and those that should take place closer to the point of delivery. However, given the obviously trivial nature of certain administrative tasks and the relatively crucial impact of technical supervisory processes on the quality of the services delivered, the inherent hierarchical relationship between administration and supervision may not provide the most useful means of distinguishing functions or determining their optimal organizational locus.

In large school systems in which a two-layered (or more) organizational structure for general program administration is required, in moderate-sized systems in which central office-building–level interaction is the issue, or in small systems in which some services may be procured from another (intermediate) agency, guidelines for identifying and understanding different functions and locating them organizationally will probably be helpful. The distinction between policy leadership and administrative management becomes noticeable in cases such as these.

When examining the full range of leadership functions associated with any organization, certain processes fall logically into the domain of the broadest, most centralized units, whereas others fit better into the directly operational level. Policy development, for example, should surely be a function of the central office. In contrast, personnel selection usually needs to be carried out by the administrators closest to the field of action. As we move from general principles for all organizations to particulars concerning education, including special education, the determination of the proper level at which each process should be conducted becomes more difficult. We could place those functions concerned with planning, development, and evaluation at the central level, leaving decentralized units with the functions of management and direct supervision. The distinction between different levels' responsibilities is blurred by the broad scope of certain concepts. For example, while planning would normally be centered around overall long-range programmatic issues, it is also important to daily operations. Similarly, the evaluation process is normally concerned with programs calling for a broad-scale central perspective, but specific elements (e.g., instructional personnel) would best be examined by the leadership personnel (managers) nearest the action.

According to this model, planning and policy development as it relates to resource allocation, curriculum, and general program evaluation has been assumed to be appropriately executed at the most central level. This would include budget development and staff allocation, as well as inservice development for existing staff. The functions of program advocacy, public relations, and interagency liaison have also been seen as central responsibilities. The focus of restructuring has of course called into question some of these assumptions. For example, the identification of needs for inservice staff development can be best performed at the local site, regardless of the source of assistance or responsibility for delivering it. The thrust of restructuring places great emphasis on site-based management. As school personnel who are accustomed to centralized control grapple with the changes that restructuring imposes, ambiguities are unavoidable.

At the local level, the operational management functions would include personnel selection and assignment, personnel evaluation, service coordination and pupil placement, instructional supervision, resource management (including such tasks as material and facility procurement), and consumer (parent) relations. Complete dichotomization, of course, would be neither possible nor desirable. Managers should not have to execute programs that they had no voice in developing. Input on policy must include the perspectives of management personnel. Conversely, local personnel should seek the counsel of central administrators as they undertake such management tasks as personnel evaluation. The crucial factor is that responsibility for each function, be fixed at one particular level, leaving as few functions as possible in an ambiguous shared domain. Even if both levels must be involved in a particular activity, the division of authority should be clear.

MAJOR ORGANIZATIONAL ISSUES

Examples of perspectives on optimal administrative structures, drawn from both recent and past events, will illustrate some important points. These examples concern large systems in which the issue of organizational structure has been deemed worthy of intensive deliberation. Certainly the effect of such structural choices is not negligible in smaller systems, but it is the larger systems that tend to have enough at stake to invest seriously in the study of organizational structure.

The Centralization Question

One issue that confronts service systems of all sizes but has been of particular interest to larger systems is that of optimal centralization. This issue is not limited to the public school sector, since any branch of a multilevel service system must face a similar question about the degree to which the several units of the lower level should operate autonomously or be controlled by the central agency. The issue is basic to state and local relationships within the educational establishment, but it is also relevant to health, welfare, and all other social services. Within the education system, however, the issue becomes even more pronounced, because local school districts typically consist of a number of units (individual buildings) with greater or lesser degrees of autonomy. Within the general educational program, despite certain centralized functions such as fiscal controls, personnel management, and broad curricular oversight, school building units have always tended to operate with considerable independence, even though the controlling bureaucracy was assumed to be in charge. The view of school districts as "loosely coupled systems" has been extensively discussed in the literature on the sociology of schools (Weick, 1976). The more recent press for site-based management, and the political rhetoric endorsing "bottom-up" rather than "top-down" management, has gone a long way toward the legitimization of grass-roots decision making.

However, meeting the special education needs of certain students calls for services that for a number of reasons may suggest a need for a greater degree of centralization. The logical press for (relative) centralization of special education is obviously justified on the grounds of the statistical minority status of the population. That is, whatever basis for optimal organizational unit size is applicable for the general school population, a different catchment base has been assumed to be necessary for students with disabilities, particularly those with low-incidence disabilities. Furthermore, apparent needs for technical expertise, specialized materials, and other factors have also led to a press for some level of centralization.

In this context, then, a series of related questions may be asked that bear directly on the centralization issue:

1. To what extent can special education be administered from the individual building level?
2. To what extent can a general school principal provide necessary program supervision?
3. What support services can best be provided from a central district level?
4. Are there certain services that can be procured only from outside of the central system?
5. What are the relevant relationships among school building enrollment, district enrollment, community resources, the incidence and degree of disability in question, and the answers to questions 1 through 4?

The answer to the centralization question can probably best be viewed as the selection of an optimal point on a continuum, rather than as a choice between dichotomous alternatives.

The Call for Site-Based Management

A significant part of the discussion about general educational reform and restructuring, as noted in Chapter 1 of this volume, has focused on the argument that large bureaucracies in educational agencies have been a barrier to change and have perpetuated ineffective and inefficient service delivery. The argument is most easily supported, of course, in large (usually urban) local school systems, in which a certain amount of bureaucracy is apparently inevitable and poor performance, if not outright abuse, is easily documented. SEAs have also been vulnerable to charges of "over-centralization" and the perpetuation of unwieldy bureaucratic structures, especially as their responsibilities for carrying out the difficult, federally imposed task of program monitoring has challenged their capacity. In small- or moderate-size local school systems there are fewer opportunities for criticism of organizational structures, simply because the lower profile of their central offices makes flaws less visible. But in any educational organization, the notion that more decisions can be made by those at the grass-roots level has gained strength. Concerning special education programs, the concurrent press for inclusion and for reduction of the scope of separate programs for students with disabilities further suggests the diminishing need for separate decision-making personnel and adds strength to the argument that more operational control should be exercised at the site of service delivery.

It is mentioned above that significant study of and changes in the organizational structure of special education has most often occurred at times of crisis in a system. The precipitation of such crises by requirements imposed by the legal system has become quite prevalent in the years since 1975, especially in the larger, urban systems. In an earlier publication a rather detailed description is provided of such an attempt at reorganization of the special education system in the city of Boston (Sage & Burrello, 1986, pp. 103–107). Precipitated by a court order concerning the system's failure to comply with legal mandates, this reorganization was comprehensive, but placed a strong emphasis on the central office structure and was not particularly concerned with enhancing site-based management. In a similar vein, the late 1970s saw a major attempt at reorganizing the relationships between the central establishment and the multiple community school districts within the New York City special education structure.

The Chicago Example   A rather different situation, one reflecting a more recent ideological thrust, can be seen in the case of the city of Chicago. As a part of a state legislative mandate to reorganize the general administrative structure of the school system in 1989–1990, and coinciding with a settlement agreement that arose out of litigation focused on the inadequacies of the special education program, a major restructuring of the long-established central bureaucracy for special education was attempted. In this instance there was a general policy move toward making principals more directly responsible for everything at the building level and giving much greater authority to Local School Councils, as opposed to the central Board of Education. At the same time, the central department of special education was down-sized, through the reassignment of certain central personnel to school-based positions and a concerted effort to ensure that local building principals would view special education as an integral part of their total school responsibilities.

The reorganization plan that was announced in 1991 and had been developed by the Associate Superintendent with the assistance of an outside consultant, with input from federal and state agencies as well as local administrators and advocates, cited the following four goals:

1. To develop an efficient central special education and support services department which is consistent with Chicago School Reform and is capable of, and committed to, assisting the schools in developing quality special education and support services.
2. To implement a system of clear accountability for regulatory compliance.
3. To develop a dynamic organizational structure which will enable the Chicago Public Schools to address system-wide issues and needs.
4. To improve the management of resources that support the Department of Special Education and Pupil Support Services. (Chicago Public Schools, 1991)

Under an *Office of the Associate Superintendent,* two *Assistant Superintendents,* one for special education and one for pupil support services, were assigned roles and functions to provide leadership for ten operational units. These included such diverse functions as compliance monitoring and quality control; staff training and development; parent training; and overseeing city-wide programs for students with low-incidence disabilities, school medical health services, programs for gifted students, and certain special projects to facilitate the capacity of individual schools to serve exceptional students within their own classrooms.

The greatest change from previous operating models, and the central thrust of the reorganization, was found in the establishment of *District Teams,* centrally organized but assigned as primary liaisons to individual schools to provide technical assistance to building-level personnel in the areas of resource acquisition and coordination, policy and procedures clarification, needs assessment, and program development. Eleven of these teams, each consisting of five or six members, were assigned the responsibility of assisting districts and schools to serve as many of their exceptional students as possible in their home schools. While this reorganization resulted in a net reduction of positions in the department, the major purpose was to shift the emphasis of professionals' work from a centralized to a school-based orientation. The students whom this decentralized focus was intended to benefit included those with high-incidence or relatively mild disabilities (Chicago Public Schools, 1991).

An interesting aspect of this structure is that the District Teams were designed to function dually under superordinates from two different branches of the organization: 1) Special Education and 2) Pupil Support Services. While this might be a step toward the ideal of having these related departments coordinate more effectively and would also provide for policy input from both, it could be anticipated that in day-to-day operations, one or the other of the leaders would assume major responsibility.

The Line–Staff Relationship

An additional variable influencing generalist authority is the emphasis on special education as an *instructional* versus a *support* service. The debate over this question is often couched in terms of degree of centrality (and therefore "clout") within the system. Since basic instruction is generally seen as the central purpose of schools, some argue that the survival of special education, especially in difficult economic times, depends on its centrality in the system as a basic instructional unit, rather than as an auxiliary service (Howe, 1981). Central-office linkage with instruction would presumably enhance the line-authority connection to principals, the persons who can have the greatest impact on the system as a whole. However, this emphasis on a hierarchy of direct control also tends to be most applicable if the total system is seen as being made up of separate identifiable units.

It is clear that, given the trend toward the inclusion of all children within the general system, the idea of achieving authority through a separate line administration for special education is out of the question. Therefore, a shared authority system is most viable, even though identification with instruction rather than special services may provide the firmest anchoring of the special education program within the mainstream. However, models have been developed that conceptualize special education as a broad, supportive service for all students and implement that concept by encompassing all of the various units of the organization that deliver the entire continuum of services. It is this type of structure that has been argued as holding the best promise for the future (Sage & Burrello, 1986).

From Integration to Inclusion

We have indicated that the process of introducing changes in the organizational structure of special education systems has been subject to multiple forces of legal pressure, professional interests, bureaucratic constraints, and political vagaries. Furthermore, some of the attempts at reorganization that are discussed here and elsewhere have been seen as "grand ideas" that failed to reach fruition or to endure long enough to really demonstrate whether the concept was sound. However, one example of special education organizational development that can be cited demonstrates an evolution and development along fairly consistent conceptual lines for a period of time; this example will be described in an effort to illustrate many of the same guiding ideological principles discussed above, but with some additional speculation on the factors that have allowed this system to move toward a goal without noticeable detours or retrogression.

The Madison Development   In an earlier work (Sage & Burrello, 1986), we included an extensive description of how the Madison (Wisconsin) Metropolitan School District (MMSD) had succeeded in moving from a traditional categorical disability model of administrative and programmatic organization to a regional plan with a special education coordinator in each geographic area to facilitate the provision of direct services to children with disabilities and to support the general school program for all students. In accordance with the continuous, long-range development endeavor of MMSD, a working document for in-house study and planning was disseminated (Madison Metropolitan School District, 1982). This document, which addressed issues concerning the mission of the *whole* system, not just that of the special education services, set forth a number of goals.

It should be noted that the plan was the product of both formal and informal interaction, over a period of several years, among the Board of Education, members of the professional staff, and the community. Two of the goals were of particular relevance to the organization of special education services and should be discussed in some detail.

The goal of establishing an integrated instructional program is based on the rationale that since a variety of options are necessary to accommodate the individual learning styles and needs of all students, the educational program must include a comprehensive but flexible range of programs and service options. Four variables that inhibit or enhance the maintenance and improvement of an integrated program were cited:

1. *Resources* The provision of equal opportunities requires unequal distribution of resources. In addition, an integrated program is generally more costly than a segregated system.
2. *Parallelism* The lack of equal opportunity, which has fostered special advocacy groups that secured special legislation and funding sources, has led to the development of special management structures and delivery systems that tend to be parallel to, rather than a part of, the existing instructional program.
3. *Advocacy* While advocacy is healthy and necessary, some specific interest groups that lead to parallelism foster lack of a sense of ownership of special programs by school personnel.
4. *Attitudes/Ownership* Lack of a sense of ownership among school personnel regarding students who differ from the norm is in part an attitudinal factor that is difficult to modify when there are parallel structures to accommodate these differences.

To pursue the goal of an integrated instructional program, it would be necessary to improve the process of integrated decision making and advocacy. To avoid the pursuit of separate, parallel programs, a process was needed for setting priorities and integrating the delivery of several alternative programs designed to address the needs of a variety of students (not just those with disabilities) within the regular instructional program. This called for a much improved system of staff development and ongoing support for the general instructional staff in the form of technical assistance from specialists and an administrative structure that would facilitate a balance between school-based and district-level service provision.

The achievement of the goal of an integrated instructional program, which would require the reorganization of the management components of the district, called for a new conceptualization of the administrative relationships. While the vertical K–12 coordination of geographic-area based programs would need to be continued, the complexity of the programs precluded the Area Directors from providing sufficiently comprehensive supervision, evaluation, and coordination of staff and program. Therefore, increased horizontal coordination was cited as being necessary to integrate various special programs into the whole. This called for additional management resources and a redefinition of the roles of existing staff.

The programs supported by advocacy efforts and special funding, which had developed parallel leadership structures, were now seen as needing to be consolidated and integrated with the mainstream organizational structure. The problem of crisis management, as a result of reduction in staff and the growing complexity of parts of the organization, also called for additional human resources, redefinition of functions, and reassignment of existing personnel. In view of these considerations, 10 objectives for the reorganization of the management structure were set forth:

1. To continue to emphasize the vertical coordination of personnel and program
2. To place additional emphasis on the horizontal coordination of personnel and program
3. To improve the supervision and evaluation of administrative staff
4. To increase administrative resources in support of the planning, coordination, and priority-setting functions of the district
5. To redefine roles of existing staff so that they can accomplish assigned responsibilities and better use the talents they possess
6. To become more humanistic and less mechanistic in the management of human resources in the district
7. To eliminate organizational parallelism through the continued integration of program
8. To maintain program advocacy where it is needed
9. To provide additional management resources to components of the organization that are becoming increasingly complex and important to the operation of the district
10. To define the appropriate functions of the principal as an instructional leader and to support staff development programs necessary to implement those functions. (Madison Metropolitan School District, 1982, pp. 24–25)

The action plan to pursue these objectives called for modifying the central administrative structure in a number of ways. The establishment of a Department of Integrated Student Services, to replace the former Department of Specialized Educational Services, is of greatest importance to the concepts with which we are concerned.

The conceptual underpinnings and rationale for this new department and the scope of responsibilities it encompassed were explained in the planning document:

Continued advocacy is important to providing programs for exceptional children. However, it is important that those programs be integrated into the total instructional program and not be parallel to it. Present attitudes in the staff and community regarding the Specialized Educational Services Department seem to reinforce the concept of parallelism. It is almost impossible to place programs that meet the special needs of children within the SES Department because of the perception that all programs in the Department deal with children who are handicapped. Therefore, the name of the SES Department will be changed to the Department of Integrated Student Programs, and programs coordinated by the Department will be expanded. These programs will include the alcohol and drug abuse program, family change task force, student support services including health, the talented and gifted program, and others. In addition, the Director of the Integrated Student Programs Department will take on additional responsibility for supervising and evaluating principals of elementary schools wherein there is a large program dealing with the special needs of children. (Madison Metropolitan School District, 1982, p. 26)

As indicated earlier, the most striking aspect of this example of organizational change, beyond the rather significant conceptual expansion and integration of special education, is the fact that steady growth was to be maintained, consistent with a basic theme, over a long period of time. This may raise the question of why Madison, as compared with many other systems, has provided a more favorable climate for innovations. The size of the system (under 25,000 students enrolled), and the concomitant ease of communication and manageability of the bureaucracy can be presumed to render the system much more receptive to change than would be the case in other, larger cities. But other factors have undoubtedly allowed MMSD to be recognized as a major generator of educational innovation, particularly in special education.

The Johnson City Example A small city school district (2,900 students) in upstate New York has gained considerable recognition in recent years for two related aspects of its local programming philosophy and practice. As proponents of the outcome-based, mastery learning model for curriculum and instruction for all students, the leadership of the Johnson City system has applied the concept to children with disabilities. Furthermore, the system has embraced the ideal of including these students, even those with the most severe disabilities, within general, age-appropriate classes in the neighborhood schools they would normally attend. In 1992–1993, approximately 165 children with disabilities were included in this manner, with only 10–15 served in more restrictive settings. This school district's implementation of an inclusive philosophy is particularly notable since its size and location are of the type that the Board of Cooperative Educational Services (BOCES) in New York was designed to serve, and which are common in many localities within the state.

In Johnson City, the role relationships between the central office staff and the building-level administrators are characterized by placing major responsibility for all programs and all children on the principals, with the central office administrators acting as enablers to help the building-level personnel exercise their role. The structure for these central office functions reflects considerable overlap among four persons carrying the title of Director or Deputy Superintendent, who each report to the general Superintendent of Schools. Three of these are involved rather directly with instructional programs (the other being the district's business official), but care is taken to address the concerns of students with disabilities, those with English as a second language, and all other programs associated with external grants, in the regular instructional program. In this way, specialization among the leadership personnel is avoided and the lines between domains of expertise and responsibility are intentionally blurred. While one of the three directors is primarily responsible for the merger of special and regular education, and is therefore concerned with curriculum and instruction at all levels, the other two directors are each responsible for activities and functions that also contribute in some measure to the successful inclusion of all students, regardless of individual differences, within one integrated school environment. Figure 2 illustrates these relationships and indicates some areas of responsibility.

It should be noted that the philosophy underlying this structure includes the idea that it will remain fluid, that lines will be blurred, and that both the responsibilities of encumbents and position descriptions may shift significantly as changing needs and new opportunities for problem solving become apparent. As one of the Directors of Teaching and Learning describes it:

> I am not sure that the figure [Figure 1] will convey the spirit of collaboration and "job overlap" that actually exists . . . An outside observer of one of our central office meetings would not easily discern who was "positionally in charge." Rather, one would see direct, blunt interactions, focused on desired visions and results. How the administrative team members will be "deployed" to lead any particular project or initiative is determined, reviewed and renewed at both formal weekly meetings and daily, ongoing interactions. (A.J. Chambers, personal communication, February 17, 1993)

The fact that staff development is listed as a function under the job descriptions of each of the Directors gives a clue to the concept of leadership adopted by the planners of this central office administrative structure. The Johnson City example illustrates rather well the type of *ad hocratic* organizational response that Skrtic (1991) argues is necessary to effectively reform the traditional regular and special education systems.

In summary, the organizational structures that have been described here represent a cross-section of attempts at creative solu-

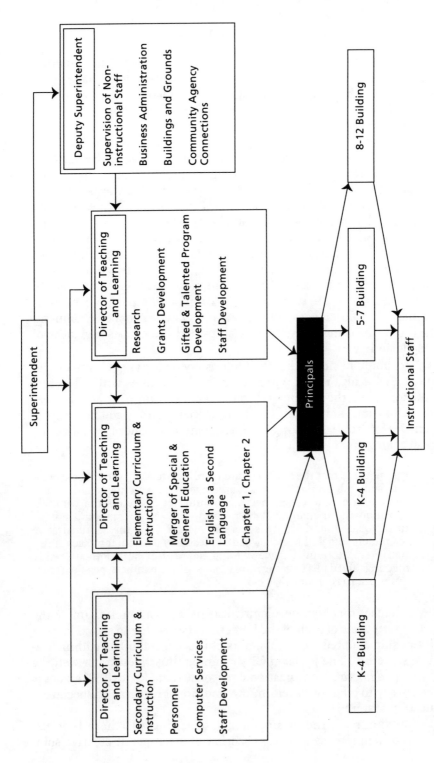

Figure 2. Administrative organization of Johnson City Central Schools.

tions to recognized inadequacies in present school system administration. Such attempts are often short lived, but those that we include represent the most ambitious attempts to put into operation a progressive theory of special education organization in systems of varying sizes. In each of the examples, planners have sought ways to balance the benefits of special identity against the merits of inclusion in order to maximize educational benefits for all students.

Burrello and Lashley (1992) have noted that to bring about "the changes which support inclusiveness in schools requires leadership with a vision which builds policy that supports a shared culture" (p. 81). The primary task is to build a joint model for the school, a way for personnel to see and believe in relationships between one another and their shared values. With the vision established, a second leadership role is that of developing policy that supports a shared culture of inclusiveness. Such a culture requires a set of beliefs that includes the following:

1. Everyone in the school is responsible for the education of each student from the school's attendance area, regardless of learning needs.
2. Everyone in the school is focused on meeting the needs of all students in a unified system of education. Labeling and separation of students are counterproductive to educational excellence.
3. All educators have skills and knowledge that should be used to support the efforts of all teachers to ensure the success of all students in typical classrooms.
4. All students benefit from participation in inclusive classrooms and schools.
5. The prevention of learning problems is the proper province of special education.
6. Assessment of students' needs is a regular part of curricular and instructional planning for all teachers and related services personnel.
7. Special education and related service personnel serve as full members of teacher teams under the leadership of the school principal.
8. Special education and related services personnel provide services to students in the context of the general school program.
9. Funding and budgeting models support the provision of services for students with special needs in the home school and local community.
10. Community human services for children are coordinated at the school.
11. Evaluation of the effectiveness of a school's program includes consideration of the post-school adjustment of students with special needs. (Burrello & Lashley, 1992, pp. 82–83)

CONCLUDING COMMENTS

If any conclusion can be drawn from this discussion of organizational principles and the examples to be found in recent practice, it is that special education should assume a broad role in the leadership of school system functions. Individualization of instruction, essential for children with special learning needs, can and should be provided for all students. Much of the necessary instructional service must be carried out within the mainstream, but teachers need assistance in the rapid assimilation and application of information as well as alternative ways to meet the multiple and diverse needs of the students.

The complexity of the task is indisputable. The educational system has been too fragmented and unorganized to meet the challenge. The problem of students who are failing in regular programs has resulted in duplication of remedial, compensatory, vocational, and special education efforts. The regular staff has been alternately threatened by and disappointed with the introduction of alternative programs for students with special needs. To confront the problem, there is a need for planning and evaluation, personnel training, and research and development. Special educators should play a major role in developing and implementing these steps. But this cannot be done without attention to organizational relationships.

Special education should be reorganized as an integral support system for all children. Initially, the shared or centralized responsibility of special education demands certain changes in roles and functions. If the schools are responsible for serving all children in the least restrictive environment, school administrators must assume responsibility for organizing, operating, and evaluating all programs for all children at the district or building level. Special educators should then plan, organize, and evaluate their contribution as a support system to the regular administrative and instructional staff. The organization should help special education to:

1. Provide support and assistance to regular education personnel to help them teach and organize instructional services for students with disabilities and others with special needs
2. Establish direct services that accommodate the unique learning and behavioral needs of students in the least restrictive environment
3. Organize building-based team efforts of parents, students, and professionals for program planning and placement of students
4. Initiate the provision of alternative settings and services at the building and district levels
5. Provide for the evaluation of students' progress and for decision points at which students can exit various programs and services
6. Provide for professional staff development to increase teacher and administrator competencies

7. Develop a field-based action research program that tests the application of basic learning principles to instruction, behavior management, and other factors that affect the mental health of students, parents, and professionals

8. Negotiate to obtain the participation of other state and community agencies in the support of instructional programs, mental health services for children, and social welfare services for parents and children

9. Provide direct consultative services to parents and students to assist them in becoming better participants in the educational planning process

10. Apply criteria derived from considerations of process and least restrictive environment to all individual educational planning and placement alternatives developed at the building or district levels

Achievement of these objectives calls for an organizational structure in which special education leadership operates on two levels and that also permits dual authority within parts of the subsystem. In policy matters, the special education administrator must participate in all aspects of the system. At the management level, the locus of operation should not be limited to particular special programs; authority must be shared with the mainstream personnel. While it takes much more than an organization chart to achieve this, and although informal relationships, personalities, and idiosyncrasies will certainly play a part, the basic concept must first be legitimized and officially endorsed if it is to be put into practice.

ILLUSTRATIVE CASE

The school district serving the city of Soda Water Springs is of moderate size, with about 25,000 students enrolled. With the election of a new school board majority and the appointment of a new superintendent last spring, the time seemed ripe for a serious reevaluation of the administrative organizational structure. As one of the key surviving central office administrators from the "old regime," Dr. Pat Karkowski, Assistant Superintendent for Instruction, has been asked to chair a committee to study alternative approaches to organizing the district and to advise the superintendent and the board as to whether the existing structure should be maintained or a new one adopted.

Pat has been advised that a free hand should be exercised, with little regard for incumbent personnel, as job descriptions for existing slots, impending retirements, and slack in the personnel budget will allow sufficient "wiggle room" to permit change if it is warranted. As the new boss put it, "If a change is needed, we should do it before the honeymoon ends!"

Furthermore, the political activity and public discussion that culminated in the election of the new board made it clear that perceptions in the community regarding various special programs, including those coming under the general rubric of special education, are "hot topics." The management of relationships between the regular and special programs must, therefore, be addressed in any recommendations. Recognizing the volatility of the situation, Pat has decided to diffuse the risk by assembling a broad-based committee to participate in the study and develop recommendations. This Organization Advisory Committee includes teachers and principals representing each level in the system, some central office directors, supervisors, and consultants and an equal number of parents and other concerned citizens. The committee is rather large, but it seems to be getting things done, and Pat's manner of handling the process has allowed the membership to feel truly enfranchised.

To help the committee understand the organization and policies currently in place, an organization chart was reviewed and analyzed, with particular attention to the structure of various special programs. It was noted that about 2,000 students are identified as having disabilities and are served through a variety of programs encompassing a wide range, from part-time attention by itinerant or resource-room teachers to full-time placement in residential settings outside of the public schools' domain. All these programs fall under the authority of a Division of Special Education, headed by a Director. The staff employed in these programs report through a line structure of departments to the division director. The management of services procured from outside of the system is also the responsibility of this Director. This responsibility includes all fiscal matters from budget development to final accounting. The authority and program relationships in this system are illustrated in Figure 3, with certain portions elaborated on to focus on the details of the special education programs.

The supervisors in the special education departments of Part-Time Programs and Full-Time Programs provide both technical assistance and evaluation and supervision of the staff employed in those programs. They are expected to have curricular and instructional expertise in special education, as well as program-management skills. The director of the Division of Special Education oversees all programs and is responsible for managing relationships between these programs and clients, both inside the system (regular teachers, principals, and other division directors) and outside of it (parents, community agencies, and taxpayers).

It was also noted that approximately 1,000 other students who are *not* identified as having disabilities receive a variety of *indirect* special services in the system every year. These services, provided by psychologists and other consultant staff, include pupil assessment, consultation with the regular classroom teachers, and counseling for parents and students who have difficulties in school but either have not yet been confirmed as having disabilities

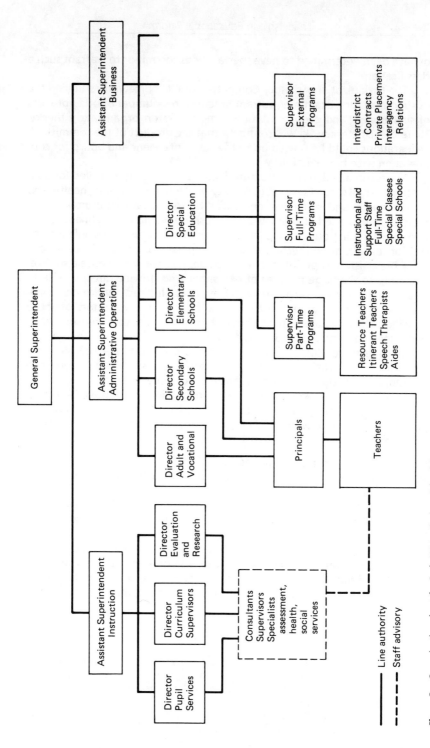

Figure 3. Organization chart for Soda Water Springs School System.

or have been determined to have special needs too minor to warrant such a classification.

The Organization Advisory Committee did its homework, studying the existing structure, examining current practices in a number of other districts of similar size, and even consulting some books on organization theory. Therefore, Dr. Karkowski was confident that the product of the committee's deliberations could be passed on to the superintendent and board for consideration with high credibility.

The recommended new structure for Soda Water Springs called for pulling together all special services (disability-related, psychological, health, and social services) under one division headed by an assistant superintendent, a position to be added at that level. This position would have a line relationship with a small group of support service administrators who would direct a staff of consultant and technical assistance personnel. Through these positions, the assistant superintendent for special services would have a staff relationship to the large number of personnel who provide direct service to students in the schools. The line authority over all direct service personnel assigned to schools would rest with the regular administrators of those buildings. The chart presented in Figure 4, which depicts these recommendations, does not include details of the Business Division, since no changes are to be made there. Both charts illustrate the distinction between line authority roles and staff consultant (supervisor/specialist) roles in regular curriculum, special education, and support service departments.

In forwarding the committee's recommendation to the boss, Pat recognized that in choosing between the existing structure and the newly proposed one, the board would have to consider a number of policy questions. For example:

What underlying values are implied by each structure?
What assumptions and perceptions about special education does each structure suggest?
What benefits does each plan promise to the consumers of services?
What benefits to system personnel can be expected from each plan?
What sacrifices does each structure entail?
What long-term effects can be predicted to result from each structure?
What are the significant fiscal considerations associated with each structure in terms of numbers and levels of positions or other service costs?
What measures can be devised to determine successful implementation?

REFERENCES

Burrello, L.C., & Lashley, C.A. (1992). On organizing for the future: The destiny of special education. In K.A. Waldron, A.E. Riester, & J.H. Moore (Eds.). *Special education: The challenge of the future* (pp. 64–95). San Francisco: Mellen Research University Press.

Chambers, A.J. (1992). *A school district's quest to fully include all students with disabilities.* Johnson City, NY: Johnson City Public Schools.

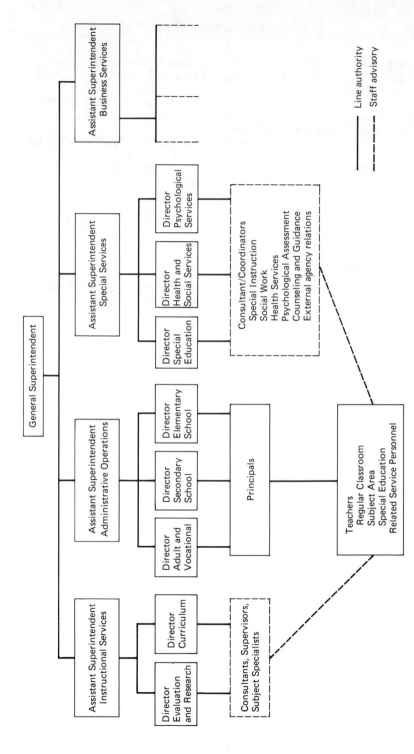

Figure 4. Proposed revised organization chart for Soda Water Springs School System.

Chicago Public Schools. (1991). *Reorganization of special education and pupil support service.* Chicago: General Superintendent's Administrative Memorandum.

Committee on Education Delivery System. (1993). *Report of the Administrative and Governance Sub-committee, South Metropolitan Association.* Homewood-Flossmoor, IL: Author.

Griffiths, D.E. (1959). *Administrative theory.* New York: Appleton-Century-Crofts.

Howe, C.E. (1981). *Administration of special education.* Denver: Love.

Madison Metropolitan School District. (1982). *A plan to maintain and improve effective schools in the 1980s.* Madison, WI: Author.

Morphet, E.L., Johns, R.L., & Reller, T.L. (1982). *Educational organization and administration* (4th ed.). Englewood Cliffs, NJ: Prentice Hall.

National Center for Educational Statistics. (1991). *Digest of educational statistics.* Washington, DC: U.S. Government Printing Office.

Sage, D.D., & Burrello, L.C. (1986). *Policy and management in special education.* Englewood Cliffs, NJ: Prentice Hall.

Skrtic, T.M. (1991). *Behind special education.* Denver: Love Publishing Co.

St. Louis Developmental Disabilities Treatment Center Parents v. Mallory, 767 F.2d 518 (8th Cir. 1985).

Stephens Associates. (1979). *Educational service agencies: Status and trends.* Burtonsville, MD: Author.

Weick, K.E. (1976). Educational organizations as loosely coupled systems. *Administrative Science Quarterly, 21*(1), 1–19.

6

Issues in Fiscal Policy

The financing of special education has sometimes been viewed as an issue separate from the mainstream of educational finance. This view has, of course, been sustained to the degree that the delivery of special education and related services and the organizational mechanisms for such delivery have been segregated from the general educational enterprise and identified instead with other social service systems. The factors regarding the status of special education and its relationship to the general education system that have been discussed in the preceding chapters are also manifested in financial relationships and policies. Therefore, to understand fiscal issues in special education, we must look first at the broad field of educational fiscal policy as a whole.

It would be inappropriate to attempt even a cursory coverage of educational finance in this chapter. However, there are a few underlying concepts from the literature and common understandings concerning educational finance that are relevant to the special education delivery system. It is also clear that as the philosophic and conceptual basis for the increased integration of special and general education has developed and gained wider acceptance in recent years, certain issues that had been seen as primarily applicable to special education interests have come to also have significant implications for general educational fiscal policy.

Therefore, this chapter initially deals with a few of the more relevant concepts that constitute basic principles of fiscal policy in both general and special education. After establishing the factors necessary for optimal policy in general, we discuss some specifics regarding the evolution of special education support systems, particularly those dealing with sources of revenue, and some considerations in the distribution of revenue. This will lead us to an examination of known facts about the costs of special education. Finally, we will examine recent developments in state-level special education fiscal policy on resource distribution and discuss the merits of the various methods currently utilized.

BASIC CONCEPTS

Since about 1970 there has been an acceleration of interest and activity surrounding general educational finance policy reform. In a manner that parallels the progressive thrust in policy development in special education, judicial, legislative, and regulatory activity throughout the United States has focused on improving upon existing policies for the support of public education. This activity has emphasized different objectives and widely varying mechanisms for the pursuit of those objectives. This variety is a function of political, economic, and general social forces, some of which parallel those forces that have brought about other (nonfiscal) changes in special education policy.

It is generally recognized that three strongly held values influence public policy in America: "*Equality, efficiency,* and *liberty* are viewed by an overwhelming electoral majority as conditions that government should maximize" (Guthrie, Garms, & Pierce, 1988, p. 22, italics added). It is quite obvious that these three abstract goals are somewhat antithetical to one another and that the exclusive pursuit of one would be at the expense of the others. Priorities among the three are a matter of ideological preference. Persons concerned with educational policy are continually faced with the need to maintain the dynamic equilibrium among these values, "with the balance at any particular point being fixed as a consequence of a complicated series of political and economic compromises" (Guthrie et al., 1988, p. 23).

As with all other issues in educational policy, government at the state level is the major influence on fiscal policy. It is generally accepted that in financing public schools, states have traditionally been responsible for the adequate provision of education, efficiently delivered, and with at least a token concern for equality. The focus of reform initiatives in the 1970s, consistent with other social trends of the time, turned much more attention to the issue of equality or equity. In spite of extensive controversy, debate, and discussion in the policy literature, accompanied by the adoption of fiscal policies by states that purport to address *adequacy, efficiency,* and/or *equity,* these terms have not yet been appropriately defined. It is also evident that the definition of *liberty* or freedom of choice is also subject to varying interpretations. Below, we define these concepts and present illustrations of how they are manifested in special education policy.

Adequacy in School Finance

In the literature on educational finance, adequacy has usually been defined as the provision of learning services that are sufficient to meet a certain goal. Since goals have tended to be poorly specified, the question "how much is enough?" has been difficult to answer. Chambers and Parrish (1982) state that "since there is no social consensus as to the specific outcomes that should result from public education and the technological relationships between educational resources and outcomes are not well understood, it is our contention that the issue of adequacy in educational provision cannot be objectively resolved" (p. 1).

Certain goals are sufficiently concrete and universally accepted that the adequacy of services designed to meet them is readily recognized. Most would agree that lack of access to a school constitutes an inadequacy. Similarly, the amount of time over which schooling is available (in hours, days, and years) has also become *somewhat* standard. Such measures of resource input have been generally accepted as at least one determinant of an adequate education. But when questions arise as to the appropriate number of students per teacher or the extent of support services that should be provided in a school, the standard of adequacy is much more debatable and is generally resolved through an interplay of political and economic forces, with no one claiming to have a definitive answer to the question "how much is enough?" However, the focus on resource input does permit a calculation of total expenditure per student, which can be compared from one time or place to another, thereby providing a type of global indicator of *relative* adequacy. It is assumed that (other things being equal) a greater per-pupil expenditure in one educational system than in another can be associated with a higher likelihood of positive outcomes. While outcome remains the true measure of adequacy, resource input is a more quantifiable proxy. While measures of attainment, achievement test scores, and similar standardized assessment instruments have long been accorded some status as indicators of general education system performance, the specific concentration on minimum competency testing as a graduation requirement in many states is also indicative of an increased focus on outcomes.

The concept is more complicated, however, when major variations in pupil needs are introduced. Regarding both input and outcome, it is recognized that students with disabilities or other special circumstances must be considered in accordance with a different standard. While most states have acknowledged differences in resource input allocation (often in terms of weights or ratio indices purported to be determined objectively), the magnitude of the resource differentials are to a large extent a reflection of values and political compromises, rather than of the objective realities of pupil needs. On the outcome side, a different standard of adequacy is reflected in the adjustments to competency testing procedures that are made in some states for students with certain disabilities. The whole concept of the individualized education program (IEP) implies a different threshold of adequacy in special education programs, as compared with that applied to the general school population. The concept of *appropriate* education, as specified in the federal law, suggests more than a guarantee of a mere minimum standard. The courts have in many cases acknowledged that the resources needed to provide an appropriate education for individuals with disabilities may require a sacrifice in the services provided for the rest of those in the school system.

It should be noted that such considerations are relevant only to the resource input element of the definition of adequacy. The courts, as well as other policy makers, have until recently tended to steer clear of specifying outcomes, especially in cases in which a high degree of pupil variance is anticipated. In the case of *Rowley*, discussed more fully in Chapter 3, the crux of the issue was the determination of what constituted an *adequate* amount of service to meet the legal requirement of an appropriate education. The service (a sign language interpreter in the classroom) called for in the IEP carried obvious fiscal implications for this and similar cases, which the school system argued were not necessary. The ruling of the U.S. Supreme Court in favor of the school system was based to a large extent on the finding that the child was making average progress in school without the additional service. This decision reflected a greater emphasis on objectively observable outcomes than on less-tangible projections of how much more Amy Rowley might have been able to achieve if accorded the opportunity to learn that the additional services would have provided.

In summary, it is clear that adequacy has been an imprecise and dynamic standard. Despite numerous attempts to deal with the concept in laws, regulations, court rulings, and policy statements, definitions remain ambiguous. As additional responsibilities are assumed by public education, additional commitments of resources are necessary. Changing expectations among consumers, school professionals, and members of society at large cause constant shifting in fiscal support. More critically, the affect of fiscal policy on efficiency and equity must also be considered.

Efficiency in School Finance

Economic efficiency is generally defined as attaining the maximum amount of output for each unit of input. In American education the focus on efficiency has varied greatly over time. At the turn of the century, significant attention was given to scientific management, in which attempts were made to reduce schooling to a series of principles that could enhance learning and reduce costs. This era of the "cheaper by the dozen" mentality, time and motion studies, and efficiency experts in the schools has been well documented (Callahan, 1962). Again in the late 1960s, the "accountability movement" that accompanied the rapid upsurge in federal social programs and the concurrent competition for available resources generated a renewed interest in demonstrating efficiency.

Much of the time, however, other forces have apparently had greater influence on educational fiscal policy. During the rapid growth period of the 1950s and 1960s, the simple need to accommodate the expanding school population effectively eclipsed efficiency considerations. But in the 1970s, declining enrollment, accompanied by high inflation, spurred an interest in mechanisms for holding the line on spending. Three types of measures have been used by various states: 1) statutory limits on per-pupil revenues collected or spent, 2) tax-rate limits, and 3) annual votes on local district budgets. These measures have been viewed primarily as keeping expenditures down, while having only a limited effect on the achievement of true efficiency.

A somewhat more promising approach to efficiency can be seen in the various technical–industrial models that were applied to education as a part of the accountability movement of the late 1960s. The basic facets of accountability are fixing responsibility for reaching specified educational goals, measuring precisely whether goals have been reached and, in some instances, calculating the costs of reaching them. The models borrowed from military, industrial, and commercial institutions, such as "management by objectives" (MBO), planning-programming-budgeting systems (PPBS), and performance contracting, have been given attention at various times, but have seldom enjoyed long-term support. The utility of any of these models in the educational setting depends on the degree to which the goals of the system can be specified, the products measured, and the actual costs of various resource inputs compared. Given the value conflicts over the basic purposes of education, it is very difficult to secure agreement on just what should be measured.

Within special education, the adoption of the IEP as a major platform of service delivery policy exemplifies a type of accountability; it
has not been seen as a vehicle for cost-effectiveness analysis, however, and its implementation has generated some concerns regarding
its possibly being interpreted as a performance contract. Policy statements from the federal level have been necessary to establish that
teachers could not be held legally liable for children's failure to attain
IEP goals. This limitation on the scope of accountability reflects the
type of professional resistance to the idea of efficiency that has been
found consistently in education. It is generally recognized that the
fears of teachers regarding measures of productivity are justified,
given the ambiguity surrounding the goals of schooling and the inadequacies in the art (or science) of measurement. Perhaps the bottom line in professional reactions to accountability is the perception
of an infringement on professional autonomy. Recognition that
teaching, at its best, is an individualized process places a high value
on the exercise of discretion and professional judgment in deciding
what the student's pace should be, and which goals should be targeted. This factor tends to make most mechanisms for accountability
difficult for the professional to accept. The situation is ameliorated
considerably by the IEP, in which both goals and the methods of measurement of their attainment are agreed upon in advance by all parties concerned. However, the emphasis in IEP compliance is usually
more on inputs than on progress toward outcomes, since professionals believe that they should not be held accountable for the attainment of outcomes that can be subject to so many uncontrollable
variables. The general idea of evaluation schemes as a means of guaranteeing efficiency still generates professional resistance.

Equity in School Finance

The pursuit of "equality" as a societal value in America has usually
translated into "equality of educational opportunity." Since virtually
no one would argue that education should or could be absolutely
equal for each individual, the variance in interpretations has revolved
around the possible meanings of "equal opportunity." In its most
simple form, it could be interpreted as nothing more than *equal access* to whatever has been established as the state-supported minimum program or foundation of support. A more reasonable interpretation takes into consideration the varying characteristics of
learners and includes the belief that *equal treatment* is possible only
when the system provides unequal resources as a means of compensating for the unequal needs of various students. It is this concept, of
course, that provides the rationale for special education, compensa-

tory education, and a few other specially funded programs. Still another interpretation employs the idea of *equal outcome*, based on the assumption that school achievement is so crucial to "life chance" that the school must be responsible for bringing virtually every student to at least some minimal level of desired performance. While this interpretation is generally recognized as being beyond the reasonable reach of educational systems, either technically or fiscally, there are some elements of the idea that can be seen in the recent *outcomes education* movement, as well as in efforts to set minimum competency requirements and in the "standard raising" rhetoric of the various task forces and reports assessing education in America in the 1980s.

The term *equity* has become the most accepted expression for the concept of equal educational opportunity, and in view of the variety of possible interpretations, several elaborations of this term have been developed. Equity is recognized as having a number of dimensions. From the perspective of the student, equity can mean either the assurance of equal funding per student or the assurance of enough dollars to provide comparable programs, given differing student needs and disparate costs for services. But the concept of equity can also be viewed from the perspective of the taxpayer, from which the appropriate objective may be to pursue either an equal burden for the support of education or a comparable burden, given differences in wealth and certain other relevant factors.

Experts in educational finance have adopted the term *horizontal equity* to express the concept of "equal treatment of equals." This is of course most applicable in cases in which conditions justify placing a high priority on reconciling existing differences in levels of fiscal support that have no rational basis. The term *vertical equity* is used to express the idea of "unequal treatment of unequals," which is most relevant in the determination of appropriate support for programs for students with varying special needs. However, both horizontal and vertical equity can also be applied to the taxpayer's perspective, from which variation in ability to support the educational system is the key consideration.

The major school finance reform efforts of the 1970s and 1980s had the predominant objective of equalizing differences in educational expenditure that result from differences in taxable wealth per student among a state's school districts. While the general principle of equalization—to adjust at the state level for differences in school districts' capacities to generate revenue—had been a part of most states' school finance policy since early in the century, progress toward achieving true equity remained fairly limited. The impetus for serious challenge of the status quo was a series of lawsuits in various states that could be attributed to a rising consciousness regarding civil rights to fair treatment.

The Serrano case (*Serrano v. Priest*, 1976) and litigation in other states that followed it established the principle of *fiscal neutrality*, which basically states that the support of public education must not be a function of local wealth but of the wealth of the state as a whole. But the focus on the school district and the taxpayer, rather than on the varying needs of students, in the courts and in the most common application of the principle of fiscal neutrality is consistent with long-standing ideas regarding public support of education. The concept of vertical student educational equity—employing different treatment of children on the basis of their circumstantial needs—is not only of more recent origin, but also tends to be more difficult to pin down with sufficient clarity to satisfy policy makers.

However, the post-*Serrano* pursuit of fiscal neutrality for the taxpayer and for the school district as a whole has been the focus of litigation in many states. It appears that the development of practical responses to the objective of vertical equity (the unequal treatment of unequals) in general educational finance must to a large extent be attributed to the demonstration of significantly varying needs for resource inputs for students with disabilities to receive a "fair share" of society's offerings. The differing needs of special populations that are now recognized and factored into most state fiscal policies include those of other groups, such as the economically disadvantaged, native Americans, and bilingual students. The categorical grants, pupil weighting, and other revenue distribution mechanisms that are described in some detail in a later section of this chapter were first utilized in the special education programs of many states.

Liberty in School Finance

The prominence of the value of liberty in the American culture has usually been expressed as the freedom to choose. The dispersal of governmental authority across the three branches (judicial, legislative, and executive) and various levels (federal, state, and local) is believed to enhance the maintenance of liberty. It is readily recognized, however, that the pursuit of that value, perhaps most concretely manifested in the existence of many thousands of small local school districts, increases the risk of both inefficiency and inequity (Guthrie et al., 1988).

Freedom of choice in education has been an issue before the courts and in legislative proposals for most of this century. The debate has primarily centered on the role of private versus public schools, as affected by governmental actions on compulsory education, regulation, and fiscal support. In recent decades the freedom of choice debate has leaned toward the libertarian value of exercising a preference for a certain kind of educational program, whether in a public or privately operated institution, and whether because of religious or other qualitative attributes. The right to make such choices has been supported by the U.S. Supreme Court.

Governmental financial support for such a choice, however, has remained clearly constrained by the Constitution. The major proposals aimed at overcoming that barrier have included mechanisms to allow public aid to go through the child or his or her family, rather than directly to the private school. These proposals have focused on either of two plans—educational vouchers and tuition tax credits.

Educational Vouchers   Levin (1980) has described the history of the concept of educational vouchers as a major mechanism for supporting freedom of choice. The first modern proposal for the use of vouchers for the purchase of educational services was advanced by Milton Friedman (1955), whose plan suggested a government-supplied allocation that the parent could use to pay for a specified level of tuition at any approved school. A very well-developed model was incorporated in the "Initiative for Family Choice in Education" proposed in California by Coons and Sugarman (1978). During the 1980s the Reagan–Bush administration supported the development of a number of alternative plans that were designed to promote choice, with the objective of creating competition as a means of improving the quality of schooling, as well as appealing to the general preference for liberty.

The relationship between voucher alternatives and key social dilemmas has been discussed by Levin. A major point is that most plans would appear to encourage "separation and stratification of students according to parental commitments and orientations and by tailoring curricula to appeal to and reinforce these parental concerns" (Levin, 1980, p. 250). This would certainly have a negative effect on the generally desired preparation for democracy. It also appears that the expansion of choices and market responsiveness that the voucher system would create would be much greater for upper-income groups than for lower-income and minority populations, which in turn would lead to even greater class stratification than that in present school systems. In summary, voucher systems would cause public support to be used to promote outcomes that conflict with some important social purposes of schooling. The recognition of these concerns was a major factor in the opposition to voucher plans, despite legislative activity in their support in certain individual states.

It should be noted that despite these negative considerations, a type of educational voucher system has been quite generally applied to a small minority of the school population for some time. Children with disabilities whose needs have been perceived to be too complex to handle within the public system have been authorized in many states to receive financial aid to cover the costs of attending private schools specially equipped for that purpose. The predominance of this alternative varies among states and regions of the country, but virtually every state, even before PL 94-142, had allowed for state or local funds to be expended for tuition to private schools. The private school provision within PL 94-142 considerably increased the tendency in most states to utilize that option. The requirement that all costs of educational services be at *public expense*, prohibiting additional educational charges to be assessed on parents, eliminates some of the problems that arose during debates over other voucher proposals. The availability of public funds for private school placement is not routine, however; it requires initiative on the part of the parent and school district. It has been noted that there is a much greater likelihood that families of higher socioeconomic levels will pursue the necessary procedures to secure such placements for their children. Federal data indicate that the greatest proportion of due process hearings regarding services have been concerned with parental requests for private placements. State regulations generally include controls at both the state and local levels to prevent unjustified assignments and tuition grant payments to private schools. However, it seems evident that in an area of ambiguous pupil needs and agency capacity for service provision, the private alternative is given the benefit of the doubt. The Supreme Court's ruling on *Florence County School District # Four v. Carter* (November 9, 1993) affirming the circuit court's decision that the school district must reimburse the parents' cost for private schooling, even though the school selected was not approved by state officials and did not meet all federal regulations, further illustrates the weight given to parent choice in these matters. Again, this demonstrates the application of the value of freedom of choice.

Tuition Tax Credits The appeal of family choice as a means of enhancing liberty in education has also found expression in federal and state tax policy. While proposals for tuition tax credits had been advanced by Senators Moynihan and Packwood in the late 1970s, the major thrust for this idea came about as a part of the Reagan administration's offensive for educational reform in 1983. Jensen (1983) points out that the chief reservation regarding tuition tax credits, even among advocates of the concept, rested on constitutionality. Since most private schools are sectarian, it was feared that such a policy would involve indirect government support of religious activities. The U.S. Supreme Court has ruled on many questions regarding state aid to private schools over the years, and the "wall of separation" between church and state has provided the basis for its decisions on such matters.

The Supreme Court's decision in the Minnesota case of *Mueller v. Allen* (1983) appears to be a significant departure from past rulings. The ruling that a Minnesota law was constitutional, even though it provided a tax deduction for tuition, was based on the fact that it was available to all citizens, regardless of whether the tuition (and certain other educational costs) was paid to public or private schools. It has been noted by those who strongly oppose such policy, particularly the American Federation of Teachers, that since public school students pay no tuition and have minimal educational expenses, such provisions are, in fact, a benefit only to those attending private schools. For those who fear any additional erosion of the public school system, the price of such supports of freedom of choice and libertarian values is simply too high.

Summary

The four major values that influence the development of general fiscal policy in education in the United States provide a backdrop against which past and prevailing approaches to the support of special education services can be better understood. The concepts of adequacy, efficiency, equity, and liberty have been discussed above as they have acted upon educational policy, and in certain instances as they have been manifested in special education. These understandings should also serve as a good platform for considering current and future developments in special education fiscal policy.

SPECIAL EDUCATION FINANCE

Policy development in both educational finance and special education service delivery has undergone intense scrutiny and a significant amount of change in the past decade or two. Both arenas of policy interest have been the focus of extensive judicial system activity, as well as legislative and regulatory consideration. It is not surprising that special education concepts have been found to be particularly relevant as general educational finance is debated or that basic fiscal issues become a central focus when overall special education policy is on the public agenda. McCarthy and Sage (1982) have noted that the concerns of educational finance have perennially focused on "determining (defining, identifying) (a) the total need for service, (b) the source and amount of total resources, and (c) an acceptable means of distribution between resources and needs" (p. 414). Attempts to address these concerns always involve achieving a balance between the pragmatic pressures of political reality and the idealistic demand for fairness or equity. The concept of *fiscal neutrality* has become an important consideration from the perspective of resource generation (the taxpayer) and is more recently being introduced into the student-need side of the equation. While it has been generally recognized that services for certain children (e.g., those with disabilities) cost more per child than do general education programs, and that the burden of meeting such costs should be spread broadly across governmental jurisdictions, the great variety of students' needs has not been sufficiently addressed in existing financial formulas:

> Special education requires a focus on individual pupil needs; general education fiscal systems, based on average group needs, are insufficiently flexible. Furthermore, it can be assumed that existing special education fiscal systems do not provide adequately flexible programming and that there is a need to develop systems which do. Flexible programming can occur only when decisions are not dependent upon fiscal influences and appropriate resources are provided for each child's unique or unequal needs. That is, we must approximate fiscal neutrality in order to achieve true equity. (McCarthy & Sage, 1982, p. 415)

Criteria for Policy Development

The criteria on which special education finance policy is based have changed over time as the public perception of special education has evolved. At one point, special education was seen almost as a charity, and funding was viewed accordingly. As legislation became more standardized, state funding came to be seen as the primary source of support for special education. Finally, as special programs have come to be seen as a basic part of every school system's responsibility, state funding has come to be used more for assisting and equalizing, rather than providing the foundation of such programs. Key considerations in formulating financial policy that have been suggested by Hartman (1992) are:

1. *Equity* for both the student and the taxpayer. Formulas must accommodate differing student needs and various levels of local wealth.
2. *Educational programming* that is appropriate. Funding should discourage improper classification and labeling of students and encourage least restrictive placements.
3. *Rationality and simplicity* to permit ease of understanding by all stakeholders.

4. *Comprehensiveness* of services and programming in relation to need.
5. *Flexibility and responsiveness,* to permit enough latitude to accommodate local circumstances and allow for changes as needed.
6. *Stability,* to permit accurate predictions of necessary funding and assurance of support for programs.
7. *Accountability and cost-effectiveness,* to track state funds and local expenditures. Procedures should encourage cost containment and cost effectiveness.
8. *Efficiency* in the effort required to maintain and manage the system.
9. *Adequate funding levels,* to ensure that the overall funding mechanism is sufficient to provide appropriate programs.

While the specifics of the states' methods are varied, all special education funding is based on the assumption that support must be drawn from a broader base than that used to fund general education. To elaborate, whatever combination of local, state, and federal financial support exists for the education of the mainstream of the population, that portion of the population defined as having special needs will require more support from the less localized levels of government. The rationale for this assumption is that:

1. Children with special needs are by definition a minority group, a small but significant proportion of the whole population.
2. The exact proportion of students with special needs will vary significantly from one subcategory of special education to another, and from one location to another, without regard to local economic ability to provide support.
3. The cost of educational services to meet special needs will be proportionately greater than the costs of serving children at large at an uncertain and varying ratio based on: 1) geographic locale, 2) subcategory of special need, and 3) the particular patterns of service delivery employed.

Some specific factors that would seem to be of primary importance when trying to create policies for optimal fiscal supports from the state for special education in local school systems can be identified from an analysis of the relevant literature. These include considerations concerning variations in the nature of the population to be educated, their identified needs, the models of service delivery to be utilized, the governance structure under which the services are organized and operated, the resources available to the organizational unit, and the costs of given resources in particular localities.

McCarthy and Sage (1982) have elaborated on each of these factors as they affect financial distribution policies.

Population Characteristics   Demographic data from a variety of sources make it clear that variations in population density, socio-economic status, and cultural characteristics are associated with variations in the need and/or demand for special education. While such factors may not create major differences in the incidence of severe disabilities, their effect on the proportions of students with mild disabilities who are identified as requiring services is pronounced. But these relationships are not necessarily directly proportional. High-density population (urban central cities) as well as very sparsely populated and economically depressed rural regions may both have greater service needs than suburban areas. The size of a system (pupil enrollment) may interact with other factors such as the efficiency of the delivery system and degree of client sophistication to affect the demand for service. It has been well recognized that a magnet effect occurs in areas in which services are well developed, and this effect is directly proportionate to consumer awareness. Overall, it is clear that fiscal support requirements are affected by basic population characteristics.

General educational finance policy in most states has reflected awareness of (if not full accounting for) this source of variation. It is generally recognized that urban centers have a disproportionate share of students with special needs as a function of economic disadvantage and poor health conditions. The concept of *municipal overburden* in school finance encompasses a number of factors, with special pupil needs as a major consideration.

Individual Needs   While population factors influence the needs of a community in the macro sense, the needs of individual students for special instruction and related services is a function of the process of developing the individualized education program. The predominant special education funding systems throughout the states have tended to link varying amounts of extra state aid to varying categories of disabling conditions, the assumption being that the cost differential between regular educational services and those for various disabilities could be computed (on the average) and provide a basis for reasonable support. Early examples of studies of the costs of special education, such as the 1970 effort by the National Educational Finance Project, approached the matter in this way (Rossmiller, Hale, & Frohreich, 1970). This assumption was much more valid when special education services tended to be largely standardized among all members of a group, but the introduction of the IEP, to the extent that its intent is realized, offers an opportunity and a mandate for much more detailed identification of individual needs. This, in turn, should translate into more prescriptively determined services.

Service Delivery Options   The result of IEP planning is expected to be a prescription for particular services, delivered in accordance with models designed to best provide for identified needs. A major consideration in such prescriptions is the degree of intensity of specialist personnel service called for in the IEP. It is recognized, however, that a similar level of labor intensity may be packaged in various ways and that these variations may have an effect upon the total fiscal support required. It should be noted that even if financial support formulas are devised to render the level of service fiscally neutral, allowing decisions concerning placement and prescribed services to be made independent of local cost considerations, accountability for expenditures must be mandated at some level of regulatory control. Within the realm of related services, even more than with special instruction, major cost variations can be expected as a result of fine distinctions in decisions regarding the differences among appropriate, optimal, and ideal programs. This was the central issue in the *Rowley* case and will be a consideration in virtually all instances of complex service needs. The most recent studies of special education costs, which will be discussed later in this chapter, have attempted to address the many variations in service delivery options in ways that were not possible in the earlier efforts.

Governance Structures   The variety of organizational units that may assume responsibility for special education services are described in Chapter 5. The relationship of the influence of such organizations to fiscal support considerations is also significant. The assumption that students with low-incidence disabilities need to be drawn from a broad catchment area has been the rationale for the use of intermediate school districts, state-operated residential programs, and private schools as alternatives to regular local school systems. Economy of scale and the notion of concentrating expertise for the benefit of thinly dispersed student populations have been important considerations. However, this has frequently had unforeseen fiscal impact:

> Different laws and regulations covering operation, and more important, the funding of such different organizational units have led not only to programmatic variation, but in some cases to rather clear fiscal incentives for choosing to place a pupil in one or the other alternative governance units. It may prove economically more viable for the local school system to send the pupil to an intermediate cooperative facility or to a private school than to provide the appropriate service locally. As long as equally appropriate services are obtained either way, there is no problem. However, it has been charged that placement decisions may be

strongly influenced by the fiscal advantage of one type of unit over another. Where that is the case, the need to correct the funding scheme to more clearly achieve fiscal neutrality is obvious. (McCarthy & Sage, 1982, p. 417)

This issue is particularly sensitive when the fiscal impact on the placement decision results in the provision of services in more restrictive environments than would be the case under purely neutral circumstances. A specific example of such a situation had been cited in New York, where for a long period of time the state support system for services delivered through boards of cooperative educational services and through private placements yielded a smaller net cost to local school districts than would have been the case if services had been provided internally.

Resource Variation and Availability In addition to the variables discussed above, which tend to be focused on students and the relationships between them and on the educational system provided, another major consideration is aggregate quantity of revenue-producing wealth. This factor determines the capacity of the system to purchase the necessary resources for the general as well as the special education program, and must be included as a fiscal policy consideration in all funding schemes. The heavier cost impact of each child with a disability, as compared with those of other pupils in the system, and the need for flexibility in the support of special education accentuate the roles of resource neutrality and taxpayer equity as necessary, though not sufficient, foundations for special education fiscal policy.

Resource variation can also be manifested in the availability of certain components that are necessary for an adequate program but are distinct from the general wealth of the community. For example, the availability of appropriately trained personnel may vary, despite general wealth, and constitute an important consideration in the total support system. Some urban and rural communities may have to pay a premium to procure personnel who would be readily available elsewhere. This has been particularly noted in the case of certain related services personnel, such as occupational and physical therapists. Other, less-tangible resources, such as enriching community facilities, volunteer personnel, and university training program personnel, may also help determine what a program can provide for a given cost.

Cost Variations The calculation of differences in costs from one system to another for standard units of resources has been included in the development of general school finance schemes in many states. Much of this variation is based on general consumer price indices or similar cost-of-living measures. This factor is probably most significant in salaries for teachers, but it can also be seen in the costs of transportation, food service, maintenance, and so on, and may be attributable either to labor union strength in a locality or to the value-related practice of paying higher salaries simply in hopes of attracting and retaining superior personnel. A totally accurate interpretation of the significance of some of these conditions may be difficult to achieve. It has been argued, for example, that while certain uncontrollable cost variations (e.g., cost of living) should be taken into consideration in a distribution formula so that the state could assist those localities with heavier cost burdens, the fact that a particular locality *chooses* to pay its teachers more to enhance quality is a matter that is locally controlled and does not justify the fiscal support of the rest of the state. At the same time, urban centers may find the high cost of maintaining buildings in densely packed, high-vandalism areas to be unavoidable; likewise, the tax burden for police and fire protection and social welfare are all part of municipal overburden. However, the degree to which such factors should be included in general state education fiscal policy continues to be a source of debate. The 1982 decision of New York State's highest court in *Levittown Union Free School District v. Nyquist* and the subsequent refusal of the U.S. Supreme Court to review the case would seem to suggest that the municipal overburden argument is not compelling.

Fiscal Policy Outcomes   A study of key policy influencers in New York State regarding the potency of the six variables described above, which took place at a time of major political activity in the legislature, the regulatory bodies of the executive branch, and the state courts, specifically addressed the issue of how to secure the optimal special education fiscal policy for that state. Conclusions summarized by McCarthy (1980) suggested that while perspectives on the importance of the six factors were greatly influenced by respondents' professional roles, geographic location, and organizational affiliation, as well as by currently volatile political issues, it was agreed that fiscal neutrality and least restrictive environment were inextricably related. Furthermore, the relationship between fiscal incentives and choices among various governance structures for service delivery constituted a significant source of non-neutrality in the state's existing policies. It was agreed that variations in needs and in resources were the most important considerations in the pursuit of an optimal policy, and that these two components of equity were frequently in conflict with political reality. It was also made very clear that despite all attempts to pursue fiscal policy rationally and with due regard for all of the balancing variables, the bottom line tended to remain primarily a political judgment of how many dollars could be captured out of the total public budget at any given time.

Approaches to Funding Formulas

It is important to remember that in spite of pervasive federal involvement in special education in recent years, fiscal support for the system remains chiefly a state and local function. With appropriations consistently falling short of congressional authorization in IDEA, as with most federal education laws, it can be anticipated that federal participation in the total funding structure could never reach the proportions that were foreseen by legislators. Given this modest input from the federal level, the major question remains how the state can best distribute funds to partially or totally equalize the cost differentials between regular and special education services in local school systems. Various approaches to making these distributions are used among the states.

Hartman (1992) discusses six types of formulas used to distribute state funds to aid local districts. Although this typology is useful for comparative purposes, the formulas are not mutually exclusive, and in actual practice many states utilize a combination of approaches. The types may be classified as follows:

1. **Flat grant** or **straight sum**   This funding model is probably the simplest, since the same amount is provided per student, without regard for variations in wealth and cost of services. Because it is clearly nonequalizing, it is currently not commonly used.
2. **Unit**   Funding is determined on the basis of units of service provided (e.g., instruction, administration, and transportation), with varying amounts allocated to support each unit. This may include salaries and all other operating expenses. The model has the advantage of eliminating the need to label students to obtain funding, but if allowances are not made for differences in the costs of resources, it also becomes nonequalizing.
3. **Personnel**   Funding is focused only on the personnel costs of the unit of instruction provided and may be limited to salaries alone. This could be a flat amount per teacher, but if the actual costs of personnel are considered, it becomes more equalizing. It has the advantage of placing less emphasis on the labeling of students, and makes it easy to trace funds for purposes of ensuring accountability.
4. **Percentage**   State aid is provided for a percentage of eligible costs, which may include personnel and other approved expendi-

tures. The effects of this model depend on the proportional relationship of state to local funding, and the particular types of expenditures that are covered. Differences in the costs of resources are accommodated, but if no caps on expenditures are enforced, districts that choose to spend more can receive inequitable shares of state support.

5. **Excess costs** Funding is provided by full or partial reimbursement (up to a specific ceiling) of expenditures that are in excess of those for regular pupils. This model has the possibility of being the most fiscally neutral, especially if *all* excess costs are reimbursed. There are fewer incentives for inappropriate classification and placement of students, but the model requires complex pupil and cost accounting if it is to remain neutral and equitable.

6. **Weighted student** Funding is based on a count of pupils served, with a weighting factor (usually varying according to types of disability or types of service) employed. The model requires labeling of students as being eligible for service, but when the applicable weight is attached to the level of service, rather than to the specific type of disability, the emphasis on classification is reduced. In states that base their *general* aid to local districts on counts of student enrollment or attendance (and most states do), this model provides a high degree of compatibility between the general and special education funding systems. The potential flaw in the scheme is the difficulty of ensuring that the weight differentials used are an accurate reflection of true costs.

Hartman also describes a more recent development, the *resource cost model*, in which the costs for all of the resources necessary to operate a program could be estimated and program units defined in terms of these costs. Then numbers of units could be established on the basis of class-size standards and state aid to a district determined according to an established proportion of total enrollment or by actual enrollment in such programs. A pure form of this model has not yet been implemented, but elements of it can be found in a number of states' policies. A study by O'Reilly (1989) that attempted to classify states according to the major attributes of their special education finance formulas showed that some form of pupil weighting was the most prominent method (17 states), with excess cost model being next (14 states), followed by a flat grant per teacher or classroom unit (11 states).

In discussing the relative merits of the various funding methods, Hartman suggests that the types can be grouped into three general categories according to the main factor used for allocation. Under this scheme, the major types would be resource-based formulas, child-based formulas, and cost-based formulas. Some of the incentives and disincentives of each type can be anticipated.

Resource-Based Formulas Placing the emphasis on the resource supplied, such as the teacher or other personnel, rather than on the pupil, has the advantage of focusing on the source of the cost. It is less likely to cause overidentification of pupils ("bounty hunting"), since the link between childcount and dollars is indirect. In the many states where the basis for general support is the teacher unit, such an approach to special education funding has the advantage of compatibility with the total system. However, it tends to require considerable regulatory activity by the state in order to determine the proper quantity of units to authorize, the minimum and maximum allowances of pupils per teacher, and all other costs and benefits of service delivery. This also probably translates into local district accounting and reporting requirements, which can be burdensome.

To the extent that state regulation may be desirable (e.g., to reinforce selected programmatic alternatives), a resource-based approach can be quite effective. However, such an approach can discourage local innovation. Furthermore, if the formula is based too specifically on the teacher or special class unit, it can also discourage mainstreaming efforts. Given the variety of current and newly developing programming alternatives, the increasing variety of possible staffing approaches, and the wide geographically based range of salaries and other cost factors, a resource unit system providing a flat rate for each employed person will probably fall short of equitably compensating for actual service costs. An advantage, however, may be the way in which the funding formula is linked to program and fiscal planning.

Child-Based Formulas Pupil unit formulas, whether straight sum or weighted, are most likely to cause over-classification. However, in the many states that use pupil enrollment or attendance as the basis for general state aid, such a scheme for special education may be almost mandatory for reasons of compatibility and political acceptance. A straight sum or single weight for all disabilities probably carries the most potential for misuse, since it can encourage identification of borderline cases that will be relatively inexpensive to serve, yet will yield the same state support as those individuals having more extensive (and more expensive) needs. This also constitutes an incentive for underserving the more needy. If differential weights or dollar amounts are provided for certain programs, it can encourage placement into programs that provide the most funds, regardless of need, thus confounding least restrictive environment considerations. If the differential weights are accurately adjusted so that state supports closely match real costs (i.e., are fiscally neutral) and a sufficient number of levels of support are included, the funding approach can prove to be a definite facilitator of optimal programming. However, such precision is difficult to maintain as a matter of statewide policy and will most certainly require complex accounting procedures at both local and state levels to keep track of the amounts of time spent by students in each type of program alternative. Such accounting and fine-tuning requirements may well prove themselves to be politically lethal in most states.

Child-based formulas in general provide good accountability as to the numbers of students served, although the expenditures per child are not as easily tracked. The variations in resources assigned to individuals must be accounted for if complete tracking of funds is an important consideration. However, aggregate tracking of funds may be sufficient for most purposes.

Cost-Based Formulas Cost-based formulas are theoretically fiscally neutral if excess costs are *fully* reimbursed. However, fiscally prudent policy makers are rarely sufficiently trusting in local practitioners to provide an unlimited ceiling on claimable expenditures. Percentage formulas that call for local systems to share in whatever expenditures are documented tend to be more acceptable in the compromises drawn between state and local obligations for program support. Reimbursement of excess costs up to an established ceiling per child or per instructional unit appears to be a reasonable method. All cost-based approaches have the advantage of minimizing the labeling of children and also permit maximum flexibility in programming alternatives, since the expenditures may not necessarily be tied to specific resources. They, therefore, have potential for enhancing program development and choice for each student. However, such formulas do carry fairly complex cost accounting requirements and approval procedures, constituting an administrative burden at both local and state levels. The greater the state share in the formula, the more stringent these are likely to be. Whether this factor outweighs the benefits of approximating fiscal neutrality is a matter that must be answered within the context of each state's specific political climate.

Viable Compromises One general aim of special education fiscal policy cited above is the facilitation of programmatic flexibility, which demands that financial considerations do not overbalance the process of determining which services are appropriate for each student. This translates to fiscal neutrality from the perspective of both the service recipient (student) and the resource provider (taxpayer). In the search for optimal solutions, policy changes in various states in recent years have increasingly taken into consideration the recognition of differentiated levels of service intensity (and therefore costs) rather than the over-simplistic use of a single weight or rate, and yet have also avoided any misconceived (pseudo precise) focus on disability classifications. This has resulted in some schemes that are seen as employing too much accounting complexity, due to so many different weights being associated with the varieties of classifications and programming options. It has also caused distress over the loss of familiar classifications and doubts about the fiscal neutrality of the assigned weights to the approved levels of service and options. A significant strength in the New York policy is the combined use of an approved excess-cost concept with a variable weighted pupil-attendance unit based on the intensity of the services provided rather than on disability classification. The adoption of that approach represents a sophisticated blending of concepts that capture at least some of the benefits of a more optimal plan, reduce focus on disability classifications, move a good way toward fiscal neutrality, yet walk the narrow line of political acceptability. It is probable that such compromises will continue to provide incremental reform in special education funding in many states.

Policy Recommendations   Concurrent with the push for more extensive inclusion of special education service within the mainstream is the recognition that existing funding structures have tended to foster continued separation of the general and special education systems. A positive statement addressing this issue can be found in a policy recommendation by the National Association of State Boards of Education (1992), which emphasized "redeployment of educational resources, focusing on creating greater support in the classroom":

> State boards, with state departments of education, should sever the link between funding, placement and handicapping label. Funding requirements should not drive programming and placement decisions for students. (p. 30)

A similar recommendation was incorporated within a policy statement of the Council of Administrators of Special Education (1993), which set forth an *Agenda for Creating a Unified Education System*. One of the ten issues cited and policy recommendations advanced in the publication encouraged that "Funding systems that support a unified system emphasize shared resources for all students without label, penalty or prejudice" (p. 18).

The discussion of the recommendation noted that some states are implementing or considering new funding formulas that allow unified sytems to emerge without the loss of crucial revenue resources.

But underlying any policy and system for the finance of special education is the assumption that the actual cost can be determined, or estimated with some degree of accuracy, and that these costs can be linked to the comparative costs of educational programs in general.

Determining the Costs

It is readily accepted, intuitively, that special education services will cost more than the services that are ordinarily provided for typical students. The foundations for early attempts at establishing rational funding policies were based on rough estimates of what the differences in costs would be. With the increasing sophistication and universality of special education, it was recognized that greater precision in identifying sources of costs, as well as comparisons to other programs, would be desirable. Many small-scale studies have been carried out in individual states, but comprehensive nationwide studies have been conducted on only three occasions.

The first comprehensive source of such data was obtained as a part of the National Educational Finance Project (Rossmiller et al., 1970), which gathered information from 24 school systems across five states. These data guided state fiscal policy makers for over 10 years. A major improvement was provided by a second study by the Rand Corporation (Kakalik, Furry, Thomas, & Carney, 1981), which used data drawn from 46 localities in 14 states, covering 50 local school systems and 57 intermediate or cooperative service organizations. This study employed a very detailed and sophisticated data collection and analysis procedure that permitted interpretation from a great variety of perspectives concerning a number of classifications. The general findings, for the purpose of state funding policy, were not very different from those of the earlier study. In both, the average per-pupil cost of special education was slightly more than twice that of regular education. However, the range in cost figures among the 13 categories of disability recognized by federal definitions, and across 10 different service delivery models or placements identified in the Rand study, was great enough to make the average cost index rather meaningless. It was clear that certain types of programs for certain types of disabilities might be only slightly more expensive than regular education, while others could be five or six times as costly.

In acknowledgment of the need for better data, the Congress mandated another study in the 1983 amendments to the Education of the Handicapped Act. A contract with Decision Resources Corporation (DRC) resulted in a study of expenditures and enrollments in special education and related services in 60 school districts across 18 states during the 1985–1986 school year. Data from the study were summarized and reported in the Eleventh Annual Report to Congress (U.S. Department of Education, 1989).

The DRC study used a somewhat different classification system for types of programs, considering as *resource programs* all services delivered for less than 15 hours per week, regardless of whether services were provided within the regular class or in "pull-out" settings. *Self-contained programs* were those of 15 or more hours per week, regardless of whether services were provided within regular schools or in special day schools. The other classifications were *Pre-school programs*, those serving children from birth through age 5, regardless of the amount of time per week; *Residential programs*, serving children of ages 3–21, public or private; and *Home/hospital programs*, those provided for children who were unable to attend school due to disabilities or related conditions. The study also isolated *supplemental services*, such as vocational programs, assessment, adaptive physical education, and a range of *related services* such as occupational therapy, physical therapy, speech-language therapy, psychological services, school health, social work, guidance, and counseling. DRC also documented expenditures for *support personnel* such as administrative staff, community liaisons, attendance officers, and research and evaluation staff.

The distribution of expenditures, by major component, were reported for the total population served, across all models of service delivery. This distribution is shown in Table 1.

The overall average annual expenditure across all programs for the 1985–1986 academic year was $3,649 per student for the special education services provided. This must be added to the average costs of regular education programs for the same students, which was $2,686, for a total cost averaging $6,335. Comparing this to the previous Rand study of 1977–1978 shows a 10% increase in expenditures over the 8-year period, after adjusting for inflation. Table 2 breaks down these figures by type of program.

It should be noted that the figure for resource programs represents the expenditure for special instruction only, and does not con-

Table 1. Distribution of special education expenditures by major component

Instructional programs	62%
Assessment	13%
Support services	11%
Related services	10%
Transportation	4%

Source: U.S. Department of Education (1989).

Table 2. Average per-pupil expenditure for different instructional programs and supplemental services

Instructional program	Expenditure
Resource program	$ 1,325
Home/hospital	3,117
Preschool	3,437
Self-contained	4,233
Residential	28,324
Supplemental service	
Related services	592
Adaptive physical education	615
Assessment	1,206
Special vocational	1,444
Transportation	1,583

Source: U.S. Department of Education (1989).

sider the costs for regular instruction of these students; in this sense, it represents a supplemental cost. By contrast, the instructional program expenditures in the other settings are much more inclusive, since they include all instructional costs. It is especially significant that the Residential program figure is the total of all tuition, which includes instruction, all other educational costs, and residential costs as well.

The study also broke down per-pupil expenditures across types of disability, and distinguished between self-contained and resource programs. Table 3 displays this data. The lower costs in certain categories within resource programs is a reflection of the lesser proportion of the school day spent in that program.

The major item of interest in examining special education costs is usually comparison with the costs of regular programs. The average per pupil cost for students who received no special education for the year of the study (1985–1986) was $2,780. The DRC study pointed out that while certain components, such as instruction, support services, and transportation are applicable to both regular and special education, other components, such as assessment and related services, are peculiar to special education alone. This, of course, causes the distribution among the components to vary considerably. Since assessment and related services alone constitute 23% of total costs for special education programs, this leaves a smaller proportion for the other components, such as transportation and support services.

In order to show how the relationship of special to regular education expenditures vary across different programs, the study broke down these figures as shown in Table 4.

Table 3. Per-pupil expenditures for different disabilities by program type

Disability	Self-contained	Resource
Deaf-blind	$20,416	NA
Deaf	7,988	NA
Autistic	7,582	NA
Speech impaired	7,140	647
Multihandicapped	6,674	NA
Visually impaired	6,181	3,395
Hard of hearing	6,058	3,372
Orthopedically impaired	5,248	3,999
Seriously emotionally disturbed	4,857	2,620
Other health impaired	4,782	NA
Mentally retarded	4,754	2,290
Learning disabled	3,083	1,643
Noncategorical	3,684	1,731
All conditions	4,233	1,325

Source: U.S. Department of Education (1989).

In comparing the costs of regular and special education, the *ratios* of expenditures derived from the DRC data are perhaps the most relevant figures to consider. As Table 5 illustrates, the data from this study are consistent with the findings of earlier studies (with the exception of data on preschool and residential programs, as no earlier study addressed these subjects).

The differences between regular and special education costs, whether expressed in absolute dollar amounts or in ratios (or, more often, indices), have been routinely defined and described as *excess*

Table 4. Average per-pupil expenditures for special and regular education by type of program

Program type	Special education	Regular education[a]	Combined special regular education	Per-pupil excess cost[b]
Resource	$2,463	$2,780	$5,243	$2,463
Self-contained	5,566	1,347	6,913	4,133
Preschool	4,750	973	5,723	2,943
Residential	29,108	389	29,497	26,717
All programs	3,649	2,686	6,335	3,555

Source: U.S. Department of Education (1989).

[a]Portion of regular education expenditures allocated to special education students while they are being served within the regular education program or as students in general.

[b]Combined regular and special education minus $2,780 (the average per pupil cost for a regular student).

Table 5. Ratio of total expenditures per pupil with a disability to total expenditures per pupil without disabilities

Student placement	Ratio
Resource programs	1.9
Self-contained programs	2.5
Preschool programs	2.1
Residential programs	10.6
All programs	2.3

Source: U.S. Department of Education (1989).

costs. In attempting to arrive at a rational basis for state fiscal support policy, it is important to keep in mind the difference between *supplemental* and *replacement* programs. Hartman (1990) pointed out this distinction when suggesting an alternative way of viewing the concept of excess cost that would be a significant improvement over the traditional one. He proposed that excess costs should be defined in terms of programs and services, rather than expenditure differences. According to his scheme, two classifications would be identified: 1) supplemental programs and services provided *in addition to* the regular program, and 2) replacement programs and services provided *instead of* the regular program, with the criterion for replacement being that students spend more than half of their total time in school in the special education program. In this way, all costs of supplemental programs would be considered excess and funded in accordance with whatever the state system dictated. In replacement programs, costs would be *partly* excess (i.e., the difference between the special education instruction cost and the regular cost). But only those services that were replaced would be included in the regular cost calculation, which would be limited to instruction only. The cost attributable to school-wide or district-wide operations would apply to all students and therefore not affect excess cost. The allocation of costs for noninstructional programs and services would be determined by the same criteria. Hartman points out many advantages to this approach, suggesting that it is simple, easily understood, requires less record keeping in the areas of pupil attendance and cost accounting, and would tend to provide a financial incentive for inclusion, since programs would be freed from the need to generate FTE pupil counts.

While the data on expenditure history generated by these studies provides some assurance that the attempts at rationalizing state support systems are roughly appropriate in terms of pursuing equity, it is also clear that there are so many variables that the achievement of perfect fiscal neutrality is not likely. A major problem highlighted by

Sage (1992) concerns the funding of services that lie somewhere between *related services* and *medical treatment*. A number of court rulings have dealt with this subject, but the issue of responsibilities shared between Medicaid, other third-party insurers, and public school systems are quite complex. As more children with severe medical conditions are being educated in regular school settings, the question of who will pay for the very expensive services required becomes more important. Attempts at the federal level to pool resources between the Office of Special Education Programs (within the Department of Education) and Medicaid and other funded programs within the Department of Health and Human Services hold promise.

At the time of the DRC cost study, it was noted that there were three sources of federal support to local school districts. By far the largest source was EHA-B funds, the basic assistance authorized by PL 94-142, which constituted 91% of all federal funds. Others were the ECIA Chapter I funds authorized under PL 89-313 and the Vocational Education Act set-aside for students with disabilities. In the districts studied, the EHA-B funds averaged only 6% of total local expenditures. Of that contribution, 79% went to instructional services and 21% to support services. It is evident that the proportion of funding from the federal level, as compared to state and local resources as a whole, leaves financial resources a major concern at the point of service delivery.

SUMMARY

On the basis of observations of existing policies and practices among the states and the concepts cited throughout this chapter, certain considerations may be set forth as key criteria for state-level policy makers. Moore, Walker, and Holland (1982) cite the following as essential to optimal special education funding schemes:

Compatibility with other state funding policies and practices   Approaches that do not differ significantly from existing general methods tend to be accepted more easily.

Rationality and simplicity   Formulas that are easily understood, logical, and contain straightforward relationships among the key policy elements have a clear advantage.

Ease of modification   The ever-changing rates of inflation, relative costs of resources, and so forth make it important for funding formulas to be self-adjusting or easily changed as circumstances require.

Minimized misclassification Formulas must avoid incentives that might influence the classification of children into certain categories that entail other than optimal programming choices.

Reinforcement of least restrictive placement choices To the extent possible, funding schemes should support other existing programming objectives.

Avoidance of stigmatizing labels The practice of basing funding on service options rather than disability classifications permits a reduced emphasis on labels.

Accommodation of varying student needs across districts Funding approaches should allow for the fact that different localities may experience quite different incidence rates of students requiring various types of service.

Accommodation of cost variations Costs of standard units of resources may vary considerably within a state, and formulas should allow for these differences.

Adjustments for fiscal capacity Since a major portion of special education finance remains a local responsibility, each district's capacity to support education in general must be considered in any funding formula.

Funding predictability Funding formulas must make it possible to predict total support needs, both at the local and state level. Stability within the system is an important attribute for planning and ensuring adequate support.

Containment of costs The funding approach must ensure that unforeseen circumstances will not overwhelm available resources. Ideally, the system should reinforce efficiently operated programs.

Minimized reports, record keeping, and state administration Funding formulas are most acceptable and successful when they make minimum demands on administrative personnel at both local and state levels.

It should be noted that trade-offs are necessary. That is, while a simple formula may be desirable, it will also be less likely to distinguish well among varying districts' needs. The more stability and cost containment that is ensured, the less capability there is to accommodate the full range of costs.

Some general fiscal policy considerations that seem to be critical to flexible programming have been suggested by McCarthy and Sage (1982):

> Since funding methods have a high capability for creating implicit incentives and disincentives for particular programming decisions, provisions should exist to make service options as "cost neutral" as

possible. While it is recognized that fiscal neutrality in the pure sense can never be fully attained, it is important for policy influencers to consciously pursue neutrality as a major goal.

The pursuit of fiscal neutrality should take into consideration the potential variations in levels of service, types of service models, and governance structures within which services are delivered. Each of these factors has impact both individually and interactively on the attainment of fiscal neutrality.

Since variations in need result from geographical population differences, distribution policies allowing for regional variations should be recognized.

Densely populated urban areas with a disproportionate number of special needs students might best be aided by a different formula than the rest of a state, using an "urban multiplier." The unique problem resulting from a particular geographic location should not constrain flexible programming.

A provision for variations in system costs for factors such as personnel and facilities, occurring as a result of geographic location, should be part of general school finance formulas.

Since it is the pattern of service delivery that most affects variations in costs, aid should be based on levels of services rather than the types of handicapping conditions or diagnostic label. This at least facilitates programming flexibility.

Since variations in resources are generally the result of the differences in property wealth among school districts, a different and more equitable measure of a district's wealth should be established, such as the inclusion of a personal income factor or a combination of both wealth and income.

The complexity of the overall funding scheme should be minimized to enhance general political acceptability.

Fiscal policy is subject to a wide variety of understandings and interpretations, even among persons with considerable familiarity and sophistication with education policies and practices. (pp. 418–419)

It is evident that recent fiscal policy changes in a number of states have reflected a recognition of these considerations, but it is equally clear that much room remains for continued development and reform.

ILLUSTRATIVE CASE

The legislature of the state of Equitania has for some time been in search of a fiscal policy that would ensure that the distribution of funds from the state level to local school districts will be fair to everyone—the taxpayer (rich or poor) and the student (regardless of varying needs). For general school programs, the state aid formula now provides about 50% of the average per-pupil expenditure in districts of average wealth. In very poor districts, the state share (aid ratio) can be as much as 90% (but no more), and in very wealthy districts the state share can shrink to 10% (but no less). The total state aid to each district is calculated by multiplying the aid ratio times the average enrollment in the district during the second month of the school year by a figure equal to the previous year's state-wide average per-pupil expenditure. This formula seems to be fairly satisfactory for the average pupil.

But it is not quite so clear what should be done to allow for variations in pupil need. At present, Equitania is operating under a procedure that allows districts to report the enrollment of all students with disabilities in two different ways—first as part of the total general enrollment and then separately, for an additional allocation. This additional aid is calculated for each district on the basis of the average expenditure per atypical student (in that district) minus the average expenditure for all students in the district. Seventy-five percent of this "excess cost" for special education is then reimbursed by the state, regardless of the relative wealth of the district. This policy has seemingly facilitated the growth of special education programs in the state, allowing districts to spend whatever is required to deliver adequate service without too much strain on local budgets.

A state Task Force on Equity and Efficiency has been meeting during the past year, and one of the chief items on its agenda is examining the way in which the state formula handles variations in student needs. It has been noted in some of the testimony collected by the task force that the policy may be too liberal (thereby threatening efficiency), since there is no cap on what a district may spend and still receive 75% reimbursement by the state. Others complain that very wealthy districts, which rightfully receive only 10%–15% state aid for their general school programs, are not only spending imprudently for students with disabilities, but are also labeling more kids in order to "clean up" at the 75% rate. These charges are advanced mostly by those in poorer districts, who see the present policy as being inequitable, since it clearly benefits wealthy districts more than poorer ones. Fiscal conservatives on the task force have noted that there ought to be more stringent accounting requirements to differentiate between the programs and resources provided for students with severe problems and needs versus those provided for students at only minor variance from the average. Some parent advocates have agreed that given the lack of differentiation, districts are prone to focus on those who are easiest to serve and give insufficient attention to the "tough cases."

A proposal for change in the special education funding formula has now been advanced by one subcommittee of the task force. This proposal calls for abandoning the 75% excess-cost reimbursement and applying the same state aid ratios (based on local district wealth) to special education as are used for the general support program. However, special education services would be differentiated and assigned varying weights. The proposed weights and program specifications (expressed in comparison to typical students, who count as "1") are as follows:

SERVICE TYPE	PERSONNEL LOAD	WEIGHT
Full-time special class (mild)	Class enrollment limited to 15	2.0
Full-time special class (moderate)	Class enrollment limited to 10	3.0
Part-time resource or consultant teacher	Maximum load = 20 students; instructional groups limited to 4 pupils	7.5
Itinerant teacher/therapist	Maximum load = 50 students; service groups limited to 3 pupils	10.0

According to the proposal, all weighted enrollments would be calculated as "full-time equivalents." Pupils receiving part-time services would be counted at the higher weight only for that proportion of the day or week for which the special service was received; they would be weighted as "1" while in regular school programs.

Reaction to the proposal has been mixed. Some observers note that while the change would excuse local districts from separate accounting for special education expenditures, it would add complications to pupil enrollment accounting. Others point out that while these weightings may allow for services delivered in groups of 3–15 students, it does not provide for those students who require individual instruction or various related services. The following are some specific questions addressed to the task force in the first public hearing on the proposal:

How would the "weighted enrollment" concept (as opposed to the present "excess cost" concept) affect taxpayer equity?

Would poor and rich districts be affected differently?

Would the proposed weights for various special education programs really provide "fiscal neutrality" in terms of pupils getting the services they need?

How would this formula affect the development of the consultant teacher model?

How could the formula be extended to include students who require even more intensive services? What weight would be appropriate for one-to-one instruction?

How would the change affect the classification of children as disabled?

How would total state-wide expenditures for special education services be affected?

Enrollment is calculated only in October of each year. How could pupils whose special education services change later in the year be appropriately accounted for?

In preparation for the next public hearing, task force members are hoping to have some answers ready. Are answers possible? What should they be?

REFERENCES

Bernstein, C.D., Hartman, W.T., & Marshall, R.S. (1976). Major policy issues in financing special education. *Journal of Educational Finance, 1*, 299–316.

Callahan, R. (1962). *The cult of efficiency.* Chicago: University of Chicago Press.

Chambers, J.G., & Parrish, T.B. (1982). *The issue of adequacy in the financing of public education: How much is enough?* Stanford, CA: Institute for Research on Educational Finance and Governance.

Coons, J.E., & Sugarman, S.D. (1978). *Education by choice.* Berkeley: University of California Press.

Council of Administrators of Special Education. (1993). *CASE future agenda for special education: Creating a unified education system.* Albuquerque, NM: Author.

Education for All Handicapped Children Act of 1975, PL 94-142. (August 23, 1977). Title 20, U.S.C. 1401 et seq: *U.S. Statutes at Large, 89,* 773–796.

Education of the Handicapped Act Amendments of 1983. PL 98-199. Title 20, U.S.C. 101 et seq: *U.S. Statutes at Large, 97,* 1357–1375.

Florence County School District # Four v. Carter [950 F.2d 156; (4th Cir. 1991), aff'd___U.S.___(November 9, 1993)]

Friedman, M. (1955). The role of government in education. In R.O. Solo (Ed.), *Economics and the public interest* (pp. 123–144). New Brunswick, NJ: Rutgers University Press.

Guthrie, J.W., Garms, W.I., & Pierce, L.C. (1988). *School finance and education policy: Enhancing educational efficiency, equality and choice.* Englewood Cliffs, NJ: Prentice Hall.

Hartman, W.T. (1990) Supplemental/replacement: An alternative approach to excess costs. *Exceptional Children, 56,* 450–459.

Hartman, W.T. (1992). State funding models for special education. *Remedial and Special Education, 13*(6), 47–58.

Jensen, D.N. (1983). *Tuition tax credits: Has the Supreme Court cleared the way?* Stanford, CA: Institute for Research on Educational Finance and Governance.

Kakalik, J.S., Furry, W.S., Thomas, M.A., & Carney, M.F. (1981). *The cost of special education* (Rand Note N-1792-ED). Santa Monica: The Rand Corporation.

Levin, H.M. (1980). Educational vouchers and social policy. In J.W. Guthrie (Ed.), *School finance policies and practices* (pp. 235–263). Cambridge, MA: Ballinger.

Levittown Union Free School District v. Nyquist, 408 N.Y.S. 2d 606 (1978); Affirmed, 443 N.Y.S. 2d 843 (1981); Reversed, 453 N.Y.S. 2d 643 (1982); Cert. denied, 459 U.S. 1139 (1983).

McCarthy, E.F. (1980). *Policy considerations for state special education funding systems.* Unpublished doctoral dissertation, Syracuse University.

McCarthy, E.F., & Sage, D.D. (1982). State special education fiscal policy: The quest for equity. *Exceptional Children, 48,* 414.

Moore, M.T., Walker, L.J., & Holland, R.P. (1982). *Fine-tuning special education finance: A guide for state policy makers.* Washington, DC: Education Policy Research Institute of Educational Testing Service.

Mueller v. Allen, U.S. Minn., 103 S.Ct. 3062 (1983).

National Association of State Boards of Education. (1992). *Winners all: A call for inclusive schools* (The report of the NASBE study group on special education). Alexandria, VA: Author.

O'Reilly, F. (1989). *State special education finance systems, 1988–89.* Alexandria, VA: National Association of State Directors of Special Education.

Rossmiller, R.A., Hale, J., & Frohreich, L. (1970). *Educational programs for exceptional children: Resource configurations and costs* (National Educational Finance Project Study No. 2). Madison: Department of Educational Administration, University of Wisconsin.

Sage, D.D. (1992). Fiscal issues in special education: Prospects for the future. In K.A. Waldron, A.E. Reister, & J.H. Moore (Eds.), *Special education: The challenge of the future* (pp. 96–124). San Francisco: Mellen Research University Press.

Serrano v. Priest, 5 Cal. 3d 584, 96 Cal. Rptr. 601,487 P. 2d 1241 (1971); subsequent opinion, 135 Cal. Rptr. 345, 557 P. 2d 929 (1976).

U.S. Department of Education. (1989). *Eleventh annual report to Congress on the implementation of the Education of the Handicapped Act.* Washington, DC: U.S. Government Printing Office.

Vocational Education Act of 1976, PL 94-482. (October, 12, 1976). Title 20, U.S.C. 2301 et seq: *U.S. Statutes at Large, 90,* 2169–2215.

7

Outcome-Based Education and Students with Disabilities

What students should learn and how they should learn it have been topics of debate in this country ever since the inception of public education. Schools today continue to struggle with these questions and are being pressured by businesses, government, parents, and special interest groups to find the answers before the rest of the world passes them by. There is an urgency in these questions that has not been present before. Many educators believe that what and how students learn cannot be separated from the total structure of the school. Communities are taking a closer look at the total school package and are hoping to reform education in a manner conducive to educational success for *all* students.

Since the passage of PL 94-142 in 1975, educators in general education classrooms have slowly relinquished some of their teaching responsibilities to various "specialists" who are trained to meet the needs of atypical students. Be it a student who is identified as having a disability, a student who is bilingual, or a student at risk for academic failure, schools have allowed this dependence on specialists, often at the expense of potential improvements in classroom curricula and instruction for all students. Case (1992) identifies four trends that lead her to argue that school personnel must refocus their thinking about what should be taught and how, particularly with regard to students with disabilities. First, the legal mandates of PL 94-142 have driven the expansion of knowledge about students with disabilities and the development of effective interventions to help improve their learning. The research overwhelmingly suggests that traditional specialized practices are not successful in meeting student needs (Gartner & Lipsky, 1987). Second, teaching is no longer "intuitive," but research-based, which implies that there are methods of teaching that have been proven to be effective for all learners. Third, changes in lifestyles and family structures have decreased the amount of support that most students receive to help them achieve success in school; therefore, more and more students tend to fall behind in their academic growth and qualify for special services. Finally, because our world is changing so rapidly, teachers can no longer depend on conveying a finite body of knowledge through basic skill instruction. The body of knowledge that was relevant yesterday may no longer be so. In fact, it may not even be considered true, today. A close look at these issues increases the motivation of school personnel to consider "new" models for educating all students, including those with disabilities.

In this chapter, we argue that authentic outcome-based education (OBE) is a major aspect of the school restructuring debate and is paramount to successfully educating students with disabilities. This concept, while long embraced by many special educators, needs to be considered within an inclusive educational paradigm. It certainly must also be considered in light of the concepts of authentic assessment and demonstrative performance. The implications for one or more sets of outcome measures and their meaning for curriculum and instruction will be far reaching and will require a number of policy choices. With the lower school completion rates and higher unemployment rates for students with disabilities, rethinking the focus of curriculum and instruction within an outcome framework is certainly warranted.

THE EVOLUTION OF OUTCOME-BASED EDUCATION

The National Center on Educational Outcomes (NCEO) defines outcomes as ". . . the results of interactions between individuals and schooling experience" (Ysseldyke, Thurlow, & Shriner, 1992, p. 37). According to William Spady, Director of the High Success Network, an outcome is a ". . . culminating demonstration of learning, . . . what it is the kids actually do" (Spady, 1992–1993, p. 66). To most outcome-based educators who subscribe to OBE, outcomes include the knowledge, skills, and attitudes that students demonstrate upon graduation. "Outcomes-based education is a system that seeks to define, design, deliver and document instruction and assessment in terms of intended outcomes" (Ysseldyke, 1992, in reference to King & Evans, 1991).

OBE is not new to educators and has evolved from a variety of theories over time. There are several OBE models operating in schools. The Outcomes Driven Developmental Model (ODDM) (Champlin, 1991) and the High Success Network (HSN) Strategic Design Model (Spady, 1992) are the two predominant models in the field today. These models are both based on the premise that all educational decisions should be driven by predetermined target outcomes for all students.

Present OBE can be linked to several major educational theories, including Ralph Tyler's (1949) work on instructional objectives, Benjamin Bloom's mastery learning (Bloom, Englehart, Furst, Hill, & Krathwohl, 1956), and Glaser's work in the area of criterion-referenced measurement (Glaser & Cox, 1968). As early as 1949, Ralph Tyler identified four fundamental questions that should guide the development of curriculum and instruction:

1. What educational purposes should the school seek to attain?
2. What educational experiences can be provided that are likely to help school personnel attain these purposes?
3. How can these educational experiences be effectively organized?
4. How can we determine whether these purposes are being attained? (p. 19)

Tyler's first question is about outcomes. Both Tyler and present day OBE advocates contend that the purpose of schooling must be clearly stated and understood before curriculum or "educational experiences" can be designed and organized. Also, an accountability system, or in Tyler's words, a way to "determine whether these purposes are being attained" must be in place (p. 106). Tyler also stressed the importance of objectives in planning learning experiences: "Tyler noted the importance of objectives for systematically planning educational experiences, stating that a well-written objective should identify both the behavior to be developed in the student and the area of content or of life in which the behavior is applied" (King & Evans, 1991, p. 73). Tyler's perspective on objectives is an apparent influence in OBE today.

The work of Benjamin Bloom and his colleagues on educational objectives and mastery learning in the 1950s and 1960s also contribute to present day OBE. Bloom's 1968 essay entitled "Learning for Mastery" is often considered to be the origin of the idea of OBE (see Champlin, 1991; King & Evans, 1991; and Spady, 1992):

> Inherent in the Mastery concept was the demand to create new conditions for success by intentionally altering many time-honored and previously untouchable variables. Among these were: Time, an intentional emphasis on the affective, altering the instructional process to provide opportunities and support, re-assessed roles for both teacher and pupil, and . . . a complete overhauling of the traditional view of who and how many could become successful learners. The emerging belief that all could become successful learners was in itself a revolution. (Champlin, 1991, p. 7)

Spady contends that Bloom's mastery learning schools were more success-based than outcome-based. "The focus was on creating more success for all the learners on whatever the individual teachers were teaching" (Spady, 1992–1993, p. 66). True OBE shifts the focus to the outcomes themselves; education becomes based on and driven by carefully defined outcomes for all students.

King and Evans also contend that criterion referenced measurement is another concept that has found a place in OBE. They note that criterion referenced measurement is particularly applicable to OBE because student performance is placed on a continuum ". . . ranging from 'no proficiency' to 'perfect performance.' Along this continuum are the tasks a student must perform and the criterion level reflecting an acceptable level of performance" (King & Evans, 1991, p. 73). By viewing a student's achievements within the framework of this continuum, one can determine what a student is currently able to do and what additional experiences are necessary in order to reach the prescribed outcome.

In 1979, the Network for Outcome-Based Schools was established by a group of practitioners, including John Champlin and William Spady, who hoped to salvage the Mastery Learning approach to education. Champlin contends that the term *outcome-based education* was coined to more clearly reflect the purpose and mission of the network.

BELIEFS GUIDING AN OUTCOME-BASED SYSTEM

According to Spady and Marshall (1991), outcome-based education is founded on three basic premises:

1. All students can learn and succeed (but not on the same day or in the same way).
2. Success breeds success.
3. Schools control the conditions of success.

Spady defines an outcome as:

> a demonstration of learning that occurs at the END of a learning experience. It is a result of learning and an actual visible, observable demonstration of three things: knowldege, combined with competence, combined with . . . 'orientations'—the attitudinal, affective, motivational, and relational elements that also make up performance. (1992, p. 6)

An outcome is the demonstration that occurs after all formal instruction is completed; OBE focuses on this end result. Schools, in conjunction with parents, students, and other community members, work collaboratively to determine what they want students to know, do, and be like when they leave school. These "exit outcomes" become the driving force behind education for all students.

Spady (1992–1993) further defines outcome-based education in terms of four principles:

1. Clarity of focus
2. Expanded opportunity
3. High expectations
4. Design down

The first principle implies that all curricula, instruction, and assessment should be focused on the targeted outcomes for all students. All aspects of education are geared to "what we want kids to demonstrate successfully at the 'real' end—not just the end of the week [or] . . . the end of the year—but the end of their time [in school]" (Spady, 1992–1993, p. 66). The focus or purpose of education is clear at all times to all educators, parents, students, and community members.

The second principle allows students multiple opportunities to "learn and demonstrate, at a very high level, whatever they are ultimately expected to learn" (Spady, 1992–1993, p. 66). This principle recognizes that all students do not learn in the same way or at the same rate and that a variety of methods and contexts are necessary to maximize student learning. Time constraints are removed and outcome performance is not tied to the calendar or to a daily bell schedule. In OBE, "WHETHER students learn important things successfully is more important than the day of the year or the hour of the day it happens" (Spady, 1992, p. 8).

The third principle, high expectations, is based on the assumption that all students are ". . . able to do significant things well" (Spady, 1992–1993, p. 66). The bell curve, which is based on the expectation that some students will fail, is no longer considered valid. All students are expected to succeed in demonstrating outcomes.

Finally, the fourth principle, designing down, implies the opposite of the traditional method of designing curriculum. In a design-down model, the outcomes are established first; the curriculum is then designed backwards, always focusing on where the students should ultimately end up. The curriculum is based on the outcomes, thus the term outcome-based education. Figure 1 illustrates an example of designing down created by Norton (1993) for a student with mild to moderate disabilities.

Spady and Marshall (1991) trace the development of outcome-based education from three perspectives: traditional, transitional,

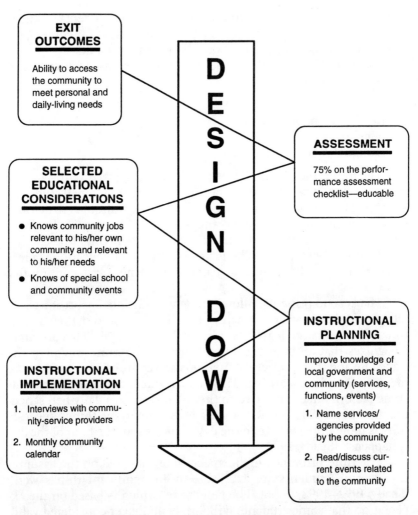

Figure 1. Example of designing down within an outcome-based framework. (Adapted from Norton, 1993.)

and transformational. They contend that most of the school personnel in the United States and Canada who subscribe to the OBE philosophy still use the traditional approach. This approach is "highly effective in improving student achievement yet, it is not, strictly speaking, outcome based" (p. 68). The school personnel using this approach develop outcomes based on the existing curriculum, determining what aspects of it are important for students to learn. Performance objectives are established and student learning typically increases even within the structure of a traditional school. But

Champlin (1991) contends that this approach affects the classroom, but not the organization of the school or district.

Spady and Marshall (1991) identify five weaknesses in this approach. First, the outcomes are limited to those resulting from small units of instruction that become ends in themselves. Second, the curriculum remains virtually unchanged, perhaps with a clearer focus, but still based on traditional content categories that usually do not relate to the real world. Also, in this traditional approach, the classroom remains the only context in which learning takes place. Student performance does not typically occur outside of the school itself. Fourth, the traditional approach does not usually address the graduate as a total person; exit outcomes that describe what a graduate should know, do, and be like do not drive the curriculum. Finally, Spady and Marshall, as well as Champlin (1991), contend that traditional OBE does not challenge the current nature and structure of schools. There is no need for schools to change their way of doing business when using this traditional approach.

Transitional OBE is "a viable approach for districts seeking to extend their vision beyond existing subject area content in defining outcomes of significance" (Spady & Marshall, 1991, p. 69). This approach, as its name implies, lies midway on the continuum between the traditional and transformational approaches. It is a viable approach because it is typically used by districts that are seeking to address higher-level competencies but are not yet ready to embark on a complete restructuring of the curricula and the schools. This approach focuses attention on the exit outcomes for all students. The school's vision targets a graduate who is competent and able to become a successful, productive member of society:

> Transitional OBE staff and community members almost universally emphasize broad attitudinal, affective, motivational and relational qualities or orientations. These schools give priority to higher-level competencies, such as critical thinking, effective communication, technological applications and complex problem solving, rather than particular kinds of knowledge or information. (Spady & Marshall, 1991, p. 69)

According to Spady and Marshall, this transitional phase soon shifts to a transformational OBE approach. Transformational OBE "represents the highest evolution of the OBE concept . . . [and] is grounded in the question: why do schools exist in this day and age?" (Spady & Marshall, 1991, p. 70). Transformational OBE is based on the four operational principles discussed earlier in this chapter (Spady, 1992/1993) and is firmly entrenched in the belief that the purpose of schooling is to provide students with the knowledge, skills, and attitudes necessary for success after leaving school:

When viewed from this future oriented, life role perspective, success in school is of limited benefit unless students are equipped to transfer that success to life in a complex, challenging, high tech future . . . Transformational OBE takes nothing about schooling today as a given . . . Instead transformational OBE districts set their existing curriculum frameworks aside when addressing the issue of future-driven exit outcomes. (Spady & Marshall, 1991, p. 70)

Spady and Marshall (1991) recommend adopting a strategic planning model that brings teams of stakeholders together to discuss future conditions of life for students and determines desired exit outcomes based on this discussion. From this point, curriculum evolves backward, always with a view toward the exit outcomes. Continuous evaluation is paramount to the success of the transformational OBE approach, as the curriculum needs to be constantly adjusted to better enable students to achieve the exit outcomes. Transformational OBE schools exist primarily for this purpose.

WHY INSTITUTE OBE FOR STUDENTS WITH DISABILITIES?

For many years special educators have professed an allegiance to OBE, according to their perception of the term. Special education programs have usually been goal driven and performance based, thus, the outcome-based emphasis is familiar to those who have worked with students with disabilities. As stated earlier in this chapter, we believe outcome-based education is fundamental to an inclusive school philosophy. In an era of nation-wide educational accountability concerns, OBE provides a new approach to teaching that professes to encompass all students and focuses on success for everyone:

OBE forces us to express what we value in education, to commit educational resources to bringing that to life in students, and—in contrast to present practice—to continue until we have succeeded. Educators become accountable for producing exit outcomes in virtually every student who enters school. (King & Evans, 1991, p. 74)

With the renewed emphasis on the least restrictive environment (LRE) and the true intent of the law, school systems find themselves scrambling for better ways to meet the needs of students with disabilities in age-appropriate environments, along with their peers. According to King and Evans, OBE is appealing to a variety of constituents—including politicians, business people, community leaders and educators—because they can latch onto exit outcomes that are quite similar to the educational goals established by most districts in the nation over the last 100 years. The difference between these goals of the past and OBE is that schools are given the autonomy to achieve these outcomes in any number of ways (King & Evans,

1991, p. 74). This freedom to establish the means, or in essence the curriculum, allows teachers the flexibility to provide educational experiences to a diverse student population in a variety of ways. Students are not required to do the same thing in the same amount of time in the same way as their age mates. They are, however, all working toward the same end result. In an OBE system, students with disabilities would be working toward the same exit outcomes as all other students and, like all other students, would work at their own pace, using strategies designed to accommodate their learning style. The true intent of PL 94-142 would be easily realized in this environment.

Students with moderate to severe disabilities can also be included in this OBE model if outcomes are broadly defined. "The primary need is for breadth and balance—meaning that the curriculum should be defined not in terms of narrow subject matter but broader areas of knowledge and skill" (McLaughlin & Warren, 1992, p. 61). The Council of Administrators of Special Education (CASE), in its Future Agenda for Special Education, advocates a unified system of educational outcomes for all students. Based on McLaughlin and Warren's research, CASE contends that this policy

> . . . allows for the formulation of a broad based set of outcomes which is applicable to all students without exception . . . This does not imply that all students are expected to learn exactly what others are learning. It does imply, however, that there are certain general expectations which all students are required to work toward even though the demonstration mode for these outcomes may vary. (CASE, Inc., 1993, p. 10)

One example of a broad-based exit outcome, as offered in the CASE Future Agenda, may be the expectation that all graduates will be literate. The degree to which students are expected to be literate may vary depending on the student's capabilities: one student may demonstrate mastery of this outcome by writing a detailed persuasive proposal; another may demonstrate literacy by effectively using an assistive device to communicate his or her needs and opinions. Students with moderate to severe disabilities may be required to work toward fewer outcomes than students without disabilities; the degree to which these outcomes are demonstrated may vary; and students may be required to perform these outcomes in multiple settings (see CASE Future Agenda, 1993, pp. 10–12).

THE IMPLEMENTATION CHALLENGE

While special educators will find many of these beliefs consistent with their past practices, the publicly centered process of establishing outcomes as well as the commitment to reporting progress toward them will be challenging. The state of Virginia has promulgated an outcome-based plan known as the Common Core of Learning. Essential to the Common Core of Learning is a set of four beliefs similar to those espoused by Spady, Champlin, and others on outcome-based education:

1. All individuals can learn successfully.
2. Success results in further success.
3. Schools create and control the conditions under which learners succeed.
4. Community, parents, and educators share in the responsibility for learning.

The major principle or characteristic of OBE is that learner outcomes are clearly delineated. The outcomes are future-oriented and focus on life skills in the context in which they will be applied. Nowhere are these characteristics more clearly presented than in the education of students with significant disabilities. The other characteristics, however—high expectations of and for all learners, and making the outcomes the sources of all other major educational decisions— have not yet pervaded any educational constituency, including state and local educational leadership. The belief that students with the most severe disabilities are worthy of our highest expectations for learning has not been pervasive.

Under an OBE model, instruction is carefully orchestrated toward the achievement of outcomes; it is characterized by its appropriateness to the learner's needs, interests, and developmental level. Finally, instruction is designed to be active and experience-based for maximum application of the skills and knowledge in the appropriate context. Again, many of these characteristics are well-grounded in the practice and research of professionals in special education. In the case of students with less significant disabilities, these characteristics of instruction and learning are often separate from the curriculum delivered in the typical classroom (where students with learning disabilities may be integrated part-time), being fully implemented in the resource classroom. Student progress in special education is often demonstrated in ways compatible with an outcome-based model. Special educators share a commitment to judge success by demonstrated achievement and application of learning, rather than becoming preoccupied with covering the content. They believe that assessment must be individualized and appropriate to the life context of the learner, rather than comparative to that of all students of the same age, or based simply upon time spent in school. Special educators also share the measurement perspective of criterion-referenced assessment that outcome-based educators hold, as well as a commitment to teaching students to demonstrate skills independently and to creating meaningful social relationships and real jobs in the competitive work place. Finally, special educators believe, as do OBE advocates, that each student should be given the time and assistance necessary to achieve desired outcomes and that there should be no limits due to traditional definitions of school, learning, or teaching.

Barriers to Implementation

What then are the barriers to implementing OBE for students with disabilities? There are a number of assumptions that educators need to discuss that shape the issues and policy options surrounding OBE and its meaning for students with disabilities. The first assumption is that the targeted outcomes for all students include students with disabilities. Many special educators fear that when advocates of OBE profess their commitment to including *all* students under their definition, they are not necessarily referring to students with disabilities. According to Ysseldyke et al. (1992), "even though most position papers and calls for standards by policy groups, legislatures, and government agencies contain language that is inclusive of all students, few of their actions follow through on the inclusive rhetoric" (p. 36). Ysseldyke et al. support this statement with a study by Anderson (1992) that suggests that most current reform efforts do not consider students with disabilities when advocating changes in the educational system. These students are still viewed as separate entities in a separate system. Ysseldyke et al. contend that all special education professionals and advocates must keep informed about local restructuring debates, particularly in regard to outcomes and accountability systems. It is imperative that the needs of students with disabilities are considered during these debates. This assumption also requires the community of stakeholders to reach a consensus on outcomes that include all students. Outcomes cannot be devised by school personnel alone. The community must be involved in the decision-making process regarding outcomes for all students, including those with disabilities, as a first step toward including the community as a partner in the educational process.

Second, one goal of outcome-based education and its accompanying focus on accountability is the improvement of student performance. Expecting all students, including those with disabilities, to be more successful requires a joint commitment on the part of all school personnel, parents, and community members who share in the education of students with disabilities. It also requires a belief that all students can and will learn with their assistance. While this is still a problem for some special educators, it is more of an issue with the community at large. Without this shared responsibility and commitment, much time will be devoted to philosophical explanations, discussions, and debate each time a student with a disability enters a classroom or other community learning site.

Third, it is assumed that some students with disabilities will continue to need specially designed instruction and other related services in order to benefit from an education program. While most typical students are able to access the curriculum without support, many students with disabilities will require adaptation, additional support, and alternative strategies to prepare them for an active and productive life after school.

Fourth, it is assumed that some students with sensory or major physical disabilities may need to pursue unique outcomes. What these outcomes are and how they will be achieved need to be clearly outlined.

Major Issues in Implementation

Several issues need to be examined when implementing an inclusive outcome-based approach (Brauen, 1993).

Issue #1   What is the framework that a state or school district will use to include students with disabilities in an outcome-based system?   In the State of Virginia Common Core of Learning, seven dimensions of living are proposed for all learners and a set of life-role performances are described that correspond to each dimension:

1. *Personal Well-Being and Accomplishment*   performances demonstrate capacity to analyze, implement, avoid, harmonize, and advocate.
2. *Interpersonal Relations*   performances demonstrate capacity to use, sustain, analyze, explore, respect, exhibit, and model.
3. *Life-Long Learning*   performances demonstrate capacity to anticipate and explore, discover, analyze, use, and modify.
4. *Cultural and Creative Endeavors*   performances demonstrate capacity to investigate and participate, accept, create and communicate, examine, and enjoy.
5. *Work and Economic Well-Being*   performances demonstrate capacity to make, collaborate, respond, accept responsibility, and explore.
6. *Local and Global Civic Participation*   performances demonstrate capacity to identify, cooperate, defend, participate, and support.
7. *Global Environment*   performances demonstrate capacity to use, investigate, and nurture.

An outcome-based framework inclusive of all students, such as the example above, requires a consensus on the outcomes that are desirable for students with disabilities. With a consensus on outcomes, illustrative indicators or benchmarks for students with disabilities are created to guide the student, family, school, and community agencies in their common pursuit of the individual's well-being.

These seven dimensions of living correspond well to the five major adult roles identified by Frey:

> These roles are characterized by the extent to which individuals care for their personal and daily living needs (**personal manager**); productively occupy their time (**productive worker**); participate as members of their communities and the world beyond (**community participant**); develop relationships and integrate socially (**social participants**); and maximize personal effectiveness and the quality of their lives (**self-actualizing individuals**). (Frey, 1993, p. 7)

In addition to the adult life roles, Frey identifies eleven behaviors for persons with disabilities that intersect with these roles:

Maintain personal health, fitness, and appearance
Manage domestic responsibilities
Complete daily living tasks
Define and fulfill career and other life pursuits
Obtain and use community resources
Follow rules and laws
Travel in the local community and beyond
Participate in social situations and settings
Build relationships and support networks
Manage personal decisions
Meet personal challenges

CASE has proposed a unifying framework that argues for the community of stakeholders to prepare or reaffirm a set of outcomes for all students. Once the framework is established, personnel from individual schools are encouraged to design alternative curricula and instructional processes for all students. Individual educational plans for all students are then created to allow for student and school accountability by setting criterion-referenced assessment measures. This framework is illustrated in Figure 2.

Issue #2   How will the outcomes for students with disabilities mesh with the curriculum for all students?   Clearly, many students with disabilities are capable of achieving the outcomes listed above, but others will need ongoing support to participate in community life and to derive satisfaction from their work and their interactions with others. The nature of their progress toward these and other outcomes related to independent living, work, and social relations outside of

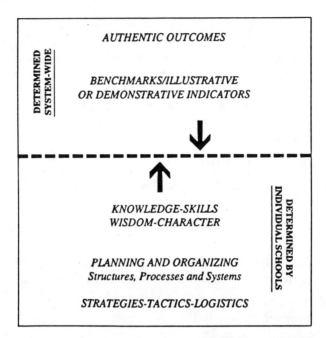

Figure 2.   Curriculum framework for a Unified System. (From CASE, Inc. [1993]. *Case future agenda for special education: Creating a unified education system.* Albuquerque: Author; reprinted by permission.)

school and work will require curriculum and instruction that is community-based as well as school-based. These curricular and instructional options may also be useful for students without disabilities. The school-based curricular planning process supports the implementation of instruction within the typical programs for all students, as well as the specific in-school modifications and community-based programs necessary to help students with disabilities meet the benchmarks or demonstrative indicators expected of them.

Issue #3   Who will be held accountable for the outcomes of students with disabilities? What unique resources are needed to support the attainment of those outcomes?   The rationale for a school-based inclusion program is that the school that a student with disabilities would normally attend is the agent responsible for the student's education. Each school's programs and services would be supplemented as necessary by district resources after a careful accounting was completed to determine what capacities were necessary to serve all identified students with disabilities. To require more specific accountability for individual student programs would be unrealistic, since personnel taking primary responsibility will often share accountability and be required to report their progress as part of the team's over-all responsibilities. In a site-managed school with its assigned or selected students, the principal and the school's system of managing student support teams would take responsibility for progress toward valued student outcomes.

Issue #4   What are the appropriate sources and measures of outcome data for students with disabilities?   Determining the outcomes and the context in which the learned behavior is expected to be demonstrated heavily influences the selection of criteria to judge student progress. Earlier, it was argued that criterion-referenced assessment is the preferred method. The sources of data that count as evidence are embedded in the outcomes and the context itself. Setting a rate or frequency for an assembly task in a manufacturing setting is significantly different from judging appropriate bus-riding behavior with a friend to and from work. The time it takes to learn the behaviors and to demonstrate the achievement of desired learning is variable, but should be noted throughout the student assessment. In short, a wide array of sources of data is expected to be used. Measures will vary in the same way as sources, depending upon the task and context.

Policy Options and Outcome-Based
Education for Students with Disabilities

Introducing OBE that is inclusive of students with disabilities involves a number of choices, some more extreme than others. Offering choices allows school districts to account for their place on a continuum of practice and local capacity to serve all students within an outcome-based context. Once an outcome-based perspective is selected, a clear statement of policy intent requires a definition of who is included when reference is made to *all students*. Once this is accomplished, district policy makers must agree to either an identical or differentiated set of outcomes for students with disabilities. These outcomes should be future oriented and publicly proclaimed. Once the outcomes are included or differentiated, the accountability system must also be determined. The second policy choice is whether the accountability system is to be grounded at the individual or system level. This includes chosing single or differentiated systems, and deciding whether to identify students with disabilities as a sub-group or to aggregate their performance with those of all other students. A conscious choice needs to be made to either continue to include a process assessment of student planning and implementation of the IEP or to move entirely to the outcomes perspective.

These broad policy choices need to be made within a vertical group of board members, cabinet-level representatives, district and school administrators, teams of regular and special education teachers, related service personnel, and students and parents. When making local policy decisions regarding outcomes, goals that are suggested, and sometime mandated, at the national or state level must be considered (e.g., National Education Goals, Curriculum and Evaluation standards of the National Council of Teachers of Mathematics, Virginia Common Core of Learning). The issue of the inclusion of students with disabilities in the outcome determination and accountability implementation process must be included in the discussion. After these policy decisions are made, a series of more technical implementation questions needs to be addressed. First, is the focus of student progress going to emphasize movement or gains in outcomes, meeting pre-specified standards, or both? Second, will the individualized education program (IEP) be the instrument of record or will data on subjects not covered in the IEP be included in the assessment process? Will the performance-based assessments sometimes be used exclusively, or always in conjunction with state-mandated competency tests? How will staff determine if the student should take the state competency examination, and will the students with disabilities be included in the aggregate? These questions must be considered in light of state and other external requirements and a realistic assessment of costs and use in the public arena.

IMPLICATIONS

According to Spady (1992), the implications will depend in large part on which of the three approaches to OBE are adopted by local schools. Traditional OBE requires the fewest number of changes in structure and curriculum. Transitional OBE requires schools to "stretch the organizational structures more, but not enough to make the school an unfamiliar place" (Spady, 1992, p. 12). It is the transformational approach that involves the most restructuring and reorganization: "Transformational OBE implies a fundamental redefinition of the form that schooling takes, the things it attempts to accomplish, and the symbols of what the institution represents" (Spady, 1992, p. 12). Spady contends that the direction in which school districts move will depend on the amount of pressure parents, community leaders, and other constituents apply in favor of preparing students for a future that is quite different from the past. He also suggests that the university plays an important role in how education is defined, another factor affecting which OBE approach is adopted.

> If future-oriented thinking and policy making prevail, and the schooling experience gets defined as preparation for life rather than preparation for more schooling, then models of Transformational OBE will come to the

fore, and traditional curriculum frameworks, content, and delivery systems will be significantly modified over time. But if the purpose of schooling continues to be defined as preparation for more schooling in the traditional content areas, then Traditional OBE and the preservation of existing content and delivery structures will emerge as the dominant pattern of OBE implementation. (Spady, 1992, p. 12)

Spady (1992) contends that regardless of the approach, several changes will automatically occur in schools once any authentic OBE model is in place. First, programs will not be confined to particular blocks of time or particular days of the week or months of the year. Students will learn in multi-age groups in systems that are more flexible and attuned to individual needs. Grading and the assignment of credits will be criterion-based and "will focus on what students can eventually learn to do well rather than on how well they do the first time they encounter something" (Spady, 1992, p. 12). Also, learning will become much more collaborative for both students and teachers, and much less competitive. Curriculum structures will change as the system responds to individual differences while working toward exit outcomes. The learning capabilities of students will be far more important to teachers than covering a certain topic in a certain amount of time. Textbooks will no longer drive the curriculum. Tracking will disappear and norm-referenced standardized testing will take a back seat to criterion-based assessment measures that focus on the outcomes that are most significant.

For students with disabilities to be included in any OBE school, several political and economic obstacles must be removed. In order for inclusive OBE to flourish, the categorical labels traditionally assigned to students, staff, materials, rooms, instructional procedures, and behavior management practices for students with disabilities must be removed. Students must become simply students, not "exceptional" students, and teachers must be simply teachers, and not special education teachers (see McLaughlin & Warren, 1992). Revising the child classification system would be a first step. In most states, the classification of students means more money for individual school districts, and thus will not be easy to eliminate. State and federal governments need to allow schools to experiment with enriched general programs based on broad, noncategorical or cross-categorical approaches. A mechanism would need to be developed whereby schools could apply for waivers to avoid having to label students in order to secure funding. In return, schools would be required to supply data showing pupils' outcomes. This would eliminate the need for extensive evaluation and identification procedures.

The IEP will need to be re-examined and redefined in an OBE system, although it has always been a goal-driven, outcome-based document that not only contains long- and short-term goals and objectives, but also indicates the person or persons responsible for providing the agreed upon specially designed instruction and other related services that the student is to receive. It is at this point however, that special education and authentic outcome-based education part company. According to Spady (1992), authentic outcomes are not tied to the calendar, are not synonymous with standardized test results, are not step-by-step instructional objectives, and are not developed around the existing curricula. Though IEP goals and objectives usually focus on what the team expects the student to do, they are often developed around the current curriculum and use standardized measures to assess performance, and a specific target date for completion is usually assigned. The IEP process has served as a tool for measuring compliance but has not included the results orientation required in an outcome-based system. Despite banks of objectives and computer assisted IEP generators, individual plans have not been aggregated to determine program success rates. The IEP has not served as a vehicle to measure student progress toward valued in-school or post-school outcomes. Thus, the IEP must be transformed to focus on broadly defined exit outcomes that have been established for all students. It must outline the services needed to meet these outcomes, not simply the amount of time to be spent in particular programs. Finally, the IEP must become the tool by which the success of specialized services are measured, and adjustments must be ongoing, as the student's needs warrant. These subtle yet important differences are noteworthy in any discussion of outcome-based education for students with disabilities in restructured schools.

The greatest implications will be for special educators themselves. They will find themselves increasingly integrated into the general education system. They will face the same pressures of accountability that all other teachers are facing. They will be required to work in collaborative situations, and their autonomy and control over programs and services for students with disabilities will diminish substantially.

The real challenge is to continue to improve teaching practices by using the best of what we currently know. Higher education will need to drastically change its procedures for training future teachers of *all* students. Those who are already teaching will need to be "retaught" to work with a variety of learners. Effective, well-planned staff development procedures must be established and sufficient time allotted for this reteaching.

The implications are also profound for the special education administrator. Ultimately, it is the special education administrator who can encourage inclusive ventures or continue to harbor programs and services from the rest of the school. As outcome-based schools develop, the expertise of the special educator will be called upon, particularly in developing goals and objectives. The special education administrator can encourage and support the staff as they venture into the world of collegiality and cooperation and can themselves enter into similar relationships with building administrators as OBE is implemented. Principals who are unfamiliar with special education terminology, regulations, and funding procedures will need assistance and support as they begin reclaiming their population of students with disabilities. Technical assistance will be necessary in developing appropriate strategies for students with disabilities to meet exit outcomes. The special education administrator can be an invaluable resource as schools move toward becoming outcome-based systems. It is clearly a matter of administrative choice to maintain the status quo or make changes that can benefit students with disabilities. Though these implications may present challenges to all administrators, we believe students with disabilities can be most successful in an outcome-based education system that is truly inclusive.

ILLUSTRATIVE CASE

Two special education teachers, Sandy and Greg, representing elementary and secondary programs for students with mild and significant disabilities, scheduled an appointment with the Director of Special Education after attending a 2-day, district-sponsored workshop on outcome-based education. As the meeting began, Pam, the director of special education, noted their excitement and apprehension.

Sandy began, "It was an honor to represent our department at the district restructuring meeting. It started a commitment to reach consensus on district exit outcomes for all students, but I'm not sure that *all* meant *all*."

Greg argued that he was not sure why he was selected, since his department in the high school worked with those students in the district who had the most severe disabilities. Greg said, "I am not sure my kids are able to achieve the outcomes that we discussed. I am afraid that the goals are still too academic in nature."

Sandy questioned Greg's interpretation. "I feel that the district outcomes are inclusive of all students. What I think you missed, Greg, is that these outcomes will be measured and demonstrated in different ways."

Pam interjected, "It's my understanding that the district exit outcomes will be the same for all students. Our concern should be determining which outcomes should be demonstrated in classes in which the students are included, rather than in the school as a whole or in the community. How would you two decide which outcomes should be demonstrated in which setting?

Each of you may have different responses to that question given the different types of students you have responsibility for.

Greg added, "Are you saying that we do not have any unique outcomes that should drive our instruction?"

Pam said, "That's right! In terms of exit outcomes, I think they are the same for all students. But there may be some enabling outcomes that are unique to a student's disability."

Sandy asked for an example.

Pam offered, "An enabling outcome might be the need of a student with a visual impairment to be taught Braille so that he or she can meet an exit outcome related to literacy. I really think the key issues are where we want the behaviors to be demonstrated, what we will accept as successful performance, and how they will be measured."

Some additional questions that the group discussed were:

Who will decide which exit outcomes will be emphasized?
How can we inform and involve parents in determining outcomes for students?
How can we adjust the IEP process to focus on exit outcomes?
What community agencies and other community resources can assist the students in meeting exit outcomes? How will outcomes affect transitional planning?
What resources do we need to ensure that all students will be successful in meeting the exit outcomes?
Do any other questions need to be resolved when moving to an outcome-based approach to education?

REFERENCES

Anderson, R.J. (1992). Educational reform: Does it all add up? *Teaching Exceptional Children, 24*(2), 4.

Bloom, B.S., Engelhart, M.D., Furst, E.J., Hill, W.H., & Krathwohl, D.R., (1956). *Taxonomy of educational objectives: Handbook I. Cognitive domain.* New York, David McKay Co.

Brauen, M.L. (1993, Month). *Outcomes-based accountability in special education: The myth and the reality.* Paper presented at CASE Public Policy Conference.

Case, A. (1992). The special education rescue: A case for systems thinking. *Educational Leadership, 50*(2), 32–34.

Champlin, J. (1991). Taking stock and moving on. *Journal of the National Center for Outcome Based Education, 1*(1), 5–8.

CASE, Inc. (1993). *CASE future agenda for special education: Creating a unified education system.* Albuquerque: Author.

Education for All Handicapped Children Act of 1975, PL 94-142. (August 23, 1977). Title 20, U.S.C. 1401 et seq: *U.S. Statutes at Large, 89,* 773–796.

Evans, K.M. (1992). *An outcome-based primer.* Minneapolis: University of Minnesota, Center for Applied Research in Educational Improvements.

Frey, W. (1993, April). *A state perspective on assessment of educational out-*

comes for students with disabilities. Paper presented at the CEC Annual Convention, Lansing, MI.

Gartner, A., & Lipsky, D.K. (1987). Beyond special education: Toward a quality system for all students. *Harvard Educational Review, 7*(4), 367–395.

Glaser, R., & Cox, R.C. (1968). Criterion reference testing for the measurement of educational outcomes. In R. Weisgerber (Ed.). *Instructional processes and media innovation.* Skokie, IL: Rand McNally.

King, J., & Evans, K. (1991). Can we achieve outcome-based education? *Educational Leadership 49*(2), 73–75.

McLaughlin, M., & Warren, S. (1992). *Issues and options in restructuring schools and special education programs.* College Park: University of Maryland, The Center for Policy Options in Special Education, and the Institute for the Study of Exceptional Children and Youth.

Norton, D. (1993, April). *Issues in putting outcome based education into practice at the district level.* Panel discussion, The Council for Exceptional Children, San Antonio.

Spady, W. (Summer, 1992). It's time to take a close look at outcome-based education. *Outcomes,* 6–13.

Spady, W. (1992/1993). [Interview with Ron Brandt] On outcome-based education: A conversation with Bill Spady. *Educational Leadership, 50*(4), 66–70.

Spady W., & Marshall, K. (1991). Beyond traditional outcome-based education. *Educational Leadership, 49*(2), 67–72.

Tyler, R. (1949). *Basic Principles of Curriculum and Instruction.* Chicago: University Press.

Ysseldyke, J., Thurlow, M., & Shriner, J. (1992). Outcomes are for special educators too. *TEACHING Exceptional Children, 25*(1), 36–50.

8

The Principal as Leader

The recent restructuring efforts in our nation's schools, coupled with trends in special education, have created new challenges for school principals. Restructuring is becoming synonymous with such terms as *decentralized governance, site-based management*, and *shared decision making*. The emerging trend in special education is to provide education for students with disabilities in classrooms with their peers. These classrooms are housed within the local school and include all students, both with and without disabilities, regardless of the types or extent of their needs. The school-level administrator is becoming the instructional leader who must design, lead, manage, and implement programs for *all* students in the school.

As educational services for students with disabilities change, there is a need to describe and analyze the role of school administrators in new ways. Leibfried (1984) suggests that the principal plays a major role in shaping teacher attitudes and overall school climate. O'Rourke (1980) and Tyler (1983) agree that there is a significant relationship between the principal's attitudes and those of the teachers: "The principal sets the tone for the staff, students, parents, and community attitude toward special students" (Bank Street College of Education, 1982, p. 2). While the influence of principals is significant, the manner in which principals use their influence in different school contexts has not been well described, nor has the relationship between the high school principal and special education management been subject to much investigation. In this chapter we look at the principal's past role in special education and the ways this role is evolving to meet the new challenges brought on by inclusive education and school restructuring.

THE EVOLVING ROLE OF THE PRINCIPAL

Where We Have Been

Throughout the 1970s and 1980s, the role of the principal in special education generated significant interest. Most of the research literature to date relates to the management practices of principals in the administration of PL 94-142 and includes detailed suggestions for implementation of the law (see Caetano, 1978; DuClos, Litwin, Meyers, & Ulrich, 1977; Gage, 1979; Payne & Murray, 1974; Smith, 1978; Vergason, Smith, Vinton, & Wyatt, 1975; Zettel, 1979). The literature supports the view that the principal's behavior toward special education programs can influence their success. Specific role responsibilities in the delivery of special education have been addressed by several researchers, and there is general agreement as to what these responsibilities ought to be. Although there is a consensus in the context of both regular and special education that the building principal has the primary responsibility for service delivery, the literature on education administration until recently provided only:

> . . . admonitions that describe what a good manager should do. The research and practice literature did not present models that describe how certain management or leadership acts actually become translated into concrete activities which help children succeed in school. (Bossert, Dwyer, Rowan, & Lee, 1982, p. 34)

The following list of "should do" suggestions is typical of the exhortative contents of literature published during the first decade following the passage of PL 94-142 dealing with the principal's responsibilities (Cochrane & Westling, 1977):

1. Principals should become knowledgable about the characteristics of children with disabilities.
2. Principals should provide information on exceptional children's education to the other members of the school community.
3. The principal should utilize special educators as support personnel.
4. The principal should consider alternative means of supporting teachers and students.
5. The principal should involve community-resource personnel in the education of exceptional students.
6. The principal should combine special-materials funds with those for the rest of the programs.
7. The principal should encourage teachers to educate children about various disabilities.

In 1975, directors of special education were asked what degree of difficulty they encountered in implementing selected components of PL 94-142. The most problematic areas were found to be the least restrictive environment (LRE) and individualized education program (IEP) requirements. Other specific difficulties cited were: deadlines for IEP completion, scheduling of personnel, and lack of clarity in federal and state laws (Keilbaugh, 1980).

Not only did the special education administrator face such tasks in implementing PL 94-142, the school principal, by virtue of his or her leadership role, also dealt with these same issues (Payne & Murray, 1974). Vergason et al. (1975) summarized this responsibility, stating that "the principal must maintain administrative authority over the day-to-day function of *all* staff within the building in order to have a coordinated, integrated program" (p. 104).

In summary, assumptions about and understandings of the role of principals in the delivery of special education initially evolved from the requirements of federal and state laws and from earlier works on the responsibilities of directors of special education.

Where We Are Heading

As schools move toward decentralization and districts focus on more inclusive programming for students with disabilities, the role of school principal is becoming one of leadership in and commitment to successfully meeting the needs of all children. Recent research by Rude and Rubadeau (1992) identified 16 "essential competencies" of building-level administrators and asked respondents to rate the importance of each in their role as special education leader. Table 1 lists these competencies in order of importance. The first five might better be thought of as part of an educational platform or an espoused theory of practice. Each of the 16 competencies suggests ownership and responsibility for all students, including those with extensive needs.

Two additional research studies take an in-depth look at the leadership behaviors and belief systems of building administrators concerning students with disabilities. These studies go beyond descriptions of espoused theories to include theories of practice (Schon, 1987). The purposes of the two research projects presented below were: 1) to describe and contrast elementary and secondary school principals' behaviors and beliefs, which are perceived by the principal and staff to influence attitudes and behaviors toward special education; and 2) to validate a theoretical framework of instructional leadership.

CONCEPTUAL FRAMEWORK

Bank Street College of Education (1982) and Burrello, Schrup, and Barnett (1988) suggest that principals of schools should display certain behaviors and accomplish specific objectives that will enable students with disabilities to become a part of the school culture. One view of necessary conditions in schools is presented by Bossert et al.

Table 1. Competency statements ranked according to total mean scores for all respondents

Rank	Competency category	Mean
1	Selection of special education staff who espouse the philosophy of integration	4.38
2	Recognizing the ongoing need for program and staff development in special education	4.37
3	Fosters the inclusion of special education students by modeling total school responsibility for all students	4.35
4	Philosophical orientation that indicates integration of special needs students benefits all students	4.25
5	Ability to recognize student learning styles and match with teaching strategies	4.25
6	Recognition of specialized instructional needs and appropriate access of technical support	4.16
7	Ability to identify and access human services organizations on behalf of students in need	4.10
8	Ability to select appropriate decision-making skills ranging from directive to delegating	4.08
9	Recognizing the importance of accountability in special education programs	4.06
10	Communication with diverse audiences such as parents, advocacy organizations, the courts, social services agencies, etc.	4.04
11	Understanding and applying the continuum of special services concept to meet the needs of all learners	4.00
12	Legal aspects of special education	4.00
13	Tolerance for uncertainty in special education situations	3.98
14	Use of technology to enhance instruction	3.73
15	Use of technology in special education to assist administrative record keeping	3.25
16	Knowledge and application of special education finance and reimbursement systems	3.17

From Rude, H.A., & Rubadeau, R.J. (1992). Priorities for principals as special education leaders. *The Special Education Leadership Review, 1*(1), 55–61; reprinted by permission.

(1982), who underscore four elements that are necessary for a school to be effective:

1. A school climate conducive to learning
2. A school-wide emphasis on basic skills instruction
3. The expectation among all teachers that all students can achieve
4. A system of clear instructional objectives for monitoring and assessing students' performance

Effective principals are able to create a climate in which the above characteristics will emerge. According to Burrello et al. (1988), if a principal is effective, there will be no distinction made between the expectations set for special and regular education students, staff, and programs. Sergiovanni (1984) identifies five forces of leadership that provide principals with a framework for examining their own behavior:

1. *Technical*—derived from best management practices
2. *Human*—derived from using social and interpersonal resources
3. *Educational*—derived from expert knowledge in matters of education and schooling
4. *Symbolic*—derived from focusing the attention of others on matters of importance to the school
5. *Cultural*—derived from building a unique school culture

As principals focus their attention more on the cultural and symbolic components, they also, through their attitudes and behavior, focus the attention of the staff and community on the importance of educating students with disabilities. The principal is vital to the establishment of a school climate conducive to educating all students (Burrello et al., 1988). "The symbolic leader by emphasizing selective attention [the modeling of important goals and behaviors] signals to others what is of importance and value" (Sergiovanni, 1984, p. 7).

Bossert et al. (1982) present a framework illustrating how the context of leadership affects the principal's management behavior and the impact of this behavior on the instructional climate and organization (see Figure 1). A contention of their model is that the behavior of the principal is shaped by personal, district, and external expectations. Student outcomes are then also affected by school climate and instructional organization. Since the principal's behavior has such an impact on school climate and the nature of instructional arrangements, his or her leadership behavior concerning special education may play a major role in the success of the special education program.

What knowledge and attitudes are needed by a principal to positively influence staff attitudes toward special education programs? Dwyer, Lee, Barnett, Filby, and Rowan (1985) have developed their framework based on the research of Bossert et al. (1982) (see Figure 2). Burrello et al. (1988), after an extensive review of the literature on special education leadership and role relationships, adapted the Dwyer framework to include special education elements as part of instructional leadership. Figure 3 illustrates the principal's responsibilities as the instructional leader of *all* students and programs in the school. Additional responsibilities that result from special education being included in the instructional framework are shown in bold type. The number of responsibilities common to both regular and special education management indicates the similarity of functions associated with the principal's instructional leadership role in each.

The adapted framework presented by Burrello et al. (1988) represents a theoretical construction of the day-to-day responsibilities of a principal concerning special education. Principals are expected to

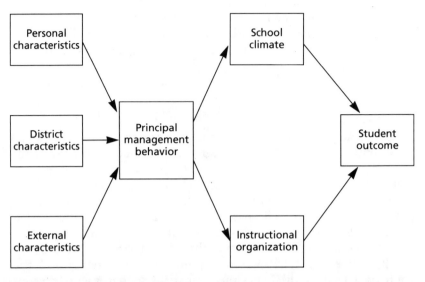

Figure 1. A framework for examining instructional management. (Adapted from Bossert, Dwyer, Rowan, & Lee, 1982.)

perform a large number and wide variety of duties throughout the school day. However, according to Murphy (1988) there are few detailed descriptions of the setting and contexts of the actual behavior of principals, particularly secondary principals. According to Burrello et al. (1988), fewer still include principals' descriptions of their involvement in special education. For these reasons, two separate research projects were undertaken to determine how principals and their staffs view their responsibilities and duties in the management of special education in local schools.

RESEARCH METHODS

The research reported on here consisted of two parallel studies—one conducted in elementary schools (DeClue, 1990) and the other in high schools (Van Horn, 1989). The two research projects resulted in five case studies—three in the elementary and two in the secondary schools. Four school districts were involved, representing urban, rural, and suburban contexts in a midwestern state. The methodological procedures used in these case studies were based on principles of naturalistic inquiry (Lincoln & Guba, 1985). A description of the principals' daily activities and interactions and school leaders' relationships with external audiences was compiled. In addition, frameworks were constructed by each principal, representing contextual

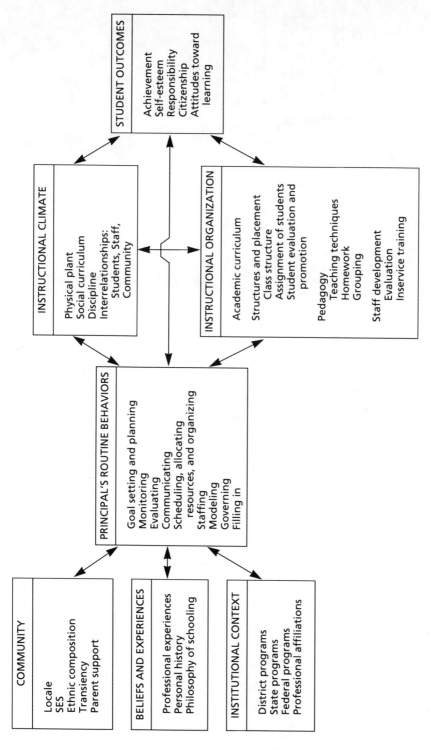

Figure 2. A framework of instructional leadership. (Adapted from Dwyer, Lee, Barnett, Filby, & Rowan, 1985.)

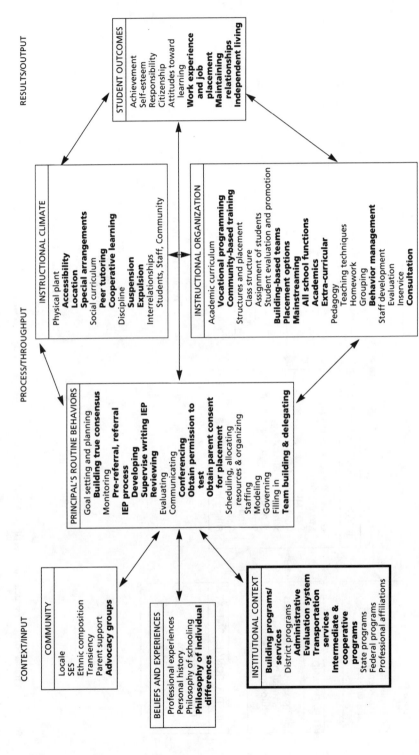

Figure 3. A framework for the principal as instructional leader in special education. (From Burrello, Schrup, & Barnett, 1988.)

factors, routine behaviors, instructional climate, instructional organization, and student outcomes.

The principals were selected from among nominations made by the special education director of each school district. After an extensive interview, the directors were asked to recommend principals who they felt were successful in dealing with special education programs in their schools. Once nominated by the director, the following criteria were used in selecting the principals:

Each setting had to include a range of types of special education programs serving students with disabilities.

The principal had to have a minimum of 2 years experience in his or her current setting.

The principal had to commit to participating in the study and learning about him- or herself and the special education programs in the building.

Data collection consisted of semi-structured interviews, observation, and document analysis. The principal, special education teachers, special education department heads, parents, and any other persons suggested by the principals and teachers were interviewed. The teachers who were interviewed were nominated by the principal. Observations of the principal and special education classrooms were conducted, in addition to a document analysis of the principals' job description, the school district's administrative handbook for special education, and any procedural guidelines for the assessment, placement, or re-evaluation of special education students. All interviews and observations took place in the school. As data were obtained, they were examined and categorized based on emerging trends. A total of 50 days were spent collecting data (10 days per site) to allow for prolonged engagement with the participants in their natural settings.

KEY FINDINGS

The following findings and conclusions are based on the data collected in the five case studies. Two frameworks were developed to provide a synthesis of data gathered from the elementary and secondary sites. The frameworks were compared with that created by Burrello et al. (1988) to determine the similarities and differences in elementary and secondary school settings. The student outcomes, instructional organization, and instructional climate sections of the frameworks are nearly identical. While the composite frameworks of the principals and Burrello et al. are remarkably similar, there are several differences worth noting.

Context Dimension

Advocacy One variation appears in the *Context* dimension from the research conducted by DeClue (1990) (see Figure 4) and Van Horn (1989) (see Figure 5) as compared to that in the Burrello framework presented in Figure 3. This dimension includes the factors *community, beliefs and experiences,* and *institutional context.* Under *community,* the principals did not feel that advocacy groups significantly affected their work at the building level. These administrators felt that advocacy groups, as a rule, have a broad agenda that extends beyond building-level issues and thus, their focus tends to be centered more on the district level, a sentiment echoed by the special education directors of all school districts. The principals felt that individual parents or organized groups of parents affected them more immediately. They did not consider these parents to be as formally organized as advocacy groups, but they did recognize the impact that they can have. For example, at one school site parents were instrumental in establishing a program for students with physical disabilities. At another site, the parents of some children with autism were involved in seeing that what they considered to be important programming needs of their children were met. These principals also felt the need for building-level support groups for parents of students with disabilities. Often such support was only provided at a district level, or perhaps the state or national level, and such groups were fairly far removed from the day-to-day concerns of these parents.

Professional Knowledge Another variation in the *Context* dimension of the DeClue and Van Horn frameworks worth noting is in the factor *Beliefs and experiences* under which the principals included the element *Professional experiences* in their framework. They believed that, as students with disabilities are integrated into regular school sites, a principal's knowledge base about disabilities is an important factor to consider. The principals in these studies were not trained as special educators, nor did they receive any coursework in special education as part of their principal-preparation programs. What knowledge about atypical students or programs they did possess had been acquired either on the job or through their own pursuit of information. In some cases, such knowledge was gained through their own personal experiences. The principals also felt that the addition of *Professional experiences* to the framework was applicable to other areas besides special education, such as programs for gifted students or for those considered to be at risk for academic failure.

Beliefs and Experiences It should also be noted that in Figure 3, the box containing the factor *Beliefs and experiences* has been shifted

CONTEXT/INPUT

PROCESS/THROUGHPUT

RESULTS/OUTPUT

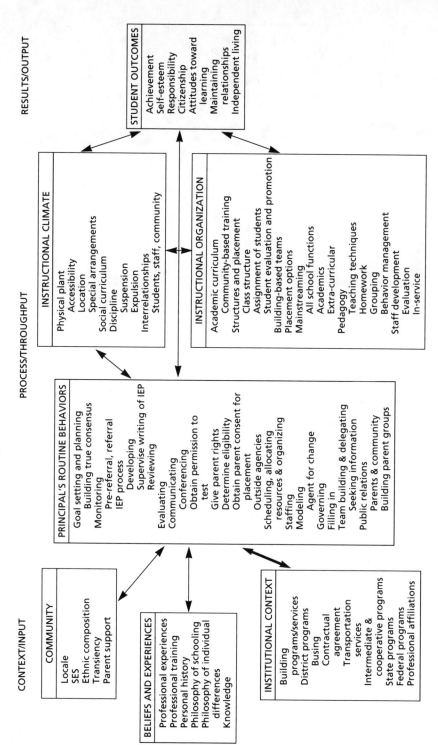

Figure 4. A framework for the elementary school principal as an instructional leader for all students. (Adapted from DeClue, 1990.)

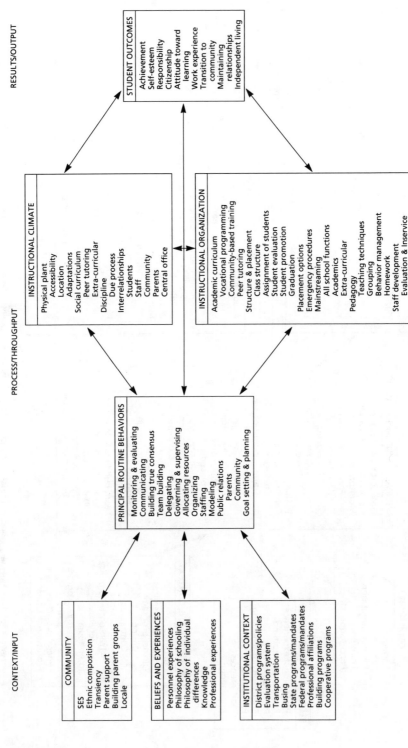

Figure 5. A framework for the secondary principal as instructional leader for all students. (Adapted from Van Horn, 1989.)

in the composite framework and is no longer aligned with the *Community* or *Institutional context* factors (See Figure 3). This shift represents the conclusion that the beliefs and attitudes of the principals toward special education were the key factors influencing their behavior toward and acceptance of students with disabilities. Principals in these five case studies consistently saw students with disabilities as being more similar to than different from typical students. They also came to understand that they had to come to know each disabled student as an individual and believed that these students had to be educated with their age-appropriate peers or they would not develop meaningful social relationships in school, in the community, or on the job. These principals' belief systems appear to be more rigid early in life and to slowly evolve later. This category appears to be the driving force for the remainder of the frameworks (DeClue, 1990; Van Horn, 1989).

Responses to Institutional Mandates   Another difference in the composite framework is the boldness of the box surrounding the factor *Institutional context* and the arrow connecting it to the factor *Principal's routine behaviors* (See Figure 4). While principals' beliefs and attitudes about special education students and programs played a major role in their acceptance of these students into their schools, it is also apparent that principals felt that district directives and state and federal guidelines often dictated the course of action concerning special education in their buildings. While most principals accepted this reactive, rather than proactive, aspect of special education, it did affect their initiating behavior. An example is the addition of *Contractual agreement* to the element *District programs*. The arrow connecting the two factors *Institutional context* and *Principals' routine behaviors* has been made bold to reflect the impact of this context on principals' behavior. Principals have reflected that they felt constrained by mandates, rules, and regulations governing referral, assessment, placement, programming, and transportation for students with disabilities.

The other conclusion drawn from the studies is that the power of law and regulation combined with principals' real concerns about due process and litigation reduces discretion in the daily functioning of the school. This *Institutional context* factor requires district compliance and results in fewer building-level alternatives. Elementary and secondary settings appear to be more alike than different in this regard (see Figures 4 and 5).

It is interesting to note that none of the principals in these five case studies indicated that his or her *Administration evaluation system* included special education in his or her own performance evaluation. When asked if they felt that they were evaluated with reference to their special education programs, principals indicated that special education was not a factor included in their overall evaluation, or that it was considered only incidentally. Principals have reported that they felt that many areas of special education programming were central office functions. They saw themselves as enablers, doing the bidding of the central office administrator of the special education or special services area, as required by state and federal law. Notice the absence of this element in either Figure 4 or Figure 5.

Process Dimension

Agent for Change   In the *Process* of the conceptual framework, elementary principals added *Agent for change* as an example of *Modeling* under *Principal's routine behaviors* (see Figure 4). They believed that in many areas, and certainly in the area of special education, their teachers sometimes needed someone to initiate thoughtful discussions about change. They also pointed out that this was not meant to imply that change was forced upon their staff members, but simply that opportunities were created for these discussions to take place and for risks to be taken. They saw themselves as support persons, especially as more and more students with disabilities were served differently and more inclusively in their schools. One example illustrates this point. When it was determined that three students from a class for those with moderate disabilities might benefit from placement in a typical homeroom, the teachers of both the special and general classes were hesitant, and so the middle school principal encouraged and facilitated the change. He was not certain that it would have occurred without his support (DeClue, 1990).

Delegation and Team Building   For secondary principals, *Team building and delegating* were highlighted under *Principal's routine behaviors*. Secondary principals built an administrative team that included assistant principals and department chairpersons. They also delegated to each department responsibilities and authority to make decisions covering curricula, discipline, scheduling, teacher evaluation, and other areas. Routine functions related to special education, such as referral and placement of students, monitoring the IEP process, and ensuring due process procedures for students with disabilities were seen by the principals as necessary for success. However, they felt that these functions were better performed by special education department heads. As suggested by Sergiovanni (1984), modeling and symbolic behaviors were key functions of principals. The support and acceptance that they displayed created an environment that allowed the department heads to function in a manner that encouraged the acceptance of special education as simply another department out of many in the high school (Van Horn, 1989).

The secondary principals also felt that an important factor in the success of the building-level special education programs was the ability of the department chairperson within the high school to act as a salesperson and negotiator, as well as to be a hard-liner when necessary. This finding is similar to assertions made by Stedman (1987): "Contrary to the traditional formula, the instructional leadership of most effective schools did not depend solely on the principal" (p. 219). The success of any program seems to depend on the department chairperson and the ability of the principal to provide the necessary freedom and resources to the department. The department chairperson can further develop the culture of the school at a more personal level. Because of the closeness of the department chairperson to the teachers and the students, this person seems to play a key role, along with the principal, in the establishment of a climate and culture that emphasize inclusion and support for all students. The informal networking and communication between regular and special education are forged by the special education department chairperson. In addition, the department chairperson acts as an advocate for the students and staff (McLaughlin, 1993; Siskin, 1990; Van Horn, 1989). Research supports the view that the existence of unique in-school communities at the department level is one of the most significant factors in teacher willingness to adapt to student diversity.

Instructional Organization

Another interesting change in the elementary principal's framework is also found in the process dimension under the factor *Instructional Organization*. Under the element *Academic curriculum, Vocational programming* has been removed (see Figure 4). While the three principals in this study recognized the importance of this type of programming for special education students, they did not feel that it was a part of their responsibilities at the elementary level. This same belief also surfaced in the results dimension of the framework under the factor *Student outcomes*. Again they recognized the importance of work experience and job placement for special education students, but they did not include it in their composite framework as they did not consider it relevant at the elementary level.

High school principals saw the need for and promoted a post-school curricular focus for all students with disabilities, especially those with more severe disabilities. They supported an *Instructional organization* that stressed vocational and community-based training leading to competitive employment and independent learning outcomes. These secondary principals went out of their way to encourage the acceptance of all students with severe disabilities by scheduling each student into a nonacademic class, typical homeroom, and extracurricular activities.

In summary, the five case studies essentially validated the research review conducted by Burrello et al. (1988). The case studies also detailed the symbolic leadership behaviors of principals, as well as the administrative practices, that promote a culture of inclusiveness. The case studies suggest similarities between elementary and secondary schools, regardless of the community demography and school district contexts. The overriding contextual issues for both elementary and secondary principals were the state and compliance issues that appear to constrain their instincts to integrate programs, services, and resources.

They also point out two major differences between elementary and secondary principal contexts. In terms of *Student outcomes*, and *Instructional organization*, principals at each level hold different expectations for performance and programming. Elementary principals in these cases were just beginning to consider community-based programming as an appropriate intervention for students with substantial disabilities.

CONCLUSIONS

Based on these five case studies, five conclusions can be drawn that have implications for school principals:

1. *The beliefs and attitudes of the principals toward special education are the key factors influencing their behavior toward students with disabilities.* The principals all displayed a positive attitude toward the acceptance of special education students and programs in their schools. This attitude was based on their own personal philosophies about the benefits to both regular and special education students when they are integrated within the same school site and program. Their positive attitude was a critical factor in creating a climate of acceptance for all students and programs in their schools. They communicated their attitude consistently in a variety of ways to students, staff, and parents and expected them to support this attitude through their own behaviors.

Research appears to support the conclusion that the attitude of the building principal toward inclusion and other aspects of special education are vital to the success of special education programs (Hyatt, 1987). Hyatt also supports the belief that the development of positive attitudes toward all aspects of the educational process, including special education, is prerequisite to the principal's effectiveness as an instructional leader. While Van Horn (1989) found high school principals' involvement to be of a more symbolic nature, the attitude of the principal is an important factor in developing a climate and culture conducive to the acceptance of students with disabilities.

2. *The most important role the principal plays in the inclusion of students with disabilities in the school is that of symbolic leader.* Sergiovanni (1984) lists five forces of leadership that are available to administrators to bring about or sustain changes necessary to improve schooling. He emphasizes that the often unnoticed symbolic force, however, is one of the characteristics of an excellent school.

The principals understood the importance of their behaviors and the symbolism attached to them. Visiting special education classrooms, seeking out and spending time with students with disabilities, and taking time to get involved in the educational concerns of both typical and atypical students were ways these principals provided a vision of acceptance of special education students and programs. The principals in Van Horn's (1989) study were indeed creating a commitment to the education of students with disabilities in their schools. Tyler (1983) points out that effective principals are very much aware of the symbolism of even the most mundane of their administrative acts, and that they use even the most ordinary occasions to demonstrate their beliefs. By embracing special education, the principals in this study conveyed to the rest of the school that students with disabilities have a place in the school (Biklen, 1985).

3. *Principals are reactive rather than proactive in the delivery of special education services.* Despite the fact that the elementary school principal is in a position to determine the day-to-day effect that PL 94-142 has on the general education program (Hanson, 1986), it is still true that the principals observed in these research investigations are generally reacting to special education decisions made outside of their schools. It was never a question of whether the special education programs would be a part of their schools, but was rather a matter of accommodating those programs once the principals learned that they were required to do so. The beliefs and attitudes of the principals about students with disabilities led them to react positively to the creation of special education programs in their schools and to create a climate of acceptance for students with disabilities.

Basically, it appears that these principals accepted the reactive nature of their part in the special education initiative. They recognize the constraints placed upon them by the interpretation of the law or central office directives. Brown (1981) points out, however, that principals can be creative within the constraints of federal and state laws. The exploration of building-level alternatives, development of working teams, provisions for mainstreaming, staff inservices, and the encouragement of interactions between students with and those without disabilities are all examples of the ways the five principals in these studies employed creativity and initiative in accommodating students with disabilities and special education programs in their schools.

At the secondary level, both principals felt that special education was no different from other departments in their schools. Yet no future plans for students with disabilities were being actively pursued. The impetus for change appeared to come from the outside—from the central office and/or state sources. It remains to be seen whether, in the future, these principals will decide to behave in a proactive manner and recruit special education programs to their schools. To date, they have followed directives and waited for new mandates; but their discretion may be increased as their commitment, ownership, and resourcefulness grow. However, special education waivers will be necessary for some aspects of inclusion to emerge.

4. *Principals rely on the central office special education staff for direct support and consultation, rather then direct involvement with building-level programs.* The principals in these studies enjoyed a great deal of autonomy in the day-to-day management of programs for students with disabilities. These principals had been nominated by the special education administrator for the studies because of their success in accommodating special education students and programs in their schools. The principals had developed a certain level of trust with the director and, therefore, were allowed to experiment with special education innovations in their schools with little involvement by the district office. The directors pointed out that there were principals in many schools who needed to be monitored more closely in order to ensure that regulations would be followed and that students were receiving an appropriate educational program.

This type of trusting relationship with the special education administration appeared to allow the principals to make independent decisions about their own students and programs, within the constraints of the law. It also meant that the principals in these studies were able to involve their own staffs in the decision-making process, which fostered a sense of ownership of the programs by the entire school. No one felt that any outside forces—such as the district office—was dictating how the program should be operated at his or her school.

The principals in these studies were quick to point out, however, that their special education director was an important source of information for them. These principals on occasion sensed their own lack of knowledge about disabling conditions or placement options, and they relied heavily on their director in those instances. Betz (1977) and Brown (1981) have suggested that the director of special education is used most frequently by principals as a source of information. It was apparent that the five principals felt that it was important to maintain a positive relationship with their directors; the special education directors, for their part, realized that they could affect special education to a large degree by acting as a facilitator to the principal (Brown, 1981).

5. *The contextual factors surrounding the school appear to make a difference in the work of the principal, but they do not appear to have a significant impact on the acceptance of special education students and programs in the school.*   Murphy (1988) points out that the district context in which principals work is a major environmental condition that has been largely ignored in studies of instructional leadership. He believes that district-level forces shape and direct principal behaviors, that district characteristics can affect the implementation of instructional programs, and that certain opportunities and constraints on the behavior of principals are created by the organizational setting in which they work. He further believes that researchers have largely ignored community influences on the exercise and interpretation of instructional leadership behaviors. Dwyer et al. (1985) believe that principals' actions are also swayed by state and federal programs.

The principals in these studies, as detailed in each case, certainly appeared to be affected by the context in which they worked. But these contextual differences mainly affected the way that each principal managed his or her time, rather than their overall attitude about the acceptance of special education students and programs into their schools. While the urban principal might spend more time dealing with the personal day-to-day needs of both general and special education students, he or she is no less accepting of special education than the rural or suburban principal. It does appear that principals' own beliefs have as much impact on their acceptance of and behavior toward special education as the contextual factors of the school or community.

IMPLICATIONS

A principal can promote acceptance of special education and of students with disabilities through modeling and symbolic behaviors that demonstrate their own feelings about inclusion. Principals should be involved with students with disabilities and display their willingness to accept such students in order to influence staff to do the same. These modeling and symbolic behaviors will set the inclusion of students with disabilities as a priority for the school.

The importance of the principal's attitude cannot be emphasized enough. The development of a positive relationship between those involved in general and special education, as well as the establishment of educating students with disabilities as a priority, can only be accomplished if the attitude of the principal is positive.

School officials responsible for the selection and professional development of principals should attempt to determine the beliefs and attitudes of candidates and search out those who are willing to assume responsibility for all students, regardless of individual differences. The need for principals who are willing to work with students with disabilities despite any fears or misconceptions must be met if special education programs are to be accepted in a school.

Beyond modeling and symbolic behaviors, the principal must also encourage staff development among both regular and special education personnel. This need for knowledge about students with disabilities is substantial, and staff members can be important sources of information to one another. Opportunities for collaborative staff-development activities can result in an increase in professional knowledge, as well as the development of a positive relationship between regular and special education personnel.

The inclusion of students with disabilities requires the principal and special education administrator to work together in identifying and developing behaviors, resources, and follow-up activities necessary to support changes in service and staff assignments such as instructional teaming. Special education administrators must assist principals in the identification of behaviors and practices that may facilitate the inclusion of students with disabilities. Special education administrators must also identify what principals need to know, what the expected outcomes are, and the best means to accomplish the goals set for school-based programs.

Special education administrators and principals need to identify building-level leadership. Decentralization and the departmental structure of high schools require many special education teachers to view themselves as agents of change in order to encourage regular educators to accept students with disabilities. Special and regular educators must communicate with each other in the identification of needs and practices.

Special education administrators must review their own evaluation process and those of principals to determine each one's responsibility for and authority over decision making. Our observations of and personal experiences with many principals suggest that there is little accountability for what happens concerning special education programs in their schools. However, with the advent of site-based management and school-level decision making, principals, along with their staff members and community councils, must become familiar with the issues that accompany a home-school policy for students with disabilities. In time, experimentation with alternative and preventive programs will emerge and change local practices within the school district as a whole. Intradistrict choice programs also need to be considered in the education of students with disabilities.

Valesky and Hirth's (1992) survey of state directors of special education indicates that preservice programs for school principals do not adequately prepare them to manage school-based programs for students with disabilities. Many states are beginning to require a general survey course for their teachers. Over the past 5 years, 32 state directors have introduced inservice training for practicing principals through the National Academy on the Principalship (CASE Report, 1993). These studies suggest principal training is a must if inclusion is to be successful.

In summary, as the paradigms of education change and district accountability for special education increases, principals, their school faculties, and district special education personnel must find new ways to use their resources in an integrated or merged system of delivery. A shared responsibility for students with disabilities that begins with principals assuming ownership of special education programs is the key to an effective education for all students.

ILLUSTRATIVE CASE

I was late for a meeting with Dale Michael, the Director of ALT, a special education cooperative unit in our area. Dale was just introducing the last of the six elementary principals when I arrived.

Dale thanked the members of the group for coming and turned to me. "Val, did you want to say anything before we begin?" I quickly offered my apologies for being late and sat down. The meeting was held in my middle school because a number of students with disabilities who had been fully included in most of their elementary schools would be advancing to my school in the next 2 years.

Dale reported that the cooperative's experience in facilitating full inclusion using Sailor's five criteria had been successful in three of the six districts in which it had been tried. While not all parents were requesting or pushing for inclusion, the expectation was that parents with students who had already been integrated would want the option of inclusion to remain available to their children. As Dale and the elementary principals discussed their experience with inclusion, I saw the handwriting on the wall. After the meeting, I approached Dale and the other principals of elementary schools that feed into my school. I quickly learned that three students with disabilities were coming to my middle school next year.

Since it was late February, I asked Dale and one of the principals well known to my staff to come to my next building-based team meeting to discuss their experiences with inclusion and its possible implications for us. During that meeting, my middle school team leaders basically concluded that the middle school philosophy that we subscribed to required a teaming concept and the heterogeneous grouping of students. We already had in place multi-level teams of teachers of grades 6, 7, and 8 who met for a common planning period. With four special education staff members serving students with learning disabilities in self-contained and resource programs and one self-contained program for students with moderate and multiple disabilities, the implications for inclusion appeared significant. Was inclusion for everyone? Were we going to do away with the current program structure? Who was prepared to begin? We had been discussing ways to include the special education staff more in our team activities; it was imperative now, especially if inclusion was going to become the operative policy of the district. The building team leaders concluded that we had better inform the staff and begin a dialogue on inclusion.

After 2 hours of discussion on inclusion with Dale and the invited elementary principal, the team leaders and I asked the staff for their observations and questions. Our staff of 30 professionals and 15 classified personnel, representing the six planning teams across grades 6 through 8, generated over 60 questions. These were categorized according to eight themes. A frequency tally was recorded for those questions that arose most often.

Staff Feedback

Themes	Questions
Definitions	What is a working definition of inclusion?
	How are the definitions of regular education initiative (REI), mainstreaming, and least restrictive environment (LRE) related to the definition of inclusion?
Benefits	How are targeted benefits chosen for the typical and disabled students in an inclusive classroom?
	Will regular students "suffer" because of inclusion?
	What benefits do teachers gain from including students with disabilities and/or special education staff in their classrooms?
Inclusion	Do we have to do this?
	Does inclusion mean integrating *all* students with disabilities, *all* day? (8)
	Does it mean one child with a disability in each class?
	Does it mean students with different disabilities included in the same class? (4)

Is inclusion more costly? (10)

Does it require additional staff? (4)

What is the number of special education students per grade level? (3)

Will inclusion work be possible with only one or two teachers per grade level? (3)

Aren't some students better educated in smaller groups?

When is inclusion *not* appropriate?

Collaborative teaching

What are some examples of co-teaching?

When co-teaching across classrooms, how many classes can a special education teacher get to in a day?

How many classes will be co-taught each day? (4)

How much planning time is needed for co-teaching? (7)

How are partners for co-teaching chosen? Are personality inventories used?

Does co-teaching require a teacher per grade level?

Will special education teachers become aides in the regular classroom?

How do we co-teach and still make ourselves available to work with selected students individually?

How do we include nonacademic teachers on the teams?

Are general education teachers expected to learn the curricula and instruction techniques used by special education teachers?

How do we schedule and distribute related-service personnel across classes? (3)

Who's the boss on the team?

Introducing inclusion

How do we begin? (3) One student at a time?

What are some strategies for changing attitudes toward inclusion? (7)

Can we experiment with both inclusion and pullout programs?

How do we encourage peer acceptance?

Can we ever achieve acceptance without labelling?

When do you involve the parents of the "typical student?" How do we deal with parents who refuse to have their child participate in an inclusive classroom? (2)

How do we schedule for planning on a daily basis?

Outcomes, curriculum, and standards

How are the outcome requirements for all students, standards, and criteria met? (4)

How are gifted students challenged in an inclusive classroom?

Are there concerns here unique to a middle and high school curriculum as compared to that of an elementary school?

Are some subjects more easily adapted to inclusion? Is science easier to adapt?

Can we evaluate the student with disabilities on our traditional report card? What about grading?

Do we include these youngsters in standardized state competency tests? All of them?

Administrative support	Will administrators allow for necessary planning time? What role will they play?
Law, rules, and regulations	Is additional legislation needed to support inclusion? Will the law require collaboration and co-teaching? Will new certification patterns be developed?

At the end of the session with the staff, the building leadership team asked me to prepare an agenda for a meeting with Dale Michael and my three elementary school principal colleagues to address staff concerns.

The Leadership Tasks

1. How would you order the questions for the discussion with your colleagues?
2. Are some of the questions non-issues?
3. Are your own concerns well expressed in the staff listing of concerns and questions? Where will you stand on inclusion?
4. What discrepancies do you see in the way you currently program for students with disabilities in your school and what might be expected with the movement to inclusion?
5. Who will be the advocate for inclusion?
6. What are the next steps you envision, depending upon whether:
   a. you support inclusion or
   b. you will hold off on your commitment to support inclusion?

REFERENCES

Bank Street College of Education. (1982). *The school principal and special education: Basic functions for principals who have special education programs in their schools with competencies needed to perform the role.* New York: Author. (ERIC Document Reproduction Service No. ED 228)

Betz, M.L. (1977). *The development of building principal's competencies in the administration of programs for the handicapped.* Unpublished doctoral dissertation, Indiana University.

Biklen, D. (1985). *Achieving the complete school.* New York: Teachers College Press.

Bossert, S., Dwyer, D., Rowan, B., & Lee, G. (1982). The instructional management role of the principal. *Educational Administration Quarterly, 18,* 34–64.

Brown, J. (1981). *The role of elementary principals in the delivery of special education services.* Unpublished doctoral dissertation, Indiana University, Bloomington.

Burrello, L., Schrup, M., & Barnett, B. (1988). *The principal as the special education instructional leader. The principal's training simulator in special education.* (U.S. Department of Education, Office of Special Education Grant number G008730038). Unpublished manuscript, Indiana University, Bloomington.

Caetano, N.P. (Ed.). (1978). P.L. 94-142: The principal and special education. *National Elementary Principal, 58*(1), 10–47.

CASE Report to Executive Committee on National Academy on Principalship on Special Education. (1993). Bloomington: Indiana University.

Cochrane, P.V., & Westling, D.L. (1977). The principal and mainstreaming: Ten suggestions for success. *Education Leadership, 34,* 506–510.

DeClue, L. (1990). *The Principal's role in managing special education programs at the elementary level.* Unpublished doctoral dissertation, Indiana University, Bloomington.

DuClos, C., Litwin, B., Meyers, L., & Ulrich, H. (1977). *Mainstreaming exceptional children: A guideline for the principal.* Westora: University of Illinois. (ERIC Document Reproduction Service No. ED 151 991)

Dwyer, D., Lee, G., Barnett, B., Filby, N., & Rowan, B. (1985). *Understanding the principal's contribution to instruction: Seven principals, seven stories.* San Francisco: Far West Laboratory.

Gage, K.H. (1979). The principal's role in implementing mainstreaming. *Educational Leadership, 36,* 575–577.

Hanson, L. (1986). *Elementary school principal's perceptions of their role regarding Public Law 94-142: The first decade.* Unpublished doctoral dissertation, Northern Illinois University.

Hyatt, N. (1987). *Perceived competencies and attitudes of a select group of elementary school administrators relative to preparations and experience in administering special education programs.* Unpublished doctoral dissertation, The College of William and Mary, Williamsburg, VA.

Keilbaugh, W.S. (1980). Special education administrators: Their perception of the degree of difficulty installing selected components of Public Law 94-142 (Doctoral Dissertation, Temple University, 1980). *Dissertation Abstracts International, 41,* 201A.

Leibfried, M. (1984, November). Improving one's attitude toward special education programs: The principal's role is instrumental. *NASSP Bulletin,* pp. 110–113.

Lincoln, Y., & Guba, E. (1985). *Naturalistic inquiry.* Beverly Hills: Sage Publications.

McLaughlin, M.W. (1993). What matters most in teachers' workplace context? In Little, J. & McLaughlin, M. (Eds.). *Teachers' work: Individuals, colleagues, and contexts* (pp. 79–103). Columbia, NY: Teachers College Press.

Murphy, J. (1988). Methodological, measurement, and conceptual problems in the study of instructional leadership. *Educational Evaluation and Policy Analysis, 10,* 117–139.

O'Rourke, A.R. (1980). A comparison of principals and teacher attitudes toward handicapped students and the relationship between those attitudes and school morale of handicapped students. (Doctoral Dissertation, The University of Nebraska–Lincoln, 1979). *Dissertation Abstracts International, 1980, 40,* 3954A.

Payne, R., & Murray, C. (1974). Principal's attitudes toward integration of the handicapped. *Exceptional Children, 41,* 123–126.

Rude, H.A., & Rubadeau, R.J. (1992). Priorities for principals as special education leaders. *The Special Education Leadership Review, 1*(1), 55–61.

Schon, D. (1987). *Educating the reflective practitioner.* San Francisco: Jossey-Bass.

Sergiovanni, T. (1984). Leadership and excellence in schooling. *Educational Leadership, 41*, 4–20.

Siskin, L. (1990). *Different worlds: The department as context for high school teaching* (Report No. P 90-120). Stanford, CA: Center for Research in the Context of Secondary School Teaching, Stanford University.

Smith, T.E.C. (1978). *High school principals attitude toward the handicapped and the work study program.* Kansas City: International Council for Exceptional Children. (ERIC Document Reproduction Service No. ED 153 353)

Stedman, L. (1987). It's time we changed the effective schools formula. *Phi Delta Kappan, 69*, 215–224.

Tyler, R. (1983). A place called school. *Phi Delta Kappan, 64*, 462–464.

Van Horn, G. (1989). *The principal's role in managing special education programs at the secondary level.* Unpublished doctoral dissertation, Indiana University, Bloomington.

Valesky, T., & Hirth, M. (1992). Survey of the states: Special education knowledge requirements for school administrators. *Exceptional Children, 58*(5), 399–405.

Vergason, G.A., Smith, F.V., & Wyatt, K.E. (1975). Questions for administrators about special education. *Theory into Practice, 14*(2), 99–104.

Zettel, J. (1979). *The impact of 94-142 upon general education administrators.* Columbus, OH: University Council for Educational Administration. (ERIC Document Reproduction Service No. ED 175 147)

9

The Special Educator as Leader

In this chapter, we return to our discussion of Newmann's criteria for restructuring (1991) and Lipp's (1992) concept of the perspective shift (introduced in Chapter 1) and their implications for the role of the special education leader. We discuss the evolution of this role that accompanies the change from a parallel to a unified or inclusive system (CASE Future Agenda, 1993, McLaughlin & Warren, 1992; Stainback & Stainback, 1984). We close this chapter by emphasizing a change in the conceptualization of educational administrators as managers prepared and socialized within a highly technical and managerial school of thought, to one of leaders as intellectual and moral actors within a symbolic and cultural framework.

UPDATING THE CONTEXT OF CHANGE

The most continuous and potent force behind the growth of special education has been the intensive lobbying efforts of parents and certain professional-interest groups. These groups have aligned themselves to expand the definition of disability, and, as a result, the number and types of students served under IDEA and its amendments have increased. In the 1990s, the addition of traumatic brain injury and autism has brought the number of federally recognized disability categories to 14. The universal inclusion of students with behavior disorders and attention deficit and hyperactivity disorders are soon to be written into the law as well. Each of these four initiatives has been developed in a time of heated professional debate over the concept of full inclusion and the Regular Education Initiative (REI). Despite the arguments of Gartner and Lipsky, (1987), Sailor (1991), and Skrtic (1991a), who contend that placement in special education programs has not had significant results as compared to placement in programs for typical students, these initiatives to recognize additional categories of disability have proceeded. The political will of Congress is un-

249

shaken by professional arguments that appear equivocal and cannot be reconciled with the political largess of meeting a constitutent request. Congress continues to ensure that dollars that otherwise might be targeted to other educational entitlements or discretionary programs are protected under IDEA. Skrtic (1991b) identifies a number of opponents of REI who make the argument for a special designation under law.

While the new Section 504 amendments stipulate that in the case of students with learning needs not identified under IDEA it is the responsibility of the general system to provide adaptive instructional services, many special educators are skeptical, believing that these students will be referred for services under existing disability categories. An assistant superintendent of secondary education in a progressive Minnesota district explained, "We stretch the definitions."

Historically, the leadership challenge of the 1960s through the 1980s was one of gaining access to or developing new services for students with disabilities in the public schools. In the 1980s, the calls for accountability, quality of services, and increased relevance of education to post-school life became the predominant leadership challenges for educators. In an earlier work, Sage and Burrello (1986) described the forces affecting the delivery of free and appropriate educational services to students with disabilities. Table 1 presents those forces, remnants of which continue to exert pressure to maintain current practices even in light of emerging changes.

Through the 1990s, the leadership challenge to educators will be to continue to meet the demands brought on by an increasing diversity of student needs and to heed advocates' calls for individual attention in times of dynamic change. The demands on the professional bureaucracy are also increasing in complexity. Trying to treat everyone equally in a political environment characterized by resource scarcity threatens bureaucratic standards of student performance. It also assumes that a stable environment will prevail over time and that the human skills necessary to teach and manage are constant across all groups involved in the enterprise. Rather than pursue standard criteria to determine which services should be provided for students with a diversity of needs, it is more appropriate to adopt a perspective that accommodates a need for novel services. Finally, a perspective measuring organizational worth solely in terms of increasing performance is limited, because in times of dynamic change the organization also needs an assessment of its capacity to adjust and adapt. In short, the question is whether personnel in the modern school can learn to problem-solve and innovate more effectively. This requires changes in services and service patterns and in relationships between

Table 1. Factors driving and restraining social change

Driving forces for change	Forces restraining change
General social climate	**Ideological factors**
Human rights	Specialized services
Civil rights	Security of segregation
Maximum feasible participation	Profesionalism
Activism	Conservatism
Consumerism	Classism
Tolerance for variance	**Bureaucratic factors**
(sex, race, religion, etc.)	Organizational maintenance
The courts	Technical mystique
Ensurance of minority rights	Job protection
Equal protection clause	Unionization
Right to education	**Pragmatic factors**
Right to treatment	Political influence
Due process	Power of identity
Nondiscriminatory classification	Visibility
Legislation	Categorical finance
State and federal	
Zero reject	
Mandatory services	
State-wide planning	
Advocacy	
Financial reform	
Manpower preparation	
Individualized education programs	
Procedural safeguards	
Least restrictive alternative	
New service models	

providers, consumers, and supporters. Skrtic (1986) has contrasted these perspectives in Table 2.

Futurists suggest that our world, our place in it, and especially our schools will need to embrace change and become more accustomed to its constantly increasing pace. According to Skrtic (1991a) one of the organizing principles of schools needs to be an ongoing adaptation perspective that will accommodate diversity rather than attempt to standardize students. This principle must also accommodate the pace of change, rather than simply classify it as a private-sector phenomena (Osborne & Gaebler, 1992). It is Skrtic's (1986, 1991a, 1991b) view that special education is based upon an adhocratic organizing principle and is therefore in conflict with the professional bureaucratic structure of the general system of education. Special education involves ad hoc groups with membership based on interest, expertise, and jurisdiction; these groups use multidisciplinary assessment data to determine student eligibility, plan individual programs, and determine the least restrictive environment in which

Table 2. Structural differences among professional cultures in school organizations

	Machine bureaucracy	Professional bureaucracy	Adhocracy
Work	Simple	Complex	Complex
Coordination	Standard processes	Standard skills	Innovation
Coupling	Sequential	Pooled/loose	Evolutionary
Product/service	Standard	Standard	Novel
Organizational measure	Performance	Performance	Problem solving
Environment	Stable	Stable	Dynamic

Adapted from Skrtic (1986).

each student can be placed. The general or regular system creates separate and parallel structures to preserve its program regularities. These separate structures are limiting those who benefit from the core curriculum and technology of instruction to a cultural elite and increasing the liabilities of an underclass of students.

With a separate system comes increasing bureaucracy and different standards that create administrative redundancies and less of a sense of ownership among teachers and administrators. While each system's processes remain intact, they function within a more loosely coupled arrangement of the schools as a whole. Students are still expected to meet separate program standards that may not allow them to compete with their peers in the typical programs. The growth of educational entitlements like IDEA and Chapter 1 programs have occurred under the assumption of a stable future. But our continued inability to restructure our country's economy to meet the challenges of the 1980s and early 1990s has led to uncertain times. Leading and managing in a dynamic environment requires a new set of organizing principles. The restructuring agenda of American business, with its economic implications, is having a major impact on schools.

Osborne and Gaebler (1992) are calling for more than the application of Total Quality Management (TQM) principles to education. They believe that TQM principles relate to: 1) an outcomes or result orientation, 2) a focus on the student and community as customers, 3) decentralized rather than centralized management, 4) prevention rather than remediation to achieve quality, and 5) a systems approach rather than an events or pattern approach. "Precisely because Deming developed his ideas for private businesses, his approach ignores other . . . principles" (Osborne & Gaebler, 1992, p. 22). Osborne and Gaebler (1992) believe TQM fails to take into account several factors that they suggest differentiate the public from the private sector. For example, they point out the issue of monopoly in the public sector, because it prevents the element of choice, which fosters competition in the private sector. They believe most public sector enterprises focus on spending, rather than earning, money. They argue that all business people know that they are in the business of making a profit, whereas public-sector employees have an unclear mission.

In addition, Osborne and Gaebler (1992) include two other principles to guide the transformation of government agencies from bureaucratic organizations to entrepreneurial ones. The concept of community empowerment and ownership, rather than leaders serving as policy makers or captains who steer rather than row the boats of practice, are among the factors that they feel will make government better. They argue that "the central failure of government today is one of means not ends" (Osborne & Gaebler, 1992, p. xxi).

Rather than following rules and procedures, public-sector employees are given the responsibility and authority to find the best way to reach a goal. Public policy makers are urged to give up managing the schools or parks department and exert their energies in determining the proper ends, rather than the means. Skrtic's concept of adhocracy is an organizational form compatible with Osborne and Gaebler's 10 principles.

Education leaders, especially in urban, and some parts of suburban, America have begun to reduce the conflict between the predominant organizing form of the general system and the ad hoc nature of the parallel special education system. New organizational and curricular forms are emerging that emulate the characteristics of adhocracies. From charter schools, to magnet and thematic schools, to microsociety curricula, school systems are empowering groups of teachers, administrators, and parents to create alternatives to the mass model of schooling for the first time in American public-educational history.

Table 3, from Burrello and Lashley (1992) presents a set of contextual forces that underlie the current context of schooling and the future agenda of special education.

The current context of trends and issues facing special education leadership personnel are rooted in the past but are magnified by current fiscal constraints. The impact of these constraints and of school equity and funding issues have increased since the early 1970s to the point where more than half the states are affected in the 1990s. Fiscal constraints and the associated aspects of special education rules and regulations have prevented the kind of sweeping innovation that characterized the development of special education in the early 1970s. The rule-and-regulation mentality that has protected special education's narrow interests is a key inhibitor of other social values

Table 3. Contextual forces leading to a paradigm shift in education

Current Forces SUPPORT EXISTING FORCES	Emerging Forces SUPPORT CHANGING FORCES
POLITICAL/BUREAUCRATIC Special Interest Special categorical services Special funding	**POLITICAL/ECONOMIC/SOCIAL** Market driven by student and parental choice Competition of private schools Generic uncertainty Changing tastes, options
COERCIVE Top-down Externally driven by state and federal mandates State & federal monitoring of professionals	**EMPOWERMENT** Professional educator taking more ownership Professional status being driven by peers
TECHNICAL Disciplinary language Disciplinary specialist teams Distinctive rules & regulations Child focused interventions Centralized & controlled by few	**INNOVATION** Common language Teacher focused teams Emphasis on similarities Organizational focused interventions Distributive and accessible to all
SYMBOLIC Pity Dependency/scapegoating Missionary/advocacy Expertise Ad hoc	**CULTURAL** All students can learn Faculties assuming responsibility for all Self-managed teams finding alternatives in an adhocracy

From Burrello, L. and Lashley, C. (1992). On organizing for the future: The destiny of special education. In K. Waldron, A. Riester, and J. Moore (Eds.), *Special education: The challenge of the future*. San Francisco: Edwin Mellen Press; reprinted by permission.

necessary in the pursuit of educational outcomes for students with disabilities. Just meeting the requirements of IDEA leaves little time or support for innovation. The federal government has been the primary source of large grants to support innovative educational programming in the past 25 years. A number of innovative practices have been supported, particularly in the area of students with the most severe disabilities (Sailor, 1991). But local innovation has slowed with increased litigation, and the paradigm of a continuum of placements has restricted creative thinking concerning the education of students with disabilities. Moving education interventions from student-driven to organizational imperatives for restructuring increases the importance of the expertise of special education personnel to the restructuring effort. The need for a collaborative work culture is increased when innovation and problem solving are encouraged and supported in order to meet the needs of vulnerable students. It is not surprising that staff members are often afraid to take on more responsibility with little support or time to learn new strategies for inclusion. As policy makers are calling for more accountability and for market-driven choice plans, the pressure escalates for the special education delivery system to support students with learning needs who might not typically qualify for specialized instructional services. Teachers in classrooms across the nation feel the demand for individualized instruction independent of a curriculum and state achievement testing system that measures success only in terms of high academic performance.

Quality and cost are subjected to new public scrutiny to determine whether special education is beneficial. Are special educators setting high expectations for the students in their programs? Do students with disabilities ever leave special education once they are referred and placed? If and when they leave, how well do they perform in the regular program? Do they get diplomas and graduate? Are graduates succeeding in post-secondary education programs? When they leave school, are they prepared for the world of work? What is the post-school adjustment rate and employability of graduates of special education programs? Are students with severe disabilities being prepared to enter competitive or sheltered employment, or none at all? Maximizing the performance and the post-school adjustment of exceptional students are the twin imperatives for those involved in special education to consider. The planning and preparation for change is slowly beginning now.

THE SPECIAL EDUCATION LEADERSHIP TASK

Building a Unified System of Education

As Lipp's (1992) discussion of the policy shift from an emphasis on viewing special education exclusively to an emphasis on viewing it inclusively suggests, the most important leadership issue in the education of students with disabilities is the need to move beyond a separate, parallel structure toward a unified system of education. The starting point for creating such a system is a policy requiring that all students have access to services that support their unique learning needs. Students with disabilities should be included under this statement in three ways. First, "all students" does not differentiate those with disabilities as a distinctive group or category. Second, "being educated in schools" describes the setting in which any student, with or without disabilities, should receive his or her education. Third, "programs and services that support their unique learning needs" requires that schools provide for the needs of even those students who are functioning well below their potential because of some unique problem in learning or inability to perform certain tasks due to an impairment. Students with disabilities should not be singled out as needing specialized educational services in order to profit from supportive or unusual in-class instructional arrangements. Inclusion requires that the school district's mission statement reflect a philosophy and a set of beliefs that establish targeted outcomes for all students, regardless of their characteristics or educational needs. Accountability for students should rest with the personnel in the neighborhood school, who must accept responsibility for educating all students, helping them to pursue established system outcomes with their age-appropriate peers. Decision making should be shared among staff, parents, and students. Special educators should never accept sole responsibility for the education of a student with a disability, independent of the regular staff of the school. Services must be provided without labels and resources be drawn from all currently identified categorical programs in order to support students as much as possible within inclusive programs. Any student should be able to receive services outside of his or her age-appropriate classroom on a short-term basis as the need is determined by the student's individual support team, which would include parents, peers, and the student him- or herself.

McLaughlin and Warren (1992) outline the factors that must underlie this policy option. School systems must express beliefs and policies that proclaim their commitment "to equal access to high quality instruction" in their home schools, leading to outcomes inclusive of all students, "regardless of their individual characteristics or needs" (p. 31). This policy assumes local-school responsibility for planning and implementing appropriate educational programs—with support, when requested, from specialized personnel—that provide services leading to desired outcomes. While a small number of students may receive specialized services outside of the home or neighborhood school, they should remain the responsibility of the school-level administration and staff.

The implications for special education leadership are profound. Having formerly developed and maintained a separate professional bureaucratic structure with clearly defined roles and responsibilities, the special educator as leader must now portray programs as inclusive, child-centered, demonstrating instructional effectiveness, and projecting a positive image concerning the education of all students. These symbolic behaviors require supporting local school programs and school-centered decision making concerning appropriate educational programs for all students (Burrello & Zadnik, 1986).

Bennis and Nanus (1985) describe symbolic leaders as communicators of purpose and vision, using words and symbols, convening others and helping them understand the mission of the enterprise. The special educator as leader in the twenty-first century must maintain an ongoing dialogue with the community of stakeholders. This requires talking to community members, in addition to parents and advocates. It requires demonstrating the relationship between education and training and the post-school contributions of students with disabilities to the community in which they live. It also requires demonstrating to parents of students without disabilities how their child's education and learning will be affected—in positive and balanced, rather than zero-sum, terms. Dispelling the assumption that students with disabilities get more attention in the regular program, and that the typical child will suffer as a result, requires developing clearly defined outcomes for all students and customized instructional arrangements to serve all students more appropriately. Local leaders need to demonstrate the positive effects of integrating and educating all students together. The benefits of cooperative learning, taking responsibility for the learning of others, expecting more of oneself than others expect, and sharing the expertise that special educators bring to students and staff are necessary conditions for obtaining the support of all stakeholders in the community.

The district's vision and beliefs need to be inclusive of all students. *All* needs to be defined by example and demonstrative indicators in order for members of the school community to understand what the term really means. Gaining the participation of students and community members with disabilities during the initial development of the vision that will guide the district and local school is an important step in ensuring that their voices are heard. During strategic planning activities, it is important to ensure that goals and objectives be developed for everyone and that they not be limited to performance criteria that require skills that are not feasibly attainable by or relevant to students with disabilities. Clearly, the goal-setting and strategy-selection process should be informed by an understanding of how special education fits into the overall mission and objectives of restructuring the schools. For example, the role of teacher-assistance teams should garner the expertise of special education professionals to prevent undesirable student behavior from interfering with student success in the classroom. Finally, modeling by the central staff is critical—principals and teachers must demonstrate the philosophy of inclusiveness among themselves, as well as encouraging students to do so.

The policy domains that are crucial to a unified system of education for all students emphasize inclusion in home school and regular program first, with specialized instructional support provided as necessary. Other policies that need attention include those governing unified outcomes, accountability and recognition/reward systems, integrated local funding, school-centered decision making and discretion concerning increased resources, and collaborative work designs for all staff.

Working with other local directors and the state department of education is necessary in examining state-level rules and regulations, some of which will need to be suspended until such time as they can be re-written to support a unified system. At least four states, Colorado, Iowa, New Mexico, and Michigan, have begun serious public debate on rule changes that will be necessary under IDEA. In preparation for that debate, the education community needs to come to a consensus on policy issues related to school restructuring and inclusion. Examining the results of model programs and their implications for rules changes is a fruitful endeavor, since policy is best informed by practice (Elmore & McLaughlin, 1988). Other areas of concern to administrators at every level include collective bargaining, funding, and the relation of rules and funding in terms of assessment, identification, placement, and personnel usage. Teacher preparation, staff development, and incentives for supporting start-up and continuing maintenance of efforts within an inclusive school and a unified system are all issues that deserve significant discussion and attention. Finally, a commitment must be made to school improvement for all students and the requirement of a full continuum of services must be met in order for the next phase of special education reform and restructuring to proceed.

Supporting Local-School Empowerment and School-Centered Decision Making

For Lipp (1992), the movement from centralized to decentralized services to support students with disabilities in their home school requires that school faculties have a clear understanding of the district policy on inclusion, including the outcomes that need to be targeted as they plan curricula and develop instructional strategies. For this perspective shift, it is important to combine the shift in power from the central office to individual schools with the shift from a specially designed central curriculum to locally designed, school-based curricula.

In a restructured school with an outcome orientation, the outcomes for all students need to include those for students with disabilities. In addition to these general outcomes, students with disabilities may also have particular sensory or physical outcomes related to their inability to perform certain tasks. Ultimately, outcomes that emphasize independent living and developing and maintaining personal and social relationships are critical to school life, as well as to life on the job. Finally, job preparation and transition to the world of work must be explicitly addressed in the school curriculum. The need to create opportunities for the socialization of students with disabilities with their peers who do not have disabilities is becoming increasingly recognized as important to their learning and to their development of a peer-support network.

These outcome needs peculiar to students with disabilities require ongoing staff dialogue and discussions, which are critical to special education staff in their interactions with typical teachers and with principals and team leaders. The special education leader's function is to create occasions for interaction to support faculties in building joint models for their outcomes, curriculum, and instruction. The Council of Administrators of Special Education (1993) prepared a model for a discussion of unified outcomes that was part of a national debate (see chap. 7, this volume). In their planning model, which is based on the CASE Future Agenda, centrally determined policy initiatives such as those defining outcomes for all students and mandating accountability systems, are matched with a set of action recommendations that are site based and require the vision and personal commitment of faculty and staff. The policy cycle needs to be recreated in the action cycle at the level on which the curriculum and instruction are adapted to accommodate differences in students. In Figure 1, the relationships between centrally determined policy and outcomes and school-based actions or responses are depicted. These cycles occur and recur, with changes in policy being made when actions can be justified as positive and appropriate to student and community needs.

Senge (1990) believes that a shared vision must ultimately attract participants because it shares elements with their own beliefs about what is desirable and significant in their mutual practice. Senge argues that enrolling people this way better ensures implementation than enrolling people through manipulation or regulations. This occurs only when the school staff have opportunities for collegial interaction and support.

Johnson (1990), Little (1981), and Little and McLaughlin's (1993) research on the teachers' workplace has shown that teachers can change their curriculum and teaching practices to accommodate diversity in the contemporary classroom when there are "school-level structures set up to foster planning and problem-solving and the con-

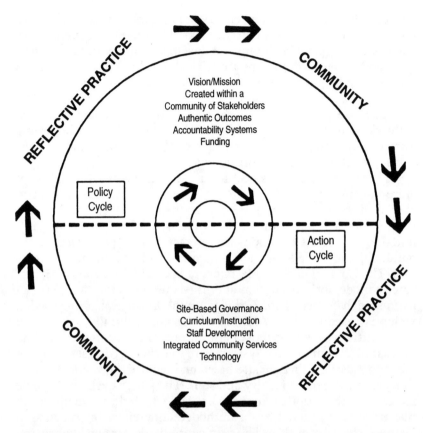

Figure 1. Policy and action cycles: centrally driven policy and locally driven actions within a community of stakeholders. (From the Council of Administrators of Special Education. [1993]. *CASE future agenda for special education: Creating a unified system*. Albuquerque, NM: Author; reprinted by permission.)

sequent development of a supportive school-level professional community and opportunities for reflection" (Little & McLaughlin, 1993, p. 13). In high schools, Siskin (1990) identified the academic department as the professional community of greatest significance to teachers' norms of practice, conceptions of task, and attitudes about teaching and students. Van Horn (1989) confirmed this finding in his study of high schools and their support for more inclusionary practices in special education. Principals and teachers alike identified the department and the department chairperson as significant forces in creating a climate of support that helped them to make it through each day, and, more importantly, allowed them to experiment with new approaches, both within and across departments, to serving students with a variety of disabilities. In studying schools in which these professional communities existed, Little and McLaughlin (1993) found that:

> cohesive and highly collegial environments are also settings in which teachers report a high level of innovativeness, high levels of energy and enthusiasm, and support for personal growth and learning . . . where teachers are enthusiastic about their work, and where focus is upon devising strategies that enable all students to prosper. (p. 15d)

In Senge's (1990) conception, such environments are the foundation for a learning organization.

Once a joint conceptual model of outcomes is created, preparing staff to share their expertise and encouraging their design of innovative ways to build on student strengths is necessary in order to move beyond ideas to action. By supporting and encouraging teachers through joint modeling, district administrators and principals need to support curriculum building and instruction that focus on active learning inside and outside of school.

The efforts of advocates for inclusion and for serving the student locally need to be supported by direct and related service personnel within the climate and instructional organization of the individual school (see Burrello, Schrup, & Barnett, 1988). The support plan of each school will evolve over time and will require ongoing negotiation concerning supportive services as the student population being served changes and, along with it, the staff's capacity to educate students with a variety of individual learning needs. Fullan (1991) and Newmann (1991) suggest that initiatives that focus on changing structures are only the tip of the iceberg. Changing practices, behaviors, and skills will require much more time, and attacking underlying beliefs calls for a significantly longer-term commitment. A minimum of 3–5 years should be allotted for the complete realization of an inclusive school philosophy.

In addition to the barriers to change discussed above, Fullan (1991) and Fullan and Stiegelbauer (1991) remind us of six components to include when initiating individual technical assistance plans:

1. Develop a clear and describable strategy for change.
2. Set the stage for evolutionary planning within a consensus-building decision-making process.
3. Be prepared to institute technical assistance at the community, school, program, or classroom level.
4. Focus primarily on building collaborative work cultures in each program or service delivery setting.
5. Keep in mind the need to negotiate between the school and district and between the school and external audiences.

6. Establish an inquiry-oriented, ad hoc problem-coping and -monitoring mindset (one that encourages reflective thinking).

Building Collaborative-School Work Cultures

Assuming an inclusive school philosophy as expressed by Sailor (1991), this change strategy can be described as adaptive, rather than programmatic, in Berman's (1980) terms. In descending order of significance, an adaptive change strategy implies complexity rather than simplicity; its designers assume an unstable rather than stable environment and conflict over, rather than consensus on, goals; and uncertainty about the technology to implement the change is an ongoing problem for those involved.

Given a commitment to support an inclusive school change strategy in the education of students with disabilities, district policy is a necessary condition, but insufficient in itself. Individual schools require a true consensus on the place of these students in the school (Burrello et al., 1988). Burrello et al. (1988), DeClue (1990), and Van Horn, (1989) found that school principals were creating a consensus within their faculties and the school community. Principals themselves need to demonstrate that students with the severest of disabilities not only have the right to an education with their age-appropriate peers, but also need to belong to the school community if they are to attain the educational outcomes necessary for independent living, developing personal and social relationships, and, for many, obtaining a job in the community. Getting a school community to move beyond an apparent and working consensus to a true consensus is best accomplished by following the advice of Hemmings and Metz (1990) and Little and McLaughlin (1993), who suggest that teachers develop different goals for their diverse students, objectives that reflect conceptions of practice rooted not in the latest fad in education, or even in state or district policy pronouncements, but in teachers' decisions about how best to respond to the students in their classrooms. "Teachers are brokers, constructing educational arrangements that acknowledge the goals of society, characteristics of the students with whom they work, their professional judgment, and the character of the workplace context" (Little & McLaughlin, 1993, p. 21).

Creating the metaphor of schools as learning communities changes the focus of intervention. The traditional view of schools as formal organizations directs the attention of school policy makers and district leaders to structures, oversight and accountability, governance, and technology. Shifting the focus to a community metaphor swings leaders' attention to:

norms and beliefs of practice, collegial relations, shared goals, occasion for collaboration, problems of mutual support and mutual obligation. Metaphors which dominate presently illuminate less the important aspects of the school workplace and relegate to shadows what matters most to teachers and teaching—the character of the workplace as professional community. (Little & McLaughlin, 1993, p. 21)

Barth (1990), Johnson (1990), Little and McLaughlin (1993), and others suggest that two key questions should guide leadership practice: 1) How can school communities be formed in which student ownership and success are collective responsibilities rather than challenges for individual teachers? and 2) How can school cultures be transformed from rigid and solitary systems dominated by norms of privacy into communities whose members share their values openly with one another, reflect constantly on practice, actively critique current situations, and invent new ways of teaching and learning? These questions can begin to be answered if we adopt a collegial culture. Little (1981) describes four characteristics of a healthy collegial environment. First, all the adult staff members in a school **talk about practice regularly**. Second, all staff members engage in **observing each other in the practice of teaching and the administration of learning settings**. Third, the faculty **actively engages in planning and designing the curriculum, structures, processes, and systems** that they will implement according to their evolving models of learning and instruction. Fourth, in a collegial environment teachers are always **teaching each other** what they know about teaching, learning, and leading.

Developing a true consensus school by school in a district requires lengthy negotiations, professional development, and technical assistance, both in the community and inside the school itself. The school's work culture can be a significant barrier to change. The two questions posed by Barth (1990), Johnson (1990), and Little and McLaughlin (1993) illustrate the necessary focus for building a collaborate work culture.

From our experience to date, introducing the concept of a collaborative work culture to support mutual responsibility for students is of paramount concern to the special educator as well as the teacher of typical children. From elementary through middle schools to high schools, many special education teachers find that they have the most to lose in this transformation. They are threatened with the loss of their identity as specialists, as well as the loss of their own students, classrooms, and independent authority over the distinct program. They fear the reduction of their professional status when integrated into the regular classroom as co-teacher. They initially question their ability to teach typical students. General education teachers across all three levels share similar concerns. They are quick to question their ability to educate a student with disabilities and they insist that the expectations for these students are significantly different than those for typical students and cannot be accommodated without special provisions outside of the general classroom. They are unwilling to be held accountable for the progress of these students while they have full classes of typical students who also require increasingly more attention and concern. Getting teachers to come to grips with setting different performance standards for students with disabilities requires extensive discussion about competition, measurement, and equity. Concerns about student progress toward outcomes measured most often by state competency tests and by meeting requirements for post-secondary education need to be addressed.

Preparing the special education staff for the change to an inclusive school philosophy must be the responsibility of the special education leader. As quickly as principals, teacher leaders, and department chairpersons are brought on board, providing teacher support becomes a shared responsibility of the full district and school leadership. The means we have found to support the paradigm or perspective shift outlined by Lipp (1992) (see pp. 21–28, this volume) is to create ad hoc, vertical groups of regular and special education teachers, related service personnel, principals, local supervisors, and parents to review the outcomes we value for all students and the means by which it is felt that they can best be achieved. A careful search of the literature, followed by critical conversations, along with visits to other school districts and schools, will assist teachers in developing a statement of beliefs reaffirming a district policy on inclusion and home-school placement.

The inclusion initiative needs to be focused on achieving appropriate outcomes for all students. This initiative should also include a commitment to increase the capacity of all staff to effectively respond to the diverse learning styles of all students. These two goals illustrate the commitment of special education to participate as partners in building a unified system that keeps provisions for the needs of students with disabilities in proportion to those of all other students. These outcomes emphasize the unique contributions of special education to the mission of the whole school. Some sample belief and collaborative-practice statements are:

For schools to become instructionally effective for all students, a commitment to "equity and quality" for all will be required.

Models that allow maximum feasible participation in the regular program must include provisions for supportive services.

Regular class teachers must assume instructional responsibility for all students, including those with a need for special education support.

School districts will have in place "systems" of support within collaborative problem-solving structures characterized by:

> Teams focusing on outcomes for all students and the different environments where these outcomes should be demonstrated—classroom, hallway, cafeteria, home neighborhood, job setting, and so forth
>
> Teams co-planning for instruction in multiple settings and measuring performance on the basis of agreed-upon criteria
>
> Teams planning and encouraging through natural peer supports in the classroom, school, and out-of-school settings
>
> Teams ultimately accepting responsibility for one another and all students they share
>
> Teams adopting a problem-solving approach and regularly reflecting on their practice
>
> Teams planning their own staff development as their need for information, reflection, and evaluation emerges

With collegial teams in place, decisions tend to be better, implementation of decisions more thorough, morale and trust higher, and adult learning more energized and prolonged. Barth (1990) concludes that there is some evidence to suggest that students' motivation increases when they cooperate and experience the same benefits that adults enjoy in a collegial work place.

The next step involves a review of current student services and placements and the targeting of less restrictive placements. The movement toward inclusion requires making extensive technical assistance available to the building team designated to provide support. It is our recommendation that as the school year begins each fall, a team workshop be provided at each school for all the teachers and related-service staff who will participate in integration programming. The objectives of the workshop should include a review of individual educational planning, the key aspects of team building, the process of conducting team meetings using student data, outcome setting for all students, making instructional arrangements, and designing instructional adaptations for integrated students. Areas suitable for co-teaching, cooperative learning, and other forms of peer tutoring and peer networking need to be identified and preparations made to accommodate parental input and gain parental acceptance. Ten full days may be required to complete these professional development activities. A commitment should also be made to provide at least 2 half-days a month for team planning and reflection. District administrators should support team planning throughout the first year in order to ensure success. Regular staff meetings should include progress reports on the team and on individual student learning to foster an ongoing sense of ownership by the school community. If this strategy is well supported and the time well used, staff will not need to set aside as much time for such meetings after the first year of implementation—quarterly reflection and problem-solving sessions should be sufficient.

To conclude this discussion of school-level collaborative work cultures, we have prepared a cycle of learning based upon the work of Senge (1990). It is our contention that district- and school-level leaders pursue a leadership odyssey. Their odyssey may have taken them through management by objectives, situational leadership theory, visioning and strategy planning technology, and most recently Total Quality Management. We have found all of these theories and practices to be inadequate for educational purposes. We have constructed a model of leadership that reflects what we have learned about managing a cycle of learning. We are proposing an alternative framework that incorporates the views of several researchers, defining leadership in education as a process of purposing and culture building (Deal & Peterson, 1990, Viall, 1984), and of developing learning communities (Barth, 1990; Johnson, 1990; Little, 1981; Little & McLaughlin, 1993), directed toward achieving authentic outcomes (Newmann, 1991) in the context of generative learning and problem solving (Senge, 1990). These four leadership purposes and their relationship to one another are portrayed in Figure 2. We offer the cycle of learning as a construct to be promoted and managed democratically. People must come to manage themselves if they are to gain control of their practice and continuously improve it over time. The leadership task is to free people from their past paradigms and to open and support their inquiry into new forms of learning and development to keep pace with the constant, rapid change that threatens to overtake us. Within bureaucratic structures, learning will continue to wane. "That structure was invented to assure domination and control, and it will never produce freedom and self-actualization. You can't get there from here" (Clark & Meloy, 1989, p. 292). The cycle of learning is based on the essential elements listed by Clark and Meloy:

Democracy
Group authority and accountability

**DEVELOPING LEADERSHIP
AND
SCHOOL CAPACITIES FOR IMPROVEMENT**

- Purposing and culture building
- Developing learning communities
- Achieving high performance outcomes
- Generating learning and decision making

Purposing and culture Building

- Enrolling stakeholders
- Developing systemically shared values and vision
- Establishing mission and objectives
- Determining truthfully what is
- Identifying the decrepancy be-tween what is and what must be
- Inviting the tension for change

Developing schools as learning organizations

- Building a community of learners
- Developing and expanding leadership of staff
- Creating and supporting team learning
- Developing productive work practices and relationships
- Integrating community resources within curriculum and instruction
- Building a baseline database for accountability
- Recognizing individual and group learning and its contribution to team and community learning
- Nurturing good tries and embracing errors

Managing the
cycle of learning

Generative learning and decision making

- Watching student, program, and organizational performance
- Questioning with confidence every practice at least annually
- Providing useful information for decision makers
- Improving all aspects of the system continually
- Generating feedback through reflective dialogue
- Checking for equity and who benefits
- Reorganizing, regrouping, and redesigning the process
- Checking for consensus and meaning internally and externally

Achieving high
performance outcomes

- Identifying significant outcomes
- Developing curriculum/ instructional strategies
- Creating authentic learning tasks and experiences
- Providing high performance learning environments

Figure 2. The cycle of learning.

Variability, generality, and interactivity in work assignment
Individual and collective self-discipline and control
Group commitment to and consensus on preferred organizational
goals and means (Clark & Meloy, 1989, p. 292)

For the special educator as leader, the model is a means to promote the creation of inclusive school cultures. The special educator
can be an active participant in creating new schools based on democratic principles and conditions that support group consensus. With a
unique perspective gained from studying and planning for the most
vulnerable of students inside and outside the schools, the special educator, as the champion of adhocracy, can focus his or her efforts on
turning schools into structures that strive for organizational diversity
through ongoing dialogue and problem solving.

Supporting Transitions and the Evaluation of
Programs and Progress Toward Valued Student Outcomes

The last of the four major special education leadership tasks is drawn
from Lipp's (1992) discussion of the perspective shift in funding, advocacy, and liaison for transitions. The changes suggested in her paradigm shift include the use of funding and accounting formulas based
on the needs of whole programs or whole districts, rather than individual students, and a shift toward pursuing funds locally, rather than
at the federal level. The advocacy shift is from an emphasis on symbolic gestures aimed at obtaining services to monitoring rights guaranteed by law. The transitions are between the home and school at
the time of student entry into the public school system and between
school and the community during transitions to independent or supported living.

Starting with funding, Lipp (1992) argues that local school personnel advocating for students with disabilities will have to fight for
more local resources for programs and services. Since state and
federal funding has not kept pace with the increasing demand for special services, the local burden that comes with identification creates
a need for more local dollars to support students with disabilities.
This financial situation pits special education administrators' needs
for resources against other district needs. Lipp (1992) also argues for
block funding and tight accounting of dollars spent in a more decentralized delivery system. Block funding will bring more resources
to the school site, but will also require more discretion in the use of
those dollars. Special educators will be held accountable for a system
to monitor how those dollars are allocated and spent. The process of
developing a system of accountability that applies to each school and

its use of dollars for students with disabilities must be tied to student services and programs. Tying dollars to services available for a school to meet student needs rather than to individual students is actually a common practice today. What will be different in the future will be the manner in which students with disabilities receive those services. For example, minutes of speech-language services typically set aside in an individual IEP may be delivered within an inclusive group of students in the classroom, rather than in an individual therapy session. What must be accounted for is student progress toward the outcomes identified in the IEP, not the process or time spent in delivery of the service. This shift in focus is the key accounting change. Staff members need support in designing computer programs that will allow for easy posting of observations and results of student performance. Aggregating performance across outcomes in those settings in which the behavior is expected to be useful will require participation by all those dedicated to serving an individual student. Annual reviews will be initiated to determine if students have access to the resources that they need to achieve the targeted outcomes of their education.

Advocacy begins with these data. If students are not making progress toward the outcomes that were set for them, parents and the special education leadership need to advocate for changes in services and service levels and examine the outcomes and the timetables for achieving them. As students progress, the school's monitoring and accountability systems may require changes in the rate and nature of instruction and support if outcomes are not being achieved.

Tasks surrounding transitions between preschool and school programs and services, between school and external agencies, and into post-school independent living and adult services require local district leadership. Regulating the flow of information from program to program requires a clear understanding of expectations, of reporting requirements, and of who is or will be responsible for what services. Gathering public-sector agency heads and identifying local representatives from each agency who will participate in student case management, service provision, and evaluation and funding involves a series of local interagency agreements. Competent state-level leadership is required to support local agency collaboration if the benefits of interagency schemes are going to be realized.

SUMMARY

It is fitting to close this chapter with Lashley's (1993) reflections on the professional discourse in the field of special education. He has created a framework that, when applied to the social practice of school administration, serves as a theory to assist practitioners and researchers alike to grasp the often "contradictory understandings of effectiveness, standards of excellence, and intentions" (Lashley, 1993, p. 4). He contends that the paradigms of social practice are divided into two major discourses. The first is driven by Skrtic's (1991b) five assumptions (see pp. 8–10, this volume), the second by the principles espoused by the proponents of inclusive education. Lashley contrasts these paradigms of practice in terms of MacIntryre's social practice dimensions (1984), which help explain why administrators pursue valued internal and external goods. These goods are the rewards and avoidance of sanctions that arise from implementing what they perceive to be good practices benefiting students with disabilities. External goods are those that accrue to the administrator personally or to the program from people and agencies outside the local schools for being in compliance or being recognized as demonstrating a recommended practice. In the Lashley model (1993), special education administrators' actions are influenced by the same type of contextual factors that were noted in Chapter 8 concerning the principal as leader: 1) personal beliefs, attitudes, values, and intentions; 2) political considerations; 3) the culture of the school district; and 4) the knowledge-base of special education. Lashley's model is presented in Figure 3.

It is our belief that local leadership is critical to advocacy. We believe Lashley has captured the dividing line between the two types of social practice employed by special educators in Figure 3. In our practice, we have repeatedly witnessed administrators agonizing over choosing to conduct their practice according to one perspective or the other. We have heard some special education leaders debate their positions on the least restrictive environment and the need to protect the continuum of services, while others have adopted a unified system and encourage the full inclusion of students with disabilities. While tradition and the administrators' personal beliefs and experiences are obviously important, the other factors that Lashley identifies—political and district-culture factors—are also relevant.

In this chapter we make clear our belief that the emerging paradigm, the perspective shift toward an inclusive school philosophy, is compatible with the underlying principles of the movement toward a general restructuring of education. We believe that administrators of special education must come to understand their own district's restructuring initiatives and find the point of interest with the emerging social practice of inclusion. It is our contention that the subtle growth and rising costs of special education within a parallel struc-

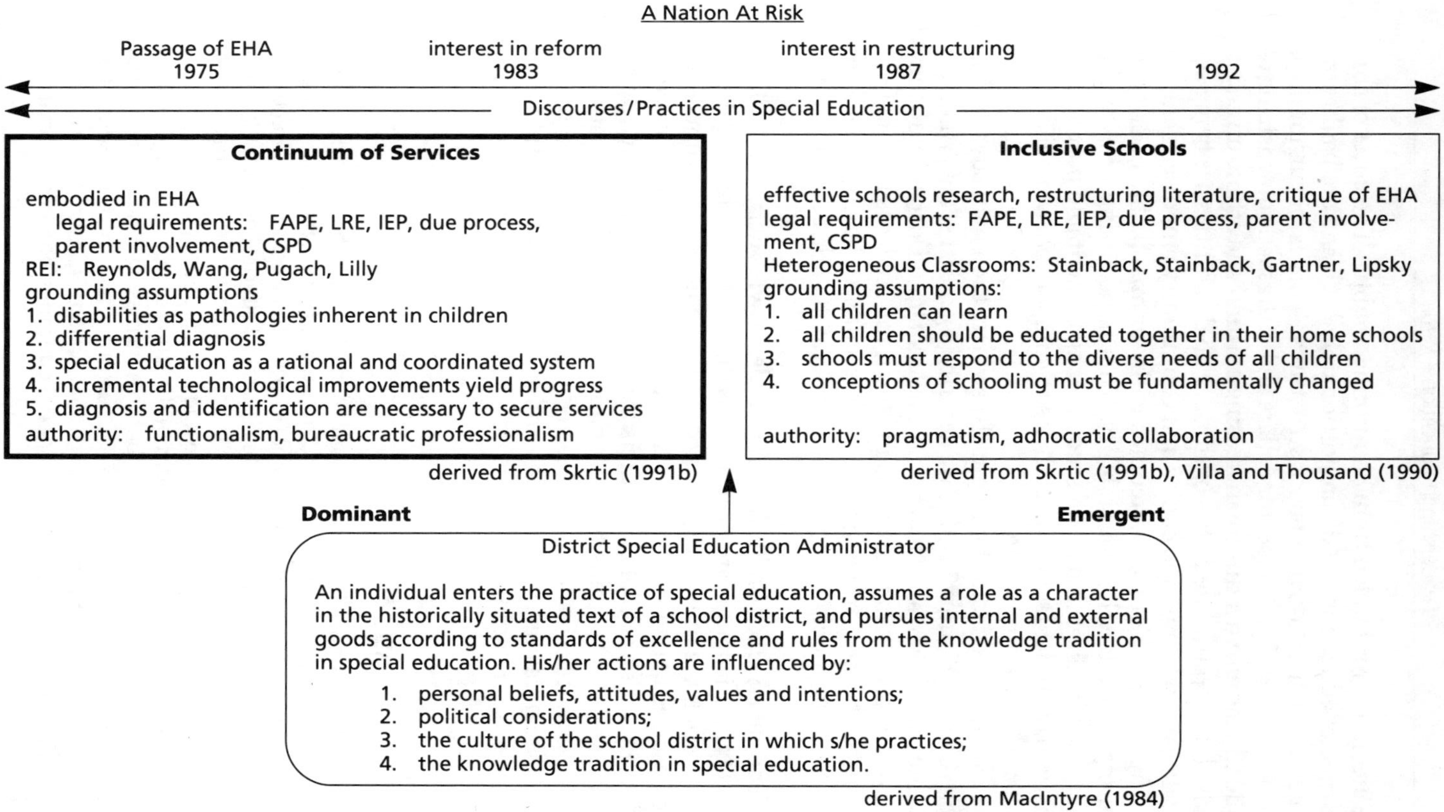

A Nation At Risk

| Passage of EHA 1975 | interest in reform 1983 | interest in restructuring 1987 | 1992 |

Discourses/Practices in Special Education

Continuum of Services

embodied in EHA
legal requirements: FAPE, LRE, IEP, due process, parent involvement, CSPD
REI: Reynolds, Wang, Pugach, Lilly
grounding assumptions
1. disabilities as pathologies inherent in children
2. differential diagnosis
3. special education as a rational and coordinated system
4. incremental technological improvements yield progress
5. diagnosis and identification are necessary to secure services
authority: functionalism, bureaucratic professionalism

derived from Skrtic (1991b)

Inclusive Schools

effective schools research, restructuring literature, critique of EHA
legal requirements: FAPE, LRE, IEP, due process, parent involvement, CSPD
Heterogeneous Classrooms: Stainback, Stainback, Gartner, Lipsky
grounding assumptions:
1. all children can learn
2. all children should be educated together in their home schools
3. schools must respond to the diverse needs of all children
4. conceptions of schooling must be fundamentally changed

authority: pragmatism, adhocratic collaboration

derived from Skrtic (1991b), Villa and Thousand (1990)

Dominant

Emergent

District Special Education Administrator

An individual enters the practice of special education, assumes a role as a character in the historically situated text of a school district, and pursues internal and external goods according to standards of excellence and rules from the knowledge tradition in special education. His/her actions are influenced by:

1. personal beliefs, attitudes, values and intentions;
2. political considerations;
3. the culture of the school district in which s/he practices;
4. the knowledge tradition in special education.

derived from MacIntyre (1984)

Figure 3. Discourse of the social practice of special education within the context of school restructuring. (From Lashley, C., 1993.)

ture are no longer hidden from an informed public. The costs of current special education are disproportionately high and are bankrupting current educational support structures. This is occurring in a time of scarcity of public-sector dollars and of dramatic downsizing of public education; in a time of increasing cultural and ethnic diversity in which the legitimate rights of those with disabilities are being acknowledged; when public choice and community empowerment are growing; when a focus on outcomes is the unmistakable priority in ensuring educational accountability. This is occurring despite the disappointing research data on student achievement and post-school transition of students with disabilities to competitive work and independent community living.

Leaders must decide for themselves where their own odyssey has taken them. In Figures 2 and 3, we describe a general set of principles and directions that all educational leaders should consider if they want to build work organizations in which the students and staff are known "to be free, to be valued, to be secure, to be challenged, to grow, to be in touch with their true selves" (Clark & Meloy, 1989, p. 291).

The social practice of educating students with disabilities along with their age-appropriate peers creates organizations that use diversity to enrich the human experience for all. Some of the practices we have described arise from the administrators' own social practice of leading inclusive schools and others from knowledge obtained by researchers who are coming to understand the unique human nature of our practice. The leadership challenge in inclusion is to point the way, create occasions for reflection and action, and get out of the way of those who are doing it well.

ILLUSTRATIVE CASE

Dana Robertson had just returned from an all-day workshop entitled *Inclusion: Equity and Excellence*, presented by a team from State University and sponsored by the State Education Department. Mo Erickson, the Director of Special Services, had also attended. As Assistant Superintendent for Instruction, Dr. Robertson had represented the South Oxford school district in lots of conferences of this sort, but this one had been especially thought provoking. The relevance of this topic, in light of the study of restructuring in which the district had been engaged, had become increasingly clear. Since Dana had been the primary leader of the Restructuring Task Force for South Oxford schools, it was fortuitous that participation in this latest state initiative on inclusion had not been limited to special education administrators in the district.

The workshop convincingly reinforced the argument that:

1. Children currently classified as special education students are not achieving all they are capable of in many existing programs.
2. These children are not being prepared for adult living.
3. The existing separate special education system is not producing the intended results.
4. Current mainstreaming practices rarely yield intended outcomes.
5. Emphasis must shift from processes of classifying and labeling students to improving instruction.
6. Special and general educators must join forces to develop an inclusive system with a focus on better outcomes for *all* students.

Dana had come away convinced that inclusion was more than a mere mechanism; rather, it was a philosophic ideal that fit the vision of a restructured education system that the South Oxford Task Force had gradually come to understand. Yes, Dana decided, this was an idea that could be contagious and whose time has surely come.

Resolutions put forth by the National Association of State Boards of Education and the Association for Supervision and Curriculum Development, as well as the Council of Administrators of Special Education and the National Association of State Directors of Special Education had all been cited as supporting the inclusion ideal.

But Dana's optimistic hope for change was dampened somewhat when one day's accumulation of mail included an unusually lengthy issue of *The Lookout*, a newsletter published periodically by the South Oxford Federation of Teachers (SOFT). This issue of the newsletter had extracted and elaborated on a number of points recently promulgated by the State Federation regarding concerns about inclusion. Some of the points (set out in bold type below) that quickly caught Dana's attention were:

1. The inclusion (or **total integration**) movement presumes that the least restrictive environment for **all** students is **always** the regular classroom.
2. Inclusion **is not a state or federal mandate**. It is not defined anywhere in law or regulation.
3. Inclusion is significantly **different** from **mainstreaming**. While mainstreaming assumes that there will be academic benefits for the student with disabilities inclusion makes no such assumption, but rests its justification on the right to physical and social participation.
4. While special education has traditionally made placement decisions based on the individual needs of a student, inclusion **disregards individual educational needs** and argues that the needs of all students can be met in the regular classroom.
5. Existing laws and regulations require that a **full continuum** of services, including **separate or segregated schools**, must remain as an available option.

The newsletter concluded with a statement that the traditional organizational structure of schools—based on grade levels, instructional tracks, and testing programs—would certainly not be compatible with an inclusion program. Therefore, the local (SOFT) leadership would continue to follow the advice of the state federation to take an active stance regarding inclusion to:

1. Monitor the plans under way in each district to be sure that any movement toward inclusion would not be at the expense of either teachers' or students' best interests.
2. Ensure that staff-development programs preceded the inclusion of students with disabilities into regular classrooms.
3. Negotiate limits on class size and/or numbers of students with disabilities who could be placed in any regular class.
4. Seek to involve parents of students with and without disabilities in the planning of any program changes or training activities related to inclusion of students with disabilities.

After some thought, Dana had to acknowledge that the Federation's statements were basically true, and it was hard to argue with some of the warnings implied in their advice. However, the tone of *The Lookout* somehow seemed disturbingly protective of the status-quo. What might this mean for the exciting ideas of the Restructuring Task Force that had crowded Dana's mind only minutes before? Was the apparent conflict simply a result of semantics, ambiguity, and fear of uncertainty? Or was it an indication of deeply rooted philosophical differences?

"Oh well. That's why we get the big bucks!" Dana concluded and picked up the phone to ask to see Mo. While Mo was coming down to meet him, Dana noted a few questions:

1. Where did the director stand on inclusion?
2. Did schools have to move to full inclusion right away?
3. Would the IEP be done away with? Or will the individual needs of students prevail?
4. How could the benefits to typical students and general education teachers be identified?
5. Wouldn't there always be a need for a "safety net" for certain students who were too disturbing and disrupting?
6. What restructuring ideas intersected with inclusive school practices?

REFERENCES

Barth, R. (1990). *Improving schools from within*. San Francisco: Jossey-Bass.
Bennis, W., & Nanus, B. (1985). *Leaders*. San Francisco: Jossey-Bass.
Berman, P. (1980). Thinking about programmed and adaptive implementation: Matching strategies to situations. In H. Ingram & D. Mann (Eds.), *Why policies succeed or fail* (pp. 205–227). Beverly Hills: Sage Publications.
Berman, P., & McLaughlin, M. (1978). *Implementing and sustaining innovations* (Research report #R-1589-8HEW). Santa Monica: Rand Corporation.
Burrello, L., & Lashley, C. (1992). On organizing for the future: The destiny of special education. In K. Waldron, A. Riester, & J. Moore (Eds.), *Special edu-

cation: The challenge of the future (pp. 64–95). San Francisco: Edwin Mellen Press.

Burrello, L., Schrup, M., & Barnett, B. (1988). *The principal as the special education instructional leader. The principal's training simulator in special education* (U.S. Department of Education, Office of Special Education Grant Number G008730038). Bloomington: Indiana University.

Burrello, L., & Zadnik, D. (1986). Critical success factors of special education administrators. *Journal of Special Education, 20*(3), 367–377.

Clark, D., & Meloy, J. (1989) Renouncing a democratic structure for leadership in schools. In T. Sergiovanni & J. Moore (Eds.), *Schools for tomorrow: Directing reforms to issues that count* (pp. 292–294). Boston: Allyn and Bacon.

Council of Administrators of Special Education. (1993). *CASE future agenda for special education: Creating a unified system.* Albuquerque, NM: Author.

Deal, T., & Peterson, K. (1990). *The principal's role in shaping school culture.* Washington, DC: U.S. Department of Education, Office of Educational Research and Improvement.

DeClue, L. (1990). *The principal's role in managing special education programs at the elementary level.* Unpublished doctoral dissertation, Indiana University, Bloomington.

Elmore, R., & McLaughlin, M. (1988). *Steady work: Policy, practice and the reform of American education* (Report No. R-1589-8-HEW). Santa Monica: Rand Corporation.

Fullan, M. (1991). *Overcoming barriers to educational change.* Washington, DC: The Office of the Undersecretary of the U.S. Department of Education.

Fullan, M., & Stiegelbauer, S. (1991). *The meaning of educational change.* New York: Teachers College Press.

Gartner, A., & Lipsky, D.K. (1987). Beyond special education: Toward a quality system for all students. *Harvard Educational Review. 57*(4), 367–395.

Hemmings, A., & Metz, M.H. (1990). Real teaching: How high school teachers negotiate societal, local, community, and student pressures when they define their work. In R. Page & L. Valli (Eds.), *Curriculum differentiation* (pp. 91–112). Buffalo, NY: SUNY Press.

Johnson, S.M. (1990). *Teachers at work: Achieving success in our schools.* New York: Basic Books.

Lashley, C.A. (1993). *Studies in the character histories of special education administrators.* Unpublished doctoral dissertation, Indiana University, Bloomington. Indiana.

Lipp, M. (1992). An emerging perspective on special education: A development agenda for the 1990s. *The Special Education Leadership Review, 1*(1), 10–39.

Little, J.W. (1981). *School success and staff development in urban desegregated schools: A summary of recent completed research.* Boulder, CO: Center for Autism Research.

Little, J.W., & McLaughlin, M. (1993). *Teacher's work: Individuals, colleagues and context.* New York: Teachers College Press.

MacIntyre, A. (1984). *After virtue: a study of moral theory.* Notre Dame, IN: University of Notre Dame Press.

McLaughlin, M., & Warren, S. (1992). *Issues and options in restructuring schools and special education programs.* College Park: University of

Maryland, the Center for Policy Options in Special Education, and The Institute for the Study of Exceptional Children and Youth.

Newmann, F.M. (1991). What is a restructured school? A framework to clarify means and ends. *Issues in restructuring schools* (Issue Report. 3–5, 16). Madison, WI: Center on organization and restructuring of schools.

Osborne, D., & Gaebler, T. (1992). *Reinventing government*. Reading, MA: Addison Wesley.

Sage, D., & Burrello, L. (1986). *Policy and management in special education*. Englewood Cliffs, NJ: Prentice Hall.

Sailor, W. (1991). Special education in the restructured school. *Remedial and Special Education, 12*(6), 8–22.

Senge, P. (1990). *The fifth discipline*. New York: Doubleday.

Siskin, L. (1990). *Different worlds: The department as context for high school teachers.* Stanford University: Center for Research on the Context of Secondary School Teaching.

Skrtic, T. (1986). The crisis in special education knowledge: A perspective on perspective. *Focus on Exceptional Children, 18*(7), 1–16.

Skrtic, T. (1991a). Behind special education: *A critical analysis of professional knowledge and school organization.* Denver: Love Publishing.

Skrtic, T. (1991b). The special education paradox: Equity as the way to excellence. *Harvard Educational Review, 6* 1(2), 148–205.

Stainback, S., & Stainback, W. (1984). A rationale for the merger of special and regular education. *Exceptional Children, 51*(2), 102–111.

The National LEADership Network study group on restructuring schools. *Total quality management: The leader's odyssey.* (1993). Washington, DC: U.S. Department of Education, Office of research and improvement.

Van Horn, G. (1989). *The principal's role in managing special education programs at the secondary level.* Unpublished doctoral dissertation, Indiana University, Bloomington.

Viall, P. (1984). The purposing of high performance systems. In T.G. Sergiovanni & J.E. Corbally (Eds.), *Leadership and organizational culture* (pp 85–104). Urbana: University of Illinois Press.

Villa, R.A., & Thousand, J.S. (1990). Administrative supports to promote inclusive schooling. In W. Stainback & S. Stainback (Eds.), *Support networks for inclusive schooling: Interdependent integrated education* (pp. 201–218). Baltimore: Paul H. Brookes Publishing Co.

10

Program Evaluation

Measuring the Merit
and Worth of Special Education

The primary evaluation questions of the 1980s were: 1) Are students being served in the public schools?, and 2) Are they being served appropriately? The first of these questions was interpreted as referring to whether the child was served under the jurisdiction of a public school entity or, if the student with a disability was in a private school, whether he or she was receiving the services from the public sector to which he or she was entitled. The second question was interpreted as pertaining to whether the student was being served according to the rules and regulations established under federal and state law. Were the student and his or her family properly informed? Was consent granted? Were multidisciplinary assessments conducted and case conference committees announced and implemented with parental involvement? Was the individualized education program (IEP) drafted and signed by all parties? Was the placement secured within the specified period, and were all due-process rights honored by the school district? More recently, questions concerning transition plans and least restrictive environment (LRE) provisions have become a part of the review process. In summary, program evaluation was and still is primarily a *compliance-assessment* process.

In the 1990s, school districts and a few states are beginning to ask questions about appropriateness that go beyond mere issues of compliance. The primary questions have become: 1) Are students with disabilities achieving the outcomes that were envisioned for them?, 2) How are students with disabilities achieving compared to their age-appropriate peers?, and 3) What are the post-school successes of students with disabilities?

Many special educators are turning their attention from questions of access and process to questions of outcomes achieved during and after school. In this chapter, we emphasize the importance of defining the context of the evaluation situation and of determining who needs to be evaluated. Determining what uses the evaluation is to serve is a critical part of identifying its appropriate focus. With the many actors surrounding the practice of special education, it is important to attend to the many stakeholders who might lay claim to programs and services for students with disabilities. We also present the most frequent types of evaluation questions posed and the sets of assumptions associated with various evaluation models and methods. We describe a set of evaluation exemplars drawn from the literature and from our own practices in local schools and intermediate units, and, in the chapter appendices, provide a list of key tasks in evaluation and a comprehensive outline of the areas that should be evaluated.

THE DEFINITION AND PURPOSES OF EVALUATION

The definition of program evaluation varies somewhat with the purposes envisioned by those conducting it. Generally, however, evaluation can be defined as "the descriptive and systematic assessment of [the] worth or merit of some object" (Schwandt, 1992). For the purposes of this chapter, the *object* of evaluation is a special education program, generally one administered from the district level. *Merit* refers to the inherent value of a program, independent of its context, while *worth* is the value of the program within the context in which it is implemented. In addition, evaluation can be classified as formative, that is, intended to provide information to improve program functioning, or summative, which means it is intended to provide information for purposes other than program development (Schwandt, 1992).

There are six potential purposes to guide and focus an evaluation of programs and services for students with exceptional needs:

1. *Program improvement* Evaluation serves as a management tool, helping the program administrator and his or her staff to make specific suggestions in the planning and implementation of a program or service.
2. *Program review* Evaluation serves as a means for top management to periodically review and audit the appropriateness of current program definition and scope and the quality of service delivery
3. *Compliance monitoring* Evaluation serves as a means for state agencies to assess whether program implementation is being conducted in accordance with state and federal laws and regulations

4. *Securing political and fiscal support* Evaluation serves as a means to secure, maintain, and increase school patronage and taxpayer support for increased school funding and participation in school activities.

5. *Policy analysis* Evaluation as policy analysis is an activity initiated by policy makers to help them decide whether to change, terminate, or reauthorize existing policies governing a program or practice (Horvath, 1985).

6. *Provision of information to the community* Evaluation is conducted to provide information about the characteristics of an education program to the community. It recognizes value pluralism and seeks to represent a range of interests in issue formulation. The basic goal is an informed citizenry, and the evaluator acts as broker in exchanges of information between different groups (MacDonald, 1974; Simons, 1987)

JUDGING THE MERIT AND WORTH OF SPECIAL EDUCATION PROGRAMS

Scriven (1973) is credited with first making the distinction between measures of merit and worth, which he called value, in evaluation (Worthen & Sanders, 1987). Evaluation theorists generally recognize the need to make distinctions between the intrinsic value (merit) and the extrinsic or practical value (worth) of a social program. Different evaluators use different methods and standards, report to different audiences, and have different intents, depending on whether their purpose is to judge the merit or worth of a program (Guba & Lincoln, 1981).

Scriven (1967) is also credited with first discussing the distinction between formative and summative evaluation. Formative evaluation is used to provide information that will help in improving a program. Summative evaluation is used to provide information about a program's utility (Worthen & Sanders, 1987). Methods and standards, audiences, and intents will also vary depending on whether the purpose of the evaluation is formative or summative.

Guba and Lincoln (1981, 1989) suggest that a 2×2 matrix with merit–worth and formative–summative dimensions be used to describe the purposes of a given evaluation. A summative merit evaluation assesses the inherent value of a program relative to expert standards, while a formative merit evaluation assesses the inherent value of a program for purposes of improving its design. A summative worth evaluation assesses program functioning in context for purposes of making decisions about its implementation, while a formative worth evaluation assesses the contextual value of a program for the specific purpose of improving its implementation.

Guba and Lincoln (1981) have argued that the relationship between merit and worth can be conceived of in three ways. The terms can either be conceived of as synonymous or independent of one another, or "worth may be treated as dependent upon some minimal level of merit" (p. 48). This third possibility has particular relevance in special education. Evaluation of merit is, at minimum, an evaluation of the compliance of the special education program with applicable regulations. Special education programs cannot be judged meritorious unless they meet legal standards; that is, their worth in the schools depends first on their compliance with state and federal requirements. Because school districts are at the mercy of these requirements when they design local programs, the debate over the validity of the assumptions that support current special education models and legal standards becomes more important as it affects state and federal requirements.

Merit Evaluation

Special education program evaluation has often been undertaken to assess the compliance of local programs with state and federal regulations. Compliance monitoring is merit evaluation; the program's design and internal consistency are judged against standards that are generally applicable. We hesitate to call the regulations promulgated under IDEA "standards upon which a group of experts agree" (Guba & Lincoln, 1981, p. 45), since there is considerable controversy over the merit of the standards, but nevertheless, the regulations are legally applicable and recognition of program merit is dependent upon their being met.

Compliance monitoring can be classified as either summative or formative merit evaluation. It is summative merit evaluation when the program is being reviewed for the purpose of warranting its compliance in preparation for a due process hearing or on-site review. In these cases, evaluation questions would include:

Does the program meet accepted standards? Are the required components for LRE, IEP, parental involvement, procedural safeguards, protections in assessment procedures, and a comprehensive system of personnel development (CSPD) in place?

Do the components of the program fit together? Are they consistent? Is there an internal logic to the program that will stand up against counter-arguments?

Do procedures for developing IEPs conflict with provisions for parental involvement?

Do provisions for parent involvement match policies on procedural safeguards?

Can the district claim to have met all requirements to the letter of the law? Can any failures to comply be justified by special circumstances?

When placements are made in more restrictive environments on the continuum of placements, but procedures for parent involvement have been followed, what arguments can be made that the LRE requirement has been met? Does policy allow for such arguments?

Do program procedures conflict with other matters of policy? For example, will the content of IEPs conflict with graduation standards?

Compliance monitoring can be formative merit evaluation when the purpose of the evaluation is to provide information that will help in improving upon the design of the program. For example, in the early days of the implementation of Part B of the Education of the Handicapped Act Amendments of 1977, special education administrators regularly evaluated their distict's progress toward compliance in order to reveal inconsistencies or lack of clarity in the procedures that they had put into place. Evaluation questions that might apply in such cases include:

How can we improve upon the design of the program?

How might procedures for parent involvement be strengthened to encourage their participation in designing the IEP? How might training plans under the CSPD be improved to increase teachers' capacities to implement IEPs?

Are procedures sufficiently clear so that teachers understand the concept of LRE well enough to participate in instructional decision making?

Are the provisions having the desired outcomes? How can the design of IEPs be improved to meet the needs of students?

Are there provisions for parent involvement that actually discourage their participation?

In what ways do program procedures interact with other matters of policy? How can such effects be mediated?

Evaluation of special education programs has historically consisted primarily of compliance monitoring. This was particularly important in the late 1970s and early 1980s, when the emphasis was on putting services for students with disabilities into place in states and in individual school districts. However, administrators and policy makers have learned that procedural compliance does not ensure that services are in place nor that the programs will produce the desired outcomes. As this circumstance has become apparent, proposals for evaluation of the worth of special education programs have been offered.

Evaluation of Worth

Although the emphasis in special education program evaluation has been on compliance monitoring to judge merit, there has been growing interest in evaluating worth, as evidenced by an example from an ongoing controversy in special education—the definition of *appropriate*. How best to assess worth is an issue surrounded by controversy. While it has been resolved legally (i.e., in terms of compliance), educators and parents continue to debate over what is the best possible program for students with disabilities. Whatever the outcome of that negotiation, the definition of *appropriateness* directly affects those who work at the point of service provision. Evaluation of appropriateness must occur at the school and classroom level. An evaluation of the worth of a program can provide a forum for resolving professional conflicts and a vehicle for dissolving the parallel system of education for students with disabilities.

IDEA requires that all students with disabilities receive a free appropriate public education in the least restrictive environment. The legal definition of *appropriate* was further modified by the U.S. Supreme Court in their decision in *Board of Education v. Rowley* in 1982, in which the Court stated that the term implies "access to specialized instruction and related services which are individually designed to provide educational benefit to the handicapped child." The Court further stated that:

> When the "mainstreaming" preference of the Act has been met and a child is being educated in the regular classrooms of the public school system, the system itself monitors the educational progress of the child. Regular examinations are administered, grades are awarded, and yearly advancement to higher grade levels is permitted for those children who attain an adequate knowledge of the course material. The grading and advancement system thus constitutes an important factor in determining educational benefit.

In its decision, the Court rejected the argument that the demand for the provision of equal education opportunity for students with disabilities implies that their program must be designed to maximize their potential. It also suggested that an appropriate program is one designed to allow the student to simply progress from grade to grade.

The Supreme Court ruling in *Rowley* prompted district administrators to design programs that would ensure that IEPs for students in their districts would meet the requirements of the "mainstreaming preference" and other provisions of the decision. The merit of these programs was tested against federal and state regulations and guidance was provided by the Supreme Court decision. Although this process resolved questions about the legality of programs, it did not resolve issues about their usefulness in providing services to students. In such cases, an evaluation of worth is in order, since the intent of the law is to provide education that meets the needs of students with disabilities, and although a program might meet the "designed to provide benefit" standard, it might not necessarily meet the student's needs.

A formative worth evaluation would assess the appropriateness of programs at the school level. Since the provisions of IDEA are implemented on a student-by-student basis, evaluation according to the definition of *appropriate* as it applies to each student and to the school program in which he or she participates can provide educators with information to improve the student's program. The procedures for attaining appropriateness may come into conflict with parent and teacher interest in providing an instructional program that meets the student's needs. The appropriateness standard implied under IDEA is the consensus among stakeholders on what should result from specialized instruction. In such a case, "designed to provide benefit" could be compared to expectations for a program that "meets the needs of the student" in order to provide information for program improvement. Evaluation questions might include:

How are the targeted outcomes for students with disabilities determined? How are they related to the planned outcomes for typical students?

How does implementation of the program meet the needs of students? What factors in the school context support programs designed to provide educational benefit?

Do school personnel understand the relationship between the legal definition of *appropriate* and the content of the IEP?

Does application of appropriateness standards result in an equitable opportunity for each student in the classroom and school?

Do students whose programs meet mainstreaming and appropriateness standards progress from grade to grade? What factors in the school and classroom support and hinder progress? Are these factors related to the appropriateness standards?

Information about the impact that the procedures might have on individual and school instructional practices would result from a summative worth evaluation. Such an evaluation could occur annually, when administrators review IEPs. Administrators and board members would use this information to make decisions about the procedures as policy in the schools. The district's efforts in conducting programs "designed to provide educational benefit" would be compared to programs that "meet the needs of the student" in an effort to inform policy makers about the impact of regulations on schools. From such information, policy statements regarding the provision of services might be developed. Questions for a summative worth evaluation might include:

What impact do appropriateness procedures have on student progress? How do the procedures affect what schools do on behalf of students with disabilities?

How has the provision of services changed as a result of the implementation of procedures aimed at achieving appropriateness?

Do teachers and parents understand the procedures and the impact that they have on the student's IEP and placement in the least restrictive environment?

What burdens do the procedures place on schools? Has paperwork increased? Is instructional time taken away from students to implement the procedures?

In the example of procedures for ensuring appropriateness, the legal standard set forth by the U.S. Supreme Court in *Rowley* must be met before other considerations about students' programs enter into the discussion. Evaluation of the procedures provides information necessary to reveal discrepancies between legal standards and program practices and between provision of services intended to meet requirements to the letter of the law ("designed to benefit") and services intended to fulfill the intent of the law ("meets the needs of the student").

Awareness of discrepancies and inconsistencies allows educators to improve programs as they affect students at the level of the school and classroom. Evaluating the worth of a special education program requires evaluators and school personnel to examine the impact that the program has on students, classrooms, and the school. Information about these effects can be used to illuminate the conflicts that occur when educators attempt to implement complex policy initiatives. Evaluation sheds light on the discrepancies between program design and program practice and on the relationships among those affected by the program. When this information is used both to improve the program and to increase the tolerance and flexibility of persons involved, evaluation has made its expected contribution.

In judging a program, both merit and worth should be considered. Focusing only on merit results in programs that are well-designed and compliant but may not be applicable in school settings. Focusing only on worth may yield a program that is practical, but that may not comply with regulations. Architects say that form should follow function. Unfortunately, much of both program development and program evaluation in special education has been concerned with the function of meeting compliance standards. As a result, the form of special education programs has been aimed at ensuring procedural adherence rather than student learning. In this case, following the letter of the law through minimal procedural compliance sometimes seems to violate the spirit of the law (see Skrtic, 1991).

OTHER CONSIDERATIONS

Political and Ethical Considerations

The practice of evaluation is fraught with political and ethical issues that can affect the evaluator both personally and professionally. Since special education programs bring together teachers, parents, and others concerned with the educational lives of children who are recognized as having difficulties, interactions among participants during the evaluation can be filled with emotion. By assessing the value of a program, the evaluator may be putting the district participants in an uncomfortable position. Because of the frequency of due-process proceedings, the evaluator may indeed find him- or herself in a position of providing testimony that a program is not in compliance or is inappropriate, in which case the district has much to lose. Finally, information about students is privileged under the confidentiality provisions of IDEA. Although this provision is waived for purposes of sanctioned program evaluation, school personnel, who are accustomed to maintaining confidentiality, may be hesitant to discuss individual students.

Setting Standards

The development of standards against which the program will be judged is an important part of evaluation. Standards may be provided by the client, or their development may be the responsibility of the evaluator. The standards used provide some insight into the underlying conceptualization of program effectiveness.

Federal documents provide standards that must be met in compliance monitoring activities (U.S. Department of Education, 1990) and individual states have adapted these federal standards in their own sets of monitoring documents. States, researchers, and professional organizations also develop standards for evaluating special education programs in areas beyond mere compliance with regulations. *Indiana's Effectiveness Indicators for Special Education* (Indiana Department of Education, 1990) provides one set of standards that has been used to provide guidance to districts undertaking evaluations of special education programs. The *Outcome Indicators for Special Education* (Frey, 1993) provide standards that could be used in an evaluation of special education curriculum and instructional practices.

Administrators and evaluators may also decide to develop a set of standards that will be unique to a particular evaluation. As evaluations are focused more narrowly, development of particular standards may include those related to compliance issues, as well as strategically chosen issues of quality. For example, an evaluation of procedural safeguards would include monitoring of compliance with the requirement of providing notices to parents about regulatory standards and qualitative assessment of parents' participation in decision making by applying some locally designed standards to data gathered from interviews with parents and teachers.

When standards are developed, the goals and objectives of the general education program should also be considered (Horvath, 1985). One intent of special education is to provide access to the general program. The degree of similarity between the goals and objectives of both programs is an important standard in evaluation. In addition, districts and schools generally have written goals and curriculum statements that do not need to be rewritten for purposes of evaluating the special education program. Educational goals are not so variable as to be unique to a given program. Finally, reviewing the goals of the general program provide a venue for a critique of those goals relative to their applicability for all students. Such an opportunity allows those involved in the evaluation of the special education program to have an impact on the general program through a formal, legitimate process.

Data Collection and Analysis

Feasibility, methodological expertise, and the questions to be answered or the issues to be addressed are some of the factors that determine the kinds of data to be collected in an evaluation. Various approaches to evaluation use different methods of data collection and analysis, based on their conceptualization of evaluation practice and the issues to be addressed in a particular evaluation. Quantitative data have been used in program evaluation to assess programs against objectives. Quantitative methodologies are perceived to be inexpensive, easy to administer, and bias-free.

As evaluators have recognized that programs are not the rational, linear entities that quantitative social science envisions, interest has developed in qualitative methods of evaluation (Guba & Lincoln,

1989). Qualitative methods yield data from which the evaluator gains an understanding of the value of a program. Value pluralism and contextual relevance are important factors to evaluators seeking to understand the complexity of a social program (Skrtic, Guba, & Knowlton, 1985).

Designers of special education program evaluation models must recognize the role of data collection and analysis strategies in addressing various types of evaluation questions. Quasi-experimental approaches could be used to assess the relationship between implementation of certain procedures and student outcomes. Standards checklists to record the frequency of particular actions are often used in assessing compliance. Interviews and examination of documents can also be used for data collection in value-based evaluation.

EVALUATION MODELS

Tracy (1984) created a descriptive matrix of six different evaluation models and approaches contrasted across a set of seven factors. These seven models, their assumptions, and other considerations are displayed in Table 1. The seven factors that appear in Table 1 are defined below.

Focus   The way in which each author places emphasis on his or her approach
Proponents   The major theoretical contributors to each approach
Purpose   The author's goal for the evaluation process
Definition   The way each author has defined the process of evaluation
Design   The content and scope of the study, consistent with both the definition and purpose subscribed to in the evaluation process
Methodology/procedures   The suggested type of activities and means of following through
Audiences   The individuals for whom the evaluation is being conducted

We now move to consider the issue of program evaluation in special education and the assumptions that we believe are significant in conducting program studies for each of the six purposes described above.

These assumptions are grounded in our perception of recommended practice in program evaluation and in the context of special education today and through the 1990s. We have derived these statements from our own practice of evaluation in urban and suburban school systems and rural cooperatives. As we suggested earlier, start-

Table 1. Overview of evaluation models

Dimensions	Objectives	System	Context	Processes	Judgmental	Naturalistic
Focus	Performance measurement	Planning, design	Input, process, and output	Formal/informal, Formative/summative	Panels, experts	Responsiveness, effectiveness
Proponents	Tyler, Popham	Provus, Alkin	Stufflebeam	Scriven	Eisner, Wolf	Guba-Lincoln, Stake
Purpose	To determine effectiveness of objectives	To decide whether to change, hold, or terminate	To provide data in context for decisions	To identify multiple roles and processes in evaluation	To provide expert judgment	To develop responsive methodologies
Definition	Process to relate objectives to behavior	Process to relate standards to performance	Process to define (etc.) data for decisions	Process to describe and judge performance data w/ goals	Process to focus on standards and professional judgment	Process to develop responsive and natural methodology
Design	Explicit and including local personnel	Provides feedback loop and information for making decisions	Directed by administrator. Use of systems approach	General structure. Evaluative from within (formative) or from without (summative)	Responsive and based on experience and training	Emergent and responsive
Methodology/procedures	Pre/post comparisons or other appropriate indices of the objectives	Reference in terms of "needs"	Varies, includes needs assessment, case studies, and advocate teams	Modus operandi analysis	Implicit use of "refined perceptual apparatus"	Naturalistic inquiry
Audiences	Teachers, curriculum developers, students, and parents	All decision makers	All decision makers	Sponsors and consumers	Anyone involved with the entity being evaluated	Anyone involved with the entity evaluated

From Tracy, P. (1984). Supportive staff and related services evaluation. In L.C. Burrello (Series Ed.), *CASE information packet series*. Bloomington, IN: Council of Administrators of Special Education; reprinted by permission.

ing is the toughest part. To assist the reader about to undertake a comprehensive program evaluation, we present our recommended outline of an evaluation in Appendix A. The assumptions presented below correspond to the six purposes of program evaluation noted earlier.

Program Improvement

1. Program evaluation is one of management's tools to encourage organizational members to accept and work toward improved practices.
2. When leaders in special education focus on results, increased evaluation activity follows.
3. Program evaluation should become a regular activity so that staff and top management come to expect it and resistance to it is reduced.
4. Staff-initiated evaluation for the purpose of program improvement is defensible and can be more easily budgeted for on a regular basis.
5. Program administrators who initiate program evaluation activities for school-improvement purposes will project a positive program image and rarely have to subject themselves or their staff to needless externally driven compliance evaluation.
6. Program evaluation should set the stage for the planning and introduction of change or the reinforcement of current practices; if staff changes are necessary, they should come after a failure to respond to offers of support in the follow-up evaluation.
7. Each program administrator on the educational management team should prepare a program and personnel improvement plan on an annual basis and be prepared to share results before each annual budget is prepared and resources allocated.
8. Each special education director should establish a nonsalary discretionary fund to support innovations and reinforce excellent staff practices documented during annual program and personnel-improvement projects.

Program Review

1. Program evaluation has been instituted in school system and university settings to give top management an external referent by which to judge their special education unit's practices.
2. Regular program evaluation is instituted to give top management a means to justify expanding or delimiting a program.
3. If top management wants to make a change in the leadership or

the practices of the program under review, they will persist until they get the kind of external evaluation that justifies their ends.

4. Program evaluation gets increasingly more difficult as the number of programs and services to be reviewed increases; the corollary to the above is that the more focused the review, the easier it is to attain the intended outcomes.
5. Program reviews will not necessarily lead to increased top management or community support unless chief stakeholder values are well understood and organizational evaluation activities are deeply rooted in them.
6. Program reviews are concerned more with the status quo than with what might be, and for that reason they tend to have limited future application.

Program Compliance

1. Compliance reviews focus on minimum criteria.
2. Compliance reviews are more concerned with what was originally intended than with what ought to be.
3. Compliance reviews are status reports.
4. Compliance reviews are concerned with the presence or absence of written statements of assurance and practice.
5. Compliance reviews are valuable as a threat to spur action because they are generally a state-agency prerogative that can lead to sanctions and withholding of funds.
6. Compliance reviews are most helpful in dealing with immature organizations or those with new top management who do not trust the local special education leadership.
7. Compliance reviews are also helpful to new special education leadership personnel who need to gain a state, as well as local, perspective on the status of their new district.

Political and Fiscal Support

1. All forms of program evaluation can be used for this purpose.
2. The degree of utility depends on the involvement of key stakeholding groups and on their particular values and concerns.
3. Program evaluation reports can make staff, as well as community members, more receptive to future patron participation and volunteer activities.
4. Sharing evaluation data with the media in parts or in a series from start to finish may encourage wider and more frequent coverage and follow-up.

5. Program evaluation data included in public information releases should focus on student progress and community contributions.
6. Students are untapped consumer evaluations and potential disseminators of what's right with the schools; program evaluators should share results with students whenever possible, so that they in turn can share results with their parents.
7. Program evaluation data should be released in group meetings that include community patrons who do not have children in the schools, as well as identified stakeholders who do.

Policy Analysis

1. Policy analysis is often initiated at the federal and state levels in response to concerns that transcend those of the local level.
2. Policy analysis is often initiated because of competition for limited human resources within education (regular, special, vocational, and higher education) and between education and other human services agencies.
3. Policy analysis is also primarily driven by issues of equity and questions concerning access to service at local, as well as state and federal, levels.
4. Policy analysis studies demand in-depth testimony from key stakeholding audiences.
5. Quantitative evidence is not sufficient to justify policy changes; qualitative evidence demonstrating effects on clients and constituents is necessary to portray the effects of current and projected policy changes.
6. The effects of policy changes are rarely immediately evident, because they demand the test of program implementation (Horvath, 1985).

Community Information

1. This type of evaluation requires a democratic approach.
2. It recognizes the value of pluralism and seeks to represent a range of interests in issue formation.
3. This approach seeks to create an informed citizenry. The key justificatory concept is the "right to know."
4. The main activity is to collect definitions of, and reactions to, the programs and services being provided.
5. The evaluator using this model operates as a negotiator between groups of stakeholders.
6. The criterion for success is the range of audiences served.

7. The report is nonrecommendatory, allowing the audiences to draw their own conclusions (MacDonald, 1974; Simons, 1987).

Below, we describe a number of ways local administrators have used evaluation successfully to create a climate conducive to school improvement. These recommendations contain both traditional and emergent responsive evaluation strategies and tactics. Keep in mind that time and costs vary with the size and scope of the evaluation.

EXEMPLARS OF EVALUATION APPROACHES AND MODELS

In this section a description of evaluation approaches and models is presented. After describing the context of federal and state monitoring systems, we present a series of local school and intermediate unit evaluation approaches. After the presentation of each model, a summary is presented within the seven-part framework used earlier by Tracy (1984) to depict differences among leading evaluation models, approaches, and proponents.

Federal and State Monitoring Systems

According to federal regulation, implementation of the provisions IDEA is a state responsibility. Program evaluation by school districts is not covered in the regulations for IDEA; rather, authority is vested in the state "to assess and insure the effectiveness of efforts to educate these (handicapped) children" [34 CFR §300.1 (d)] and to "insure that free appropriate public education is available to all students with disabilities" [34 CFR §300.300 (a)]. States provide such assurances through submission of an annual program plan, known under IDEA as the State Plan.

The U.S. Department of Education conducts program reviews "to monitor the development and implementation of [the] policies and procedures required" (U.S. Department of Education, 1990, p. 111). The components of this monitoring system include review of annual reports, State Plan review, compliance monitoring, verification of Corrective Action Plan implementation, specific-issue compliance monitoring, and complaint investigation. The purpose of federal monitoring activities is:

> to determine if SEAs [state education agencies] are implementing the policies and procedures required by EHA-B and which have been approved in the State Plan. The program review process, used by both Federal and State agencies, is the means of assuring legal accountability [that is, compliance with Federal law and applicable State law] by the Department and by States receiving funds under EHA-B *so that all chil-*

dren with handicaps receive needed special education and related services. (U.S. Department of Education, 1990, pp. 112–113, emphasis added)

State monitoring of local districts' placement procedures is provided for under the requirements covering LRE, continuum of alternative placements, placement procedures, participation in non-academic settings, placement in public or private institutions, and technical assistance and training [34 CFR §300.382 (f) (7)], as well as procedures for the review and dissemination of "significant information and promising practices" [34 CFR §300.384 (3)]. Finally, states have the authority to monitor the activities of private schools in cases in which students with disabilities have been placed there by a public agency [34 CFR §300.402 (b)].

The systems of regulations developed for IDEA led to monitoring systems that were akin to disciplinary audits. Compliance was measured through checklists of procedural safeguards, procedures pertaining to LRE, and efforts to involve parents, and by comparing the information on student IEPs with the list of requirements in state regulations. After 12 years of implementation, federal monitoring of states continues to reveal procedural inadequacies in state and local efforts to meet regulatory requirements. For example, "in eight of the ten FY 1989 reports, OSEP [the Office of Special Education Programs] monitors found instances in which SEAs were not ensuring that the contents of IEPs were consistent with EHA-B requirements" (U.S. Department of Education, 1990, p. 132). In 40% of reports, the contents of notices to parents regarding procedural safeguards were not considered to be complete enough to satisfy regulations.

Monitoring activities for IDEA consist of either document review or on-site visits to schools and districts. Documentation of compliance comes in the form of annual reports and district plans for expenditures of federal and state funds. Through periodic on-site visits, compliance with federal and state regulations is assessed by reviewing policies and procedures and by interviewing staff and parents about their participation in special education programs. Federal monitors periodically visit state departments of education and some districts (U.S. Department of Education, 1990). States have designed various methods for on-site review of districts. As reduced availability of funds has restricted the activities of state departments of special education, on-site monitoring has occurred less regularly.

State departments of education are also able to rely on other procedures required by IDEA for feedback on the performance of schools in accommodating students with disabilities. Complaint procedures and due-process hearings (34 CFR § 300.506) are required avenues by which parents and advocates can object to actions that schools take or refuse to take on behalf of children.

In responding to complaints or requests for due process hearings, districts are often required to gather information about compliance and the effectiveness of a child's program, and this process often involves issues beyond the scope of an individual child's IEP. Since the outcome of complaints and hearings often hinges on whether schools made their decisions in a procedurally correct way, LEA administrators are very careful about compliance with district, state, and federal rules. Procedural noncompliance discovered as the result of a complaint is recorded as requiring corrective action.

Noncompliance with federal regulations has three significant effects. First, compliance with regulations is a condition for receiving federal funding under IDEA (34 CFR §300.2). Second, districts that do not comply with IDEA will also not comply with Section 504 of the Vocational Rehabilitation Act of 1973, which may trigger investigations by the Office of Civil Rights and civil sanctions requiring remedies (Rothstein, 1990). Finally, noncompliance with federal regulations jeopardizes any case that a district might make in responding to a complaint lodged with the SEA by a parent or in a due-process hearing.

Special education administrators are hesitant to proceed to a due-process hearing if they are aware of compliance violations. Their hesitancy leads to a weakened position and moves many administrators to negotiate with parents concerning educational issues and program changes. This can lead to significant expense for the district if its inability to negotiate due to compliance violations results in an expensive, and possibly unnecessary, placement for a child (Hehir, 1992).

The requirement of monitoring compliance with federal regulations led state education agencies to rely on an objectives-oriented approach to evaluation. Regulations were written in terms that would allow compliance to be measurable and observable so that monitoring would show whether the basic procedural requirements for provision of services to students with disabilities were being met. In addition, the process of setting compliance standards gave states the opportunity to communicate in a clear fashion what the requirements were for implementation of IDEA and for state laws and policies based on it. The highly prescriptive standards set forth clear goals and objectives that LEAs could work toward, and monitoring based on these standards provided clear information about the status of the special education program in a given district. This axiom has been true for the evaluation of special education programs. But operating according to regulations has not automatically yielded programs that meet the needs of students (Skrtic et al., 1987).

Compliance monitoring has also had the effect of setting special education apart from regular education. Having a separate set of regulations and a separate monitoring system reinforces the parallel nature of the systems. The goals and objectives of the special education program are assumed to be those established in the monitoring system. This perception places the emphasis on program procedures, rather than on the outcomes of services provided for students.

In summary, compliance monitoring has resulted in an objectives-oriented approach to evaluation. In the early period of implementation, compliance issues tend to have a great influence on the structure and substance of a program. Possible penalties keep educators focused on compliance, and this emphasis on implementation "by the book" inhibits the efforts of educators to provide quality services for students.

Evaluation of the quality of special education programs has not usually been at the center of efforts in districts or individual schools. Upon passage of PL 94-142 in 1975, highly prescriptive federal regulations were put into place, as was the policy norm at that time (Odden & Marsh, 1990). Since special education was a relatively unfamiliar discipline to school districts, state offices of special education developed detailed and highly structured systems of regulations, not only because federal rules required specificity, but also because the state regulations provided a vehicle for teaching school personnel about the procedural intricacies of special education. These actions put the emphasis on procedural compliance rather than on program outcomes, quality of participation, or improvements in educational opportunities for students with disabilities.

One example of a state system is the Indiana State Board of Education's regulations (Article 7, Rules 3–16, January, 1992) that govern the provision of special education and related services to students with disabilities. Under "Program Planning and Evaluation" (Rule 5), each LEA is required to file a comprehensive plan with the Indiana Department of Education. In addition to the comprehensive plan, Rule 5 describes program monitoring and approval procedures, which are administered by the division of special education, as follows:

Section 2(a):
The division of special education shall monitor all public agencies that receive federal and state monies for special education to ensure compliance with and implementation of the mandates of federal and state laws, rules, regulations, and policies regarding the provision of programs,

services, protections, and a free appropriate public education to all students with disabilities in Indiana.

Section 2(b):
The monitoring activities include, but are not limited to, the following:

(1) Complaint investigations.
(2) Data collection and analysis.
(3) State or federal fiscal audits.
(4) On-site reviews of the total special education program on a cyclical or other basis.
(5) On-site reviews of portions of programs to examine one (1) or more issues.
(6) Collection of performance-based accreditation information.
(7) Due process hearing decisions. (pp. 13–14)

In addition, each LEA must provide for evaluation of the CSPD and "the training opportunities provided, both on a short-term and long-term basis" (p. 14).

Rule 6 of Article 7 requires each LEA to "provide for participation of and consultation with parents of students in special education and other community members" (p. 14), and it encourages "the establishment of a parent advisory council, committee, task force, or group" (p. 14). The purpose of such a group is not stipulated in the regulations, but its participation as a stakeholder group in program evaluation is not precluded.

In order to help LEAs "to move beyond an exclusive focus on compliance with regulations to an emphasis on outcomes and program improvement," the Indiana Department of Education, in January 1990, in conjunction with the Indiana Council of Administrators of Special Education and the Council for Exceptional Children, moved "to develop a state-wide initiative that [would] address quality in special education" by developing the *Indiana's Effectiveness Indicators for Special Education.* These indicators are based on the work of the National RRC Panel on Indicators of Effectiveness in Special Education, published by the Mid-South Regional Resource Center. *Indiana's Effectiveness Indicators* is a "merger and re-categorization of [*Indiana's*] *Effectiveness Indicators for Special Education: A Reference Tool* (National RRC Panel on indicator's of Effectiveness in Special Education, 1986) with the nine correlates or characteristics of effective schools outlined in *Indiana's Performance Based Accreditation Manual"* (*Indiana's Effectiveness Indicators for Special Education,* 1990, p. 3). *Indiana's Effectiveness Indicators for Special Education* represents an effort to include the evaluation of special education programs within the accreditation program in which all schools must participate. This effort has the effect of ensuring that special education programs are considered to be an important part of the school's offerings, and it helps to break down the barriers between general and special education that have resulted from the parallel system.

In "Correlate 5: Program Evaluation," *Indiana's Effectiveness Indicators* includes a discussion of the need for and purposes of program evaluation as an important component of effective special education programs. Program evaluation is described as follows:

> Routine and systematic program evaluations provide information for making decisions regarding the policies and processes impacting on the programs and services being provided to students with handicaps. Program evaluation is a dynamic process that includes all stakeholders (students, parents, teachers, administrators, district staff, school board, and community). It involves data collection, data analysis, presentation of results, and the development of action plans to foster improvement in programming. (p. 44)

According to the indicators listed under Correlate 5, program evaluation should be a routine activity aimed at uncovering "strengths and weaknesses for both individual and school special education programs" (p. 44). Evaluation may be formative or summative, include longitudinal studies, and/or involve parents, other stakeholders, and the local special education advisory committee. Components of the special education program that are considered include: "classroom academic and vocational programs, curriculum and IEP implementation, resource adequacy, related services, district policies and procedures for identification, evaluation, and movement of students over time, and follow-up of graduates" (p. 45). Efforts should be made to evaluate the link between the school's mission and the operation of the special education program. In addition, Correlate 5 enumerates standards that might be used in a program evaluation in the areas of instruction, goal setting and implementation, and policies and procedures.

State-Initiated Models

Purpose   To provide data in the local context in order to determine available options in formulating an action plan.

Definition   To define evaluation questions initially in the 12 areas noted below and establish acceptable performance standards.

Focus   Performance indicators of student progress and process indicators established by some form of state-level consensus. Each state suggests certain areas for evaluation, but also encourages the generation of other performance and process indicators of local interest.

Performance Indicators
1. Physical and emotional well-being, values and attitudes
2. Skills and knowledge
3. Citizenship and respect
4. Occupational competence
5. Community adjustment
6. Creative talents and interests

Process Indicators
1. Child identification and evaluation
2. Parent and public involvement
3. Facilities and range of services
4. Staff development
5. Least restrictive environment
6. IEP evaluation

Proponents Daniel Stufflebeam, Malcom Provus, and Ralph Tyler

Design Primarily survey design work, often using state-developed prototypes that are adapted by district task forces of key stakeholding groups organized and directed by the local special education administrator

Methodology/Procedures Determine sample sizes; analyze data in the form of percentages; develop trend analysis and uncover patterns; write action plan. Regional or state personnel often provide technical assistance.

Audiences Primarily decision makers and participants in the process

Other Considerations Time frame reported by users is 2–3 months. State provides prototypes or technical assistance for designing local surveys, as well as training in data collection and report writing.

Local School District Program Review Model

Purpose/Definition/Focus To assess how the current program stacks up against the opinions of experts judged to have a national, state, and local perspective in comparable settings, and who are well-grounded in the contemporary practice of special education

Proponents Robert Wolf and E. Wisner

Design Review the district's historical and current status and respond to the circumstances with the panel's assessment of what is best practice and possible in the school district context, using the expert panel's experiences and training.

Methodology/Procedures   With the help and input of top management, the special education leader gains consensus on and initiates a negotiated set of targeted program-review outcomes with top management. Then an internal audit committee is formed, composed of all program personnel involved in special education and representatives from the community adisory board, which generates a set of questions to assess a wider range of regular and special education personnel perceptions of necessary changes. These data are provided as evidence, along with selected documents the expert panel requests of the director. The final stage of data collection is the interrogation of key staff, from top management groups to teacher aides, and site visitations to suspect programs. Data analysis begins with a derivation conference during which the panel solicits additional data when questions arise. A draft oral report follows; top management and the director tailor the report to district opportunities and constraints. The final steps include sharing the report in written form with the internal audit committee and community advisory board, and ultimately with the superintendent's cabinet. The director is then required to produce an internal management plan that includes a discussion of options and eventual sanctioning of resources as policy changes occur.

Audiences   Any groups concerned with the entity to be evaluated. Generally, a comprehensive review will involve at least top and middle building-level management, instructional and related-services personnel, and representatives from school patrons and community agencies.

Other Considerations   Time to complete the task can be broken down into director time, internal audit time, staff time, and expert panel time commitments. The expert panel should include a local peer director from a well-respected district within the state, if possible, to provide a benchmark, as well as a state department consultant and a national administrative consultant/trainer in special education.

Johnson/Gadberry Program Planning and Evaluation Model

The Johnson/Gadberry Model has been most recently discussed by the National RRC Panel on Indicators of Effectiveness in Special Education in 1986. This model is included to illustrate an evaluation process that uses pre-established categories for a district or intermediate unit that is relatively stable and needs to determine its current status in light of changing practices.

Purpose   To set up a measurement system to determine the effectiveness of program objectives

Definition   A public process of determining local values and operational objectives that can be measured against a locally defined set of standards

Focus   Goal-based program development and subsequent evaluation of a locally articulated philosophy, integrated with a set of goals and specific objectives, progress toward which can be measured by self-generated criteria

Proponents   Richard Johnson and Eva Gadberry in special education, and Ralph Tyler, James Popham, and Malcolm Provus in evaluation literature

Design   The model is explicit in terms of the factors that Johnson and Gadberry suggest the administrator consider in planning for and conducting the evaluation:

1.   Statement of philosophy
2.   Overall program policies
3.   Overall program design
4.   Overall planning and coordination
5.   Student assessment and program planning
6.   Content
7.   Method
8.   Staff
9.   Staff development
10.   Instructional resources
11.   Physical plan requirements
12.   Transportation
13.   Parent involvement and training
14.   Interagency and advocacy group collaboration
15.   Community relations and involvement
16.   Fiscal resources
17.   Component policies and procedures
18.   Total program evaluation

Each component of the model is used in the design of the evaluation, from philosophy to goals and objectives. Three criteria are used to measure goal and/or objective achievement. For each program or subprogram component, this model seeks to assess: 1) quality, 2) sufficiency of effort and resources, and 3) whether or not the program or component is cost-effective.

Methodology/Procedures   Generating criteria statements for each of the 18 components in the J/G model using the concepts of quality, sufficiency, and cost-effectiveness is one of the first key steps in using this process. With the criteria statements established, task force groups tackle four interrelated activities separately and then together to gain a consensus. The four tasks are:

1. Define "what is" currently happening using team-developed criteria statements; this task involves interviewing personnel within the systems and community patrons.
2. Define "what should be" and reach consensus on a "community" set of expectations to guide decision making.
3. Define the discrepancy between the results obtained in tasks 1 and 2.
4. Develop an action plan to reach the desired states defined in task 2.

Audiences Top management, cooperative and LEA administrators, SEA representatives, and all staff and community patrons and agencies personnel, as appropriate

Other Considerations Adoption of this evaluation process demands a deep commitment among top management and special education administrators; it is not advisable that it be implemented in a district in a crisis, but rather only in settings in which the system participants basically want a thorough review of the past and are seeking to establish a new game plan for the future. This type of planning both ensures a thoughtful study and encourages commitment and acceptance of the future. This type of planning and evaluation project demands an 18- to 24-month time frame.

Responsive Evaluation Model

Many more examples of responsive evaluation are to be found in studies of federal and state projects than in those of local school system special education practices. This example describes how an evaluation of a major SEA/LEA training project was conducted using the responsive evaluation model. The authors have used some of the naturalistic methods described below in assessing the effectiveness of evaluation efforts in a large urban school district with over 50,000 students, a large suburban district with over 14,000 students, and a large special education cooperative serving over 20,000 special education students.

Purpose To determine if task force planning and implementation of quality practices in personnel development could be effectively replicated in local school districts and cooperatives that included both regular and special educators; in short, this type of evaluation assesses the values of the project participants in terms of the merit of the planning versus the worth of the plan produced and the training actually provided.

Definition To determine what values are held by SEAs, technical assistance groups, and local planning team members and whether or not the intent of the SEA project is in fact apparent and operational in the typical behavior of the planning team and others affected by the planning and training activities in their usual situations.

Focus To assess key stakeholders' perceptions of the effectiveness of LEA planning and implementation of training projects within a statewide network supported by SEA discretionary money and a university-based technical assistance group.

Proponents Egon Guba, Yvonna Lincoln, and Robert Stake

Design The design of a naturalistic inquiry is emergent, rather than preordained like the state-initiated or Johnson-Gadberry processes. The evaluator seeks to discover the values held by multiple audiences and attempts to describe in detail the patterns (if any) in their divergent values regarding the merit of the process or the worth of the plan or training actually delivered.

Methodology/Procedures Evaluators are the chief actors in a naturalistic inquiry; the evaluator seeks to determine the general intent of the project by garnering a collection of data sources (both oral and written), including a thorough review of the grant proposal documents, letters of introduction, and letters of agreement between the parties in the interagency arrangement. From these documents an unstructured interview schedule is developed and a sample of school districts or individual schools or programs within a district that are progressing well and others that are suspect are selected. A set of 10–15 interviews are conducted with the sample of teachers and administrators selected from among both the regular and special educators' planning teams and non–team members; the sample grows as the evaluator solicits the names of others during the interviews in order to further explore unique perceptions or distinct values that emerged from the interviews with the initial sample. Plans and evaluation reports are reviewed, training sessions observed, and participants queried during and after training sessions, with the evaluator in attendance; finally, (where possible) the evaluator attends staff and planning meetings at the home site (Beatty, 1985).

Data Analysis Occurs during and after reviewing the initial interviews; the evaluator is searching for the patterns or themes that emerge. These patterns result from the dissection and reassembly of the participants' values and observations. They are shared with the participants to clarify their meaning and with others to confirm their validity. Reports consist largely of the participants' own words, giving the readers a sense of actually being there, while framing recommendations in their own context.

Audiences Anyone involved, or representative of the project or program under study

Other Considerations Time—depending upon the size of the entity being evaluated. This type of evaluation is very labor intensive.

Other Recommendations

Combining qualitative and quantitative evaluation methods, especially in large evaluation efforts, is highly recommended. In large organizations and in programs having multiple audiences, as the program implementors get farther away from the policy makers, the original intent is likely to be confounded. We recommend this combined approach, however, because it increases the scope and focus of the evaluation and consequently should be more effective. Quantitative approaches may appear to be more efficient, and they generally are, but they can miss the target by a wide margin. Qualitative approaches, while labor intensive, lead to rich descriptions of reality that build rapport and encourage acceptance of change among participants.

A second recommendation we wish to make involves the use of the work of Brinkeroff, Brethower, Hluchyj, and Nowakowski (1983) in the Evaluation Training Consortium (ETC) at Western Michigan University. The ETC has a long history in evaluation training and has produced a set of volumes that contain descriptions of the process of designing and focusing evaluations. We have included a display of one of the evaluation functions from this work, which lists key issues and questions and the key evaluation tasks that correspond to both the functions and issues. See Appendix B for the format.

SUMMARY

Education program evaluation has been conceived of as a process by which judgments are made about the merit and worth of an educational program. Judgments about special education programs have commonly focused on their compatibility with federal and state policies and regulations. Compliance monitoring has taken the form of program evaluations of special education being conducted separately from those of other district- or school-level programs, such as North Central self-studies or state performance assessments.

With the push for inclusion and a unified system of education that includes an outcome-based orientation for all students, special education evaluation will slowly become a part of the other more holistic program evaluation activities. Program evaluation will also encourage educators to address important concerns that arise when schools seek to meet the needs of all of the students. Two particular emerging issues in special education that evaluation studies should address are the relationships between students and the impact of peer teaching and cooperative learning on students' acceptance into the social group and their sense of their own efficacy. The evaluation should also examine the nature of interventions and their outcomes, as well as the roles of teachers inside and outside of the school and the relationship between interventions and post-school outcomes related to independent living, work, and social relationships. It should examine the use of technology and the organizational forms of adhocracy that are used to bring expertise together to support unsuccessful students in schools regardless of their special needs. Parental satisfaction and employer and university assessments of graduates should also be considered.

In this period of transition from separate, parallel systems of delivery to more integrated and unified systems, program evaluation models based on goal-oriented, professional management approaches will not capture the dynamic community elements that affect program development. The times require more democratic and responsive evaluation approaches that encourage the openness and collaboration that are called for in IDEA. Responsive and democratic approaches are educative and activist, and stress the value of pluralism and negotiation between stakeholders. The focus of and approach to evaluation must shift away from process and compliance and toward valued student outcomes and accountability for student performance for all.

ILLUSTRATIVE CASE

Lee Blank, the Special Education Director in Dormit Central Schools, walked back to the office after a meeting with the Associate Superintendent and a group of principals who were beginning to plan for next year's state accreditation process and North Central Association self-study. Lee reflected on the meeting, impressed by the diligence of the group and the seriousness with which they approached their tasks. But the group's total compartmentalization of the special education evaluation questions was depressing. The State of Lafayette had begun trying to alter the local school accreditation process to include special education since such a change was mandated 3 years ago. As the state's new position statement favored inclusion as a goal for all students with disabilities, the state administration, in conjunction with the State Directors' Association, was beginning to assemble a new set of evaluation questions to be part of each school's improvement process. When Lee presented the sample questions for the group's consideration, they simply said, "Lee, why don't you just include those questions as part of the district's 3-year review process for special education?"

Lee raised the following question with the group: "Since a number of you have begun to include some of our youngsters with extensive needs from the Old Westside School into every aspect of your total program, how can you carry on an evaluation of your total program and not consider the impact of those programs?"

The principals chewed on Lee's retort for about 10 minutes and then recommended that Lee convene the district's special education advisory committee and have them generate a set of questions that the individual school planning teams should consider in their instrumentation.

Lee didn't hesitate; "While I agree that input from the district committee would be valuable, it's your own staff who ought be developing the questions they think should be included in the evaluation. After all, who is going to use the data? Shouldn't it serve their purposes, and yours, first?"

The principals agreed. Then they asked that Lee sit in on their individual planning meetings. They cautioned that it was important to simply come and listen, but that Lee should also be prepared to help formulate a set of questions for the teams to consider.

What should these questions be?
What role should students play in the evaluation?
How will school-based information be gathered and used for district-level and long-range planning?

REFERENCES

Beatty, E. (1985). Qualitative responsive approaches to local special education program evaluation. In CASE Research Committee, *Quantitative vs. Qualitative: Approaches to quality special education program evaluation* (pp. 23–35). Bloomington, IN: CASE Research Committee.

Board of Education v. Rowley, 458 U.S. 176 (1982).

Brinkeroff, R., Brethower, D., Hluchyj, T., & Nowakowski, J. (1983). *Program evaluation: A practioner's guide for trainers and educators.* Boston: Kluwer-Nijhoff.

Education for All Handicapped Children Act of 1975, PL 94-142. (August 23, 1977). Title 20, U.S.C. 1401 et seq: *U.S. Statutes at Large, 89,* 773–796.

Frey, W. (1993, April). *A state perspective on assessment of educational outcomes for students with disabilities.* Paper presented at the annual convention of the Council for Exceptional Children, San Antonio.

Guba E., & Lincoln, Y. (1981). *Effective evaluation.* San Francisco: Jossey-Bass.

Guba, E., & Lincoln, Y.S. (1989). *Fourth generation evaluation.* Newbury Park, CA: Sage.

Hehir, T. (1992). The impact of due process on the programmatic decisions of special education directors. *Special Education Leadership Review, 1*(1), 63–76.

Horvath, L. (1985). A quantitative program evaluation approach to evaluating quality special education programs. In CASE Research Committee, *Quan-*

titative vs. Qualitative: Approaches to quality special education program evaluation (pp. 3–22). Bloomington, IN: Case Research Committee.

Indiana Department of Education. (1990). *Indiana's effectiveness indicators for special education.* Indianapolis: Author.

Indiana Department of Education. (1992). Article 7, Rules 3–16. Indianapolis: Author.

Individuals with Disabilities Education Act (IDEA) of 1990, PL 101-476. (October 30, 1990). Title 20, U.S.C. 1400 et seq: *U.S. Statutes at Large, 104,* 1103–1151.

Johnson, R., & Gadberry, E. (1986). *The effectiveness indicators.* Bloomington, IN: CASE Research Committee.

Lincoln, Y.S., & Guba, E. (1985). *Naturalistic inquiry.* Beverly Hills, CA: Sage.

MacDonald, B. (1974, April). *The portrayal of persons as evaluation data.* Paper presented at the annual meeting of the American Educational Research Association, San Francisco.

National RRC Panel on Indicators of Effectiveness in Special Education. (1986). *Effectiveness indicators for special education.* Bloomington, IN: CASE Research Committee.

Odden, A., & Marsh, D. (1990). Local response to the 1980's state education reforms: New patterns of local and state interaction. In J. Murphy (Ed.), *The educational reform movement of the 1980's.* Berkeley, CA: McCutcheon.

Popham, J. (1975). *Educational evaluation.* Englewood Cliffs, NJ: Prentice Hall.

Provus, M. (1971). *Discrepancy evaluation.* Berkley, CA: McCutchan.

Rehabilitation Act of 1973, PL 93-112. (September 26, 1973). Title 29, U.S.C. 701 et seq: *U.S. Statutes at Large, 87,* 355–394.

Rothstein, L. (1990). *Special education law.* White Plains, NY: Longman.

Schwandt, T. (1992). *Education inquiry methodology* (Lecture notes, Y535, Program evaluation). Indiana University, Bloomington.

Scriven, M. (1967). The methodology of evaluation. In R.E. Stake (Ed.), Curriculum evaluation. *American Education Research Association Monograph Series on Evaluation* (No. 1). Chicago: Rand-McNally.

Scriven, M. (1973). The methodology of evaluation. In B.R. Worthen & J.R. Sanders (Eds.), *Educational evaluation: Theory and practice* (pp. 60–105). Belmont, CA: Wadsworth.

Simons, H. (1987). *Getting to know schools in a democracy.* London: The Falmer Press.

Skrtic, T. (1991). The special education paradox: Equity as the way to excellence. *Harvard Education Review, 61*(2), 148–206.

Skrtic, T., Guba, E., & Knowlton, H.E. (1985). *Special education in rural America: Interorganizational special education programming in rural areas* (technical report on the multisite naturalistic field study). Washington, DC: Department of Education, National Institute of Education.

Stake, R. (1975). *Program evaluation, particularly responsive evaluation* (Paper #5 in Occasional Paper Series). Kalamazoo, MI: Evaluation Center.

Stufflebeam, D. (1983). The CIPP Model for program evaluation. In G.F. Madaus, M. Scriven, & D.L. Stufflebeam (Eds.), *Evaluation models: Viewpoints on educational and human service evaluation* (pp. 117–141). Boston: Kluwer-Nijhoff.

Tracy, P. (1984). Supportive staff and related services evaluation. In L.C. Burrello (Ed.), *CASE information packet series.* Bloomington, IN: CASE, Inc.

Tyler, R. (1949). *Basic principles of curriculum and instruction.* Chicago: University of Chicago Press.

U.S. Department of Education. (1990). *Twelfth annual report to Congress on the implementation of the Education of All Handicapped Children Act.* Washington, DC: Author.

Wisner, E.W. (1975). *The perceptive eye: Toward the reformation of education evaluation.* Stanford, CA: Stanford Evaluation Consortium, DCC. 1975.

Wisner, E.W. (1979). *The educational imagination.* New York: MacMillan.

Wolf, R. (1979). The use of judicial evaluation methods in the formulation of educational policy. *Education Evaluation and Policy Analysis, 1*(3), 19–28.

Worthen, B.R., & Sanders, J.R. (1987). *Educational evaluation: Alternative approaches and practical guidelines.* White Plains, NY: Longman.

Appendix A

A COMPREHENSIVE OUTLINE
FOR EVALUATION IN SPECIAL EDUCATION

I. *Guiding Operative Principles*
   A. When a system can operate under a consistent set of objectives, its effectiveness and efficiency are probably increased.
   B. Major objectives should be appropriately established at all levels of the system.
   C. No part of the system should view itself as being divorced from the operational framework defined by the program objectives.
   D. A person at any position in the system should know:
      1. What the systems' objectives are
      2. What his or her division's responsibilities are in meeting these objectives
      3. How those objectives prescribe, operationally, what he or she does in the system
      4. How he or she gives operational clarity to those subordinate to him or her
      5. How he or she shares personal and professional expectations and resources with peers and subordinates

II. *Organization for Service Delivery*
   A. Personnel must be of adequate quantity and quality to provide:
      1. Major policy leadership
      2. General administrative management
      3. Technical supervision/consultation
      4. Ancillary support
      5. Direct instructional service
   B. Procedures must be established, clearly understood, and consistently implemented concerning:
      1. Screening within the system
      2. Case finding outside the system
      3. Referral for evaluation
      4. Diagnostic–prescriptive services
      5. Placement in programs providing continuing instructional services
      6. Evaluation of progress in programs
      7. Changes in placement within and between programs and the mainstream

    C. Program alternatives must be available to meet varied pupil needs, considering:
1. Type of major exceptionality
2. Degree of deviance
3. Approach to instructional intervention
4. Intensity of service required

    D. Consumer involvement must be evident in parents':
1. Input on decisions regarding placement
2. Understanding of objectives of the program
3. Knowledge of pupil progress
4. Awareness of alternatives for pupils

    E. Related community agencies must be involved cooperatively with the school system in the provision of services for pupils in such areas as:
1. Health
2. Social services
3. Psychological assessment
4. Parent counseling

    F. System monitoring must be possible, in order to ensure assessment of:
1. Achievement of overall program objectives
2. Instances of unmet needs (excluded pupils, inappropriate placements, etc.)

III. *Curriculum*
    A. Curriculum will evidence:
1. Congruence with major program objectives
2. Sequence between maturational levels
3. Articulation between special and mainstream services
4. Relationship between school, home, and adult role in society
5. Community-based training activities

IV. *Physical Facilities*
    A. Facilities will reflect program philosophy in:
1. Recognition of special needs
2. Maximum feasible normalization

    B. Facilities will make provisions consistent with:
1. Variety of types of pupils served
2. Variety of instructional methodologies utilized

V. *Instructional Approaches*
    A. Teachers' activities will demonstrate:
1. Awareness of major program objectives
2. Consistency with objectives
3. Maximum flexibility to match pupil differences
4. Provision of input from home
5. Maximum relationship between present and long-range needs
6. Effective teaching practices grounded in instructional effectiveness research

    B. Teachers' characteristics will include:
1. Basic certification
2. Demonstrated competence
3. An individual development plan
4. Engagement in growth and development activities

    C. Instructional materials will be adequate in terms of:
1. Sufficient quantity to serve all pupils
2. Sufficient variety to serve all types of needs
3. Consistency with major objectives

D. Evaluation of the results of instruction will be:
   1. Systematically implemented
   2. Adequate to provide continued prescriptive guidance
   3. Transmittable to relevant targets outside the school

VI. *Outcomes*
   A. Programs will result in students who:
      1. Build healthy human relationships
      2. Participate fully in life in the community
      3. Experience minimal stigma associated with any disability they may have
      4. Have a positive self-concept
      5. Demonstrate progress in meeting individual achievement objectives
      6. Enjoy a productive occupation
   B. The global effect of programs will be to facilitate positive attitudes toward human variance in society at large.

Appendix B

KEY TASKS IN EVALUATION

Function	Key tasks
Focusing the evaluation	Determine what is to be evaluated. Identify and justify the purpose for evaluating. Define the audience (i.e., who will be affected by or involved in the evaluation). Determine what elements in the setting are likely to influence the evaluation. Enumerate the crucial evaluation questions. Decide whether the evaluation has the potential for successful implementation.
Designing the evaluation	Define the general purpose of the evaluation and decide on the proper amount of planning and degree of control. Gain an overview of the evaluation decisions, tasks, and products. Design the evaluation. Assess the quality of the design.
Collecting information	Determine the information sources to be used and the kinds of information to be collected. Decide how much information is to be collected. Determine how precise the data must be and either design or select a means to collect it. Establish procedures to maximize the reliability of the instruments and the validity of the data collected. Plan the logistics for an economical information collection procedure; try to get the most information at the lowest cost.
Managing	Select, hire, and/or train the evaluator. Draw up a formal contract or letter of agreement. Draft a budget for the evaluation. Design a time/task strategy. Monitor the evaluation, attempting to anticipate problems.

Function	Key tasks
Analyzing and interpreting data	Aggregate and code collected data. Verify the completeness and quality of the raw data. Plan and conduct an analysis of the data. Interpret the results using predetermined and alternate criteria.
Reporting	Determine to whom the results should be reported. Outline the content of the report. Decide whether reports should be written, oral, or in some other form. Plan post-report discussion, consultation, and follow-up activities to help audiences interpret and use the report. Create a schedule for the release of the reports.
Evaluating the evaluation (meta-evaluation)	Determine whether meta-evaluation is necessary, and if so, when. Select a meta-evaluator. Select or negotiate standards. Rank order standards; determine compliance.

Index

Page numbers followed by "f" indicate figures; those followed by "t" indicate tables.